From Partners To Rivals?

The Evolving Dynamics Of America And Europe

GEW Intelligence Unit

Global East-West. London

Contents

1

Introduction

An Overview of Transatlantic Relations

Background to transatlantic relations

Historically, relations between transatlantic regions stem from historical trade or colonisation activities that date back to the times when Europeans were discovering the Americas. The relationship connecting Europe to North America has greatly developed over the years while profoundly impacting global geopolitics. The transatlantic link can be defined using shared beliefs, common objectives, and a socioeconomic security network that is both interwoven and multifaceted.

Historically, as people from Europe migrated to the New World either for trade, settlement, or as a result of wars, political alliances, and cultural integrations, their thoughts and ideas travelled in the opposite direction. This in turn established the framework for transatlantic cooperation that is sustained to this day. The European nations collaborated with the United States—freed and bolstered as a global superpower in WWII—to reconstruct Europe, subsequently solidifying the importance of these relations on a political and economic scale.

Relational principles concerning democracy, human rights, the rule of law, and a market economy define transatlantic relations. Together, these values have emphasised partnership between the United States and Europe, forging unity towards a common goal. The formation of key institutions like the North Atlantic Treaty Organisation (NATO) and European Union (EU) accelerated the commitment to both collective security and economic integration, strengthening the bonds among transatlantic partners.

The transatlantic relations historical framework incorporates key milestones like the Marshall Plan that highlighted American commitment towards using resources to heal Europe's economy while integrating post-war reconstruction initiatives. The combined experiences during the Cold War also underscored the importance of transatlantic cooperation in addressing common threats and preserving peace, including the Berlin Airlift and the Cuban Missile Crisis.

In other words, the transatlantic relations context encompasses a blend of history, interconnectedness, and joint ideals. Analysing the history of these relationships and significance enables a thorough understanding of the complexities and challenges within the contemporary transatlantic partnership.

Defining the scope: Key actors and institutions

There is a nuanced interconnection of primary actors and institutions that define transatlantic relations. For example, The US State Department, the European External Action Service and the Ministries of each European Country relate to the respective government arms of every country. These officials manage the affairs and interests of their countries diplomatically on a transatlantic level where they compete and cooperate with each other.

NATO (North Atlantic Treaty Organisation) and the European Union are both International Organisations that play a significant role in transatlantic affairs. Ever since it was established, NATO has served as the central security institution for transatlantic collaborative defence relations, which underpins the mutual defence of its members, while the European Union, which is mainly a political and economic union influences indirectly through its foreign and security policy and hence, modifies its power as an actor in US-EU relations.

Outside the scope of governments and international frameworks, transatlantic relations cannot be understood without understanding the contribution of non-state actors. Cumulatively, the private sector, such as multinational corporations, and industry and professional trade associations often play the role of an economic motor and actively participate in crafting policies which directly impact the transatlantic economic relationship. People-to-people connections are also worked on by universities and other think tanks as well as civil society organisations which helps them promote shared values and principles on both sides of the Atlantic.

When studying transatlantic relations, remembering the historical context is equally important, especially during the periods immediately after the Second World War or the Cold War. For example, the Marshall Plan was one of the key developments in creating a more integrated US and Western European economy. This goes to show how the two sides of the Atlantic have worked through shifts in the international balance of power, technological progress, global challenges, in a synchronised manner which reflects the nature of this relationship.

Transatlantic relations encompass numerous institutions and actors which combine in a single web of cooperation and diplomacy. Every one of them has a distinct approach concerning the transatlantic issue, which adds to the complexity of every aspect of the United States and the European Union's relations.

Phases and stages of evolution

The evolution of transatlantic relations has always been characterised by marked phases and decisive stages in international relations development. The United States and Europe began to perceive themselves as important world powers after the Second World War, which created the basis for the strong alliances and structures that were meant to sustain cooperation between the two sides of the Atlantic. The creation of NATO in 1949, which was the first attempt at formulating a collective security alliance, represents a crucial landmark in this chain of events focusing on mutual defence and stability.

The end of the Cold War marked the start of a new era defined by the lifting of traditional geopolitical divides and the strengthening of democratic ideals, which, along with the EU and NATO, fostered the inclusion of Central and Eastern Europe within their frameworks. This transformation deepened the exploitation of democracy, human rights, and market economies while simultaneously strengthening the transatlantic community in their efforts to foster Euro-Atlantic peace, security, and regional prosperity.

The 21st century has seen unprecedented levels of transatlantic cooperation fostered in response to global security concerns. This was notably demonstrated through the joint military operations in Afghanistan during the post-9/11 counter-terrorism operations. Concurrently, the G7 and G20 provided a forum for economy, environment, and development-focused multilateral engagement, thereby deepening the transatlantic alliance's role as a cornerstone for multifaceted global problem solving.

The 2008 financial crisis was arguably one of the most testing periods for the transatlantic economy as it created a need for cohesive damage control between the U.S. and the European Union. The later discussions on the Transatlantic Trade and Investment Partnership (TTIP) sought to increase convergence productivity and strengthen the economies on both sides of the Atlantic. This, however, did not soften the complexities and sensitivities that are present in transatlantic trade relations.

What is more, the evolution of transatlantic relations has also been marked by changes in politics, leadership, and ideologies which have shifted the focus of policy goals and methods to global governance. The shift from the optimism of the Obama presidency, that embraced a renewed multilateral diplomacy and transatlantic alliance to interdependence cooperation, to a more unilateral and transactional viewpoint brought forth by Trump has vastly restructured the landscape of transatlantic cooperation and discord.

Grasping the phases of evolution coupled with the salient features of transatlantic relations aids in anchoring the major complexities in contemporary transatlantic relations and emphasises the need to look deeper into the past to find the future path of the enduring partnership.

Importance in world affairs

Transatlantic relationships, which include the partnership between the United States and Europe, are highly significant in the world affairs arena. Such ties have a profound effect on world international policies and relations, economics, security and diplomacy. The transatlantic relationship is pivotal towards defending democratic values, ensuring stability and promoting shared prosperity globally. The United States and European Union (EU) account for a significant portion of the world's GDP and trade, adding value to their collaboration beyond borders and impacting the global economy. Their military power and strategic alliances provide security and combat mutual threats, thus reinforcing world order. The powerful economies also work collaboratively in response to other international issues including climate change, sustainable development, and the advancement of human rights and democracy. The strong transatlantic relationship develops the support necessary to maintain an international system that promotes peace, prosperity, and progress.

The need to maintain basic order and tackle new challenges as one marks its importance around the world. It underscores why the significance of transatlantic ties continues to be analysed, as their comprehension is critical in explaining the myriad forces, more so at the present time, which call for underlying consideration for the stark realities that exist within international relations.

Current situation and dynamics

Analysing the condition of current relations, one could articulate them as the blend of socio-political elements intertwined with global economics. The most powerful players in this network are the US and the EU, which are the economically strongest regions in the world. Rather than restate relations which are marred by competition for who can exercise strategic dominance over 'Allied domains', the term transatlantic partnership would be more appropriate. Transformations in global power balance, persistent change of security risks, unprecedented technological progress, and increasing number of actors in the international arena have a considerable impact on the relations sustain. The combination of these factors alters the way politics, economics, and security issues are treated from the traditional West-centric viewpoint.

For the economy, transatlantic relations are still marked by interdependence and competition. The trade and investment relationships between the EU and the US continue to be significant, but recent disputes over trade relations and differences in regulatory approaches have strained economic relations. The expansion of the digital economy has created another dimension of economic interdependence in data privacy, cybersecurity, and the regulation of new technologies. All of these factors add to the evolving economic landscape influencing transatlantic relations.

Regarding defence and security, the transatlantic alliance faces a range of actively developing threats, including: terrorism, cyberattacks, global pandemics, and hybrid warfare. The North Atlantic Treaty organisation (NATO) continues to be the primary forum for cooperation on transatlantic security and is on a debate regarding burden sharing and the expansion of NATO's role which indicates the strained relations within the alliance. Additionally, the renewed competition from systemic rivals including rising powers like China and Russia poses new strategic burdens for transatlantic security and reevaluates collective defence and deterrence strategies.

The relations between the transatlantic territories are considerably sensitive to sociocultural aspects as well. The past is connected to the present through people's connections, educational, and cultural activities between the 'US' and the European Union. At the same time, social development and demographic distribution changes in both regions provide new outlooks on concepts such as shared values, citizenship, immigration, multiculturalism, and global identity. To appreciate the relations between the transatlantic societies and the impact they have on one another, one needs to have more profound insights into the sociocultural aspects of the regions.

While keeping in mind these factors, we can conclude that the transatlantic partnership has entered the stage that requires strategic shifts in behaviour as well as other unorthodox strategies in order to tackle the issues and make the most out of available resources. Understanding how these factors influence the partnership makes it easier to formulate strategies on how to further improve the partnership, ensuring that the alliance remains strong and beneficial from all sides while also ensuring that the regions are fully able to deal with the realities of world changes in the 21st century.

Core Interests and Shared Goals

Relations across the Atlantic are characterised by a myriad of core interests and shared goals that have developed with the cooperation of the United States and Europe. These relations are grounded in shared values, historical partnerships, as well as the determination to uphold and spread democratic norms for stability across the world. The primary interests and shared goals cover a wide range which serves as a framework for collaboration and commitment. One such area is security and defence whereby both sides have a stake in dealing with emerging threats, terrorism, and aiding in the collective defence of NATO allies. These shared interests have underpinned allied military interventions, intelligence cooperation, and diplomatic efforts to deter aggressive actions and defend stability and peace in regions of strategic importance. Economic prosperity and trade is also among the key components of the transatlantic partnership with shared goals for advancement, innovation, and regulatory alignment. Both the US and the EU strive towards enhancing access to markets, fostering competition, and tackling international problems such as climate change and sustainable development.

The transatlantic partnership aims to protect and advance human rights, the rule of law, and democratic governance. Through political dialogues, initiatives, and support for civil society, the US and EU form a partnership that upholds shared values and strives towards respect for human dignity, individual freedoms, and inclusive societies. Striking an equilibrium on transnational issues including public health, energy, and technological innovations demonstrates collective concern that goes beyond borders. These shared challenges require collaboration to develop research, effective communication, and capacity building to solve complex emerging problems impacting societies across the Atlantic. Generally, the primary interests and common goals serve as the foundation in the remarkable bond between the US and Europe, offering a framework for relations that rise above political cycles while capturing the essence of their intricate relations.

The Difficulties of Cooperation

Transatlantic relations, as a cooperation between Europe and the United States, have hurt the cooperation between the two sides due to shared values and interests on the United States' side. Europe has faced several challenges, and one of them is the alignment of foreign policy priorities and approaches. Empirically, it has been the case that the US unilaterally follows and implements militaristic foreign policy, while European countries put emphasis on multilateralism, diplomacy, as well as cooperative security initiatives through NATO and the EU. Such differences between policies lead each block of countries to agree to plan mergers on military interventions, sanctions and peacekeeping missions. Economic factors pose another equally important challenge to cooperation. The US and the European Union have notoriously been at conflict over trade policies, market openness or closure, and ownership of innovations. These relations were almost crippled due to conflicts on tariffs, subsidies, and trade competition which triggers the decline of transatlantic commerce, inviting tit-for-tat measures capable of blowing into trade wars. Moreover, being deeply divided over climate change, energy security, and ecology also became a problem for cooperation.

Unlike the United States, which has relatively relaxed policies that would align with the EU's agenda, the EU focuses on mitigating sustainable development, renewable energy, and greenhouse gas emissions challenges. The cited differences have thwarted collaborations towards solving global environmental issues.

The emergence of populism and nationalism has exacerbated bilateral relations on both sides of the Atlantic. There has been the rise of political movements that advocate for isolationism, protectionism, and anti-immigration sentiments, leading to increased skepticism towards international cooperation and integration. These changes have weakened the traditional transatlantic alliance and diminished the willingness to cooperate on issues like migration, refugees, and human rights. The evolution of technology and new cybersecurity threats add different layers of complexity to transatlantic relations. Disputes over digital privacy, data protection, and internet governance have become barriers to cooperation in information technology and cybersecurity. Conflicting regulatory approaches and standards make it even more difficult to align transatlantic policies on the digital economy and cybersecurity. Meeting these complex challenges involves understanding the socio-political, economic, and security factors that shape transatlantic relations. Such efforts need constructive thinking, practical solutions to neglected issues, and more cooperation based on common principles and objectives.

Strategic Engagement Opportunities

In the intricate web of transatlantic relations, there exists a plethora of opportunities for strategic engagement that could potentially transform the dynamics of the United States and Europe. One potential opportunity exists in the field of Sustainable Development and Climate Actions. While the United States and European Union focus and give attention towards the protection of the environment as well as fighting climate change, cooperation towards building renewable energy sources, advancing green technologies, carbon pricing methods, and other related efforts could become a foundation for joint work. Transatlantic partners can achieve remarkable benchmarks in environmental protection as well as economically beneficial renewable energy by combining their capabilities and resources.

Funding cooperative research and innovation activities in clean energy and climate change can stimulate scientific developments while helping to achieve a self-sustaining future. New and more promising prospects for strategy focus can be found in the areas of cybersecurity and digital governance. Given the increasing risks that cyber threats pose as well as the vast interconnectedness of digital systems within the U.S. and across the E.U., there is a shared need to address the enhancement of cyber defences, the improvement of data protection legislation and the creation of frameworks for responsible conduct by states within cyberspace. Participation in the response to cyber incidents, information exchange, and capacity development can enhance the defence capabilities of both regions against hostile cyber operations.

Harmonising regulatory approaches and encouraging public-private collaborations within the digital domain helps advance emerging technologies whilst maintaining user privacy and digital rights. The economic synergy provides profound prospects for enhancing transatlantic ties. Even with cases of divergence, there is a robust economic underpinning for the United States and the European Union to mutually increase trade relations, optimise investments, and cooperate on policy frameworks. Formulating a thorough transatlantic trade agreement alongside a bilateral investment renewal and establishing cooperative approaches to deal with global trade issues will enhance market competition and foster sustainable economic development for both sides of the Atlantic.

These collaborative actions and policies together with the joint effort to foster entrepreneurship, develop adequate human capital, and strengthen the small-to-medium-sized business sector will lead to employment and innovation growth and bolster the transatlantic economic partnership. These collaborations not only advance the transatlantic alliance but also pave a path to tackling the world's most pressing challenges. America and Europe, by leveraging the right opportunities, can greatly influence future international relations by creating a globally secure, sustainable, and prosperous realm.

Methodological approach to the analysis

With the intention of uncovering the complexities underlying transatlantic relations, a detailed and systematic approach is proposed. This analysis will use interdisciplinary methods combining international relations, political economy, history, and diplomacy. It seeks to capture the multifaceted nature of relations such as geopolitical, economic, and sociocultural issues that are integrated within transatlantic relations.

The analysis revolves around the collection and analysis of various primary sources, including, but not limited to, official speeches, policy statements, and diplomatic letters to explain and reconstruct the attitudes and motives of relevant actors on both sides of the Atlantic. Academic publications, reports from think tanks, and articles from the press constitute the secondary sources that will offer alternative viewpoints and critiques regarding the changes in the relations.

From a historical perspective, the evolution of transatlantic ties will be analysed considering challenges, achievements and turning points to understand contemporary dynamics. This transcends the past and considers historical context. This contextualisation serves as a foundation for understanding the complexities and nuances that transatlantic relations entail such as conflicts and diplomacy. Adopting a comparative analysis approach allows for the juxtaposition of the policies, strategies and priorities of the United States and the European Union, delineating points of convergence and divergence. The analysis aims to identify patterns, trends, and prospective areas of enhanced collaboration or conflict by following these parallel trajectories. A mixed methodological approach utilising both qualitative and quantitative assessments through case studies, statistical data, and other empirical evidence will be put forth to frame the arguments being presented. This blend of qualitative and quantitative methods enables a thorough exploration of all the factors that shape and influence transatlantic relations.

A prospective analysis approach will be applied along with scenario planning for foresight in trajectories and challenges transatlantic relations may face in the future. This approach sheds light on navigating through this era of transatlantic relations while offering insights to policymakers, diplomats, and scholars.

As we identified previously, the methodological approach integrates multidimensional reasoning with great depth concerning the relations between the United States and the European Union, including the rest of the world, thereby showcasing its profound understanding of international relations.

In subsequent chapters, this essay will focus on the study of Transatlantic relations from different perspectives. The allies who became strategic partners will be examined through essential historical milestones, and the framework will be laid from history to contemporary dynamics: Post 9/11 counter-terrorism efforts will be analysed from the lens of examining the cooperation – the shared security challenge's multifaceted dimensions. The impact of the 2008 financial crisis will be analysed for understanding the intricacies of economic interdependence between Euros and the United States. We will also analyse the U.S. engagement diplomacy from various angles – from Obama's Smart Power Multilateralism to Trump's Unilateral America First Policies.

While evaluating the impact of the Biden administration's attempts to rebuild infrastructure in the context of the West's growing nationalism and populism, we will simultaneously explore Transatlantic Relations. This includes their economic cooperation and competition, trade and investment policy, as well as the strategic autonomy of the EU. We will study the opposing policies of data privacy, confidentiality, taxation, and regulation, considering the geopolitical challenges from the deepening rivalry of China as well as the strengthening climate agenda for transatlantic relations.

The role of NATO as part of security concerns, changing domestic politics, and its scepticism towards globalisation, along with a host of other factors have to be considered, in addition to future projections on how to navigate an uncertain global order. Ultimately, the intricacies of US-EU relations under shifting geopolitical conditions will be deciphered through case studies of Ukraine's war and energy conflicts. Readers will grasp the multi-layered transatlantic relations, enabling them to navigate and utilise the tools of the 21st-century global geopolitical arena.

2
Historical Foundations
From allies to strategic partners

The origins of transatlantic collaboration: World War alliances

The genesis of collaboration between Europe and America was the alignment of their relations into a single coherent transatlantic relationship known as 'collaboration' for further unified systemic fighting. Strategic partnerships for military assistance between translocated the resulting links into something new were founded during the world wars. The assistance of the United States in Europe's Wars, both one and two, was a milestone not only for the United States but for the whole united front as Europe saw the prowess of coming together and aiming for the same goal, mutually beneficial partnership looking southward. The development of the League of Nations also gave a reason to further consolidate borders, strengthen ties, and set a new universal established backbone security alliances.

The interwar period is known for having both political changes and economic challenges. However, this was also the time in which efforts to strengthen transatlantic cooperation were renewed. The consolidation of transatlantic ties during the Second World War is also linked to the American entry into the conflict after the Pearl Harbor attack and her

European allies' willingness to join her. In parallel, the Grand Alliance was formed which incorporated the US, UK, and Soviet Union forging new bonds between them and entering into strife with one another, marking a new development of multilateralism. During this time the world began to understand the value of working against common threats. Because of this there was a greater focus on the collective approach to defence, deterrence, and strengthening the international system's structure which served as the foundation for the post-war order. With the termination of the Second World War the devastation of Europe led to a more coordinated effort of rebuilding infrastructure and region, hence the formation of the Marshall Plan. This American initiative sought to restore the economies of European nations and provide political support to curtail communism while at the same time appealing to a sense of shared responsibility and altruism. This economic support along with skilled labour advanced Europe's economy and strengthened transatlantic relations.

These experiences during the two world wars contributed to the development of the principles of collective security, militarising and stabilising the allies, and promoting global cooperation, all of which are vital in international relations today.

The Cold War Period: Group Defence and Retaliatory Strategy

As for the U.S. and Europe, their Cold War relations were marked by an intense competition of ideas and geopolitics. The post World War II period witnessed the rise of the US and Soviet Union as superpowers which gave birth to a divided Europe - the Eastern Bloc and Western Europe. So considering this, the US and European countries needed a strong partnership based on collective defence and deterrence strategies.

Described as one of the most prominent characteristics of the Cold War period, NATO or North Atlantic Treaty organisation was created in 1949. It is a collective alliance specialising in the defence and security of Western democracies. NATO is mainly focused on safeguarding its member countries from possible aggression by the Soviet bloc. The emphasis on the mutual defence treaty principle speaks of the union's readiness and commitment to the confrontation posed by the environment of the Cold War. NATO's deterrent doctrine gives primary importance to the ability to respond to hostile actions decisively, thereby preventing potential adversaries from armed conflict.

The balance of the militarily advanced United States with its European allies and the deployment of troops were the essential parts of the unified defence system. The presence of American soldiers in Europe is an example of the commitment to the regional security and stability via the Marshall Plan and the military assistance programmes. Greater coordination of joint military exercises as well as training enhances the level of preparedness and interoperability, which strengthens the collective will to defend the principles of collective defence.

In an environment of heightened conflicts, the shared pursuit of deterrence has taken different approaches, even to the use of nuclear capabilities. The proliferation of nuclear arms along with the nuclear umbrella supporting NATO countries underlined the need to forcibly maintain peace and prevent hostilities. The doctrine of mutually assured destruction (MAD) rests upon the understanding that the catastrophic consequences of a nuclear strike on any Member State would result in an equally destructive retaliatory response, thereby preventing any considerations of such actions by prospective challengers.

To summarise, Europe and the US bolstered their transatlantic partnership during the Cold War through collective defence and deterrence strategies implemented by the US and its European allies. The long-standing commitment to unity, shared security and aggression containment facilitated the emergence of a strategic partnership for sustained engagement amidst the challenges posed during the Cold War.

Marshall Plan: Assistance and Recovery

The aftermath of World War II created a lot of destruction in Europe's infrastructure and devastated several countries financially. The United States saw the need to provide aid in stabilising Europe's economy, which led to the formation of the Marshall Plan in 1947 which was directed by Secretary of State George C. Marshall. Alongside a name for its plan, the U.S also provided massive loans to European countries so they could recover their economy and also try to reduce the communist influence in different parts of Europe. The U.S. took on the role of a protector by providing these funds with the aim to strengthen European Powers to aid in avoiding conflicts in the future. The Marshall Plan's focal objective was to turn around the post-war economy of Europe. In response to the Plan, European countries actively collaborated to change and improve trade flows between countries.

The effects of the plan were astounding, for it triggered the recovery of Europe and set the basis for enduring transatlantic relations. By promoting economic cooperation and competition, the Marshall policy was a major factor in demolishing the obstacles in the development of relations between America and Europe. The programme did not only achieve its goals, but also served an invaluable purpose from the geopolitical perspective. It was proof of the united front of the Atlantic states, and it strengthened the position of the United States of America as a leader of the world ready to support the economic development and democratisation of its allies. The Marshall Aid Programme exemplifies the devastating effects that planned and controlled cooperation can impose on history, rendering international policies effective. Its significance is still alive today in debates concerning aid development, economic assistance, and the international partnership shedding light on its importance to global relations and diplomacy. The framework during which they were conquered stands as a reminder.

Taxonomic structures: The foundation of both NATO and OECD

Both NATO (North Atlantic Treaty Organisation) and OECD (Organisation for Economic Co-Operation and Development) have institutional frameworks that execute functions as the basis of transatlantic relations as well as inter-state relations. NATO is the original form of collective defence and security in the Euro-Atlantic region. It was created in 1949 when the Soviet Union posed a security threat, but it has since adapted to address wider concerns; currently, these include terrorism, cyber warfare, and hybrid warfare. The sustained commitment to mutual defence, as described in Article 5 of the NATO Treaty, represents the promise made across the Atlantic to face aggression and instability together. Domestic disputes regarding sharing the burden and NATO shifting its strategic focus are attempts to navigate the tension between collective security and collective vulnerability in a politically complex world.

The OECD has always been a forum for fostering economic development, trade liberalisation, and policy coordination among member countries. At first, the organisation focused on aiding with post-war reconstruction and has now expanded to include a variety of policy areas such as taxation, innovation, and even environmental sustainability. Through peer reviews and standard-setting activities, the OECD has helped align regulatory frameworks and fostered the adoption of good governance and economic management practices. The transatlantic dialogue fostered within the OECD has aided in understanding the shared challenges and opportunities that Western democracies face. Together with NATO, the OECD has served as a primary forum for dialogue and decision-making, where the US and Europe closely collaborated on issues of mutual concern. These institutions are strategically important, as their value goes beyond treaties and contracts; they showcase the commitment of both European and American countries to democratic values and form a moral backbone for defending human rights and the rule of law for the transatlantic community. Adapting to changes in the global economy and security situation while safeguarding the fundamental principles of partnership between Europe and America is crucial to sustaining the value of these institutions.

Transatlantic fault line: the conflicts in Vietnam and the Middle East

The Vietnam War and the subsequent conflicts in the Middle East marked a period of significant strain in transatlantic relations. Europe took a separate approach as compared to the Americans which led to opposing views and a rift within the Alliance. The United States' participation in the Vietnam War, especially around the steam, was the genesis of deep fractures within NATO and the United States. Furthermore, tense relations between the US and European partners emerged. While the US was dealing with a containment and intervention framework in Vietnam, the majority of European countries were against the notion, voicing their dissent in public protests and heated political debates simulating popular discontent.

Moreover, the disputes in the Middle East, especially the Arab-Israeli dispute and the Iranian revolution, reflect the differences between the United States and Europe regarding diplomacy, military action, and regional balance of power. The United States' perception of sovereign unilateral operations and their reliance on military action tend to clash with Europe's preference for coordinated diplomacy and conflict resolution. These conflicts not only illustrate the intricate challenge of maintaining transatlantic unity amid divergent approaches to foreign policy, but they have also sparked vigorous discussions centred around cardinal questions of international relations. In spite of all these issues, the transatlantic partners continue to engage in dialogue and to search for compromises to better address global security challenges, which in turn reveals the capacity to manage disagreement.

These experiences triggered reflection and new attempts aimed at resolving differences regarding the roles and responsibilities of both sides within the alliance. The conflict's fallout further strengthened the need for consultation and diplomatic coordination, paying attention to prospects and understanding strategy in a shifting geopolitical context. While the transatlantic community went through these difficult periods, it was clear that formulation of a sustainable partnership required a dialogue that was both open and constructive. Ultimately, the conflict's discord from Vietnam and the Middle East provided insight on transforming the nature of cooperation within the transatlantic framework and highlighted needed reforms towards pursuing shared objectives.

Sharpening Trade Agreements: Policies and Economic Relations

Following the volatile period of the Vietnam conflict and the Middle Eastern wars, the United States and its allies in Europe are experiencing a renewed and deepened level of their relations economically. These factors are largely attributed to the understanding of the mutual interdependence of economies, which is crucial in fostering stability and prosperity across the Atlantic.

In relation to this development, policies and agreements have emerged as important means useful in consolidating the relationship between the US and the EU. The US and EU have made an effort toward different initiatives aimed at reducing trade barriers and increasing cooperation on economic matters. These negotiations were largely aimed at increasing the access of the markets, coordination of the rules and regulations, as well as promoting competition and free trade. The Transatlantic Trade and Investment Partnership (TTIP) is one of the most notable that aimed to establish a free trade area in the world with economic advantages for both parties.

The GATT and WTO were established to address international trading issues within a regulated framework. The US and the EU were both early members, promoting market liberalisation and fair practising policies.

International policies were designed as alliances within the economic diplomacy framework. Innovation alongside entrepreneurship and technological advancements were primary targets of development policies. More recently, the discussion of international trade agreements has focused on intellectual property protection, investment promotion, and e-commerce regulation which emphasises a commitment to enhance the business development environment.

Responses to the global economic crises, including the 1970s oil shocks and the subsequent recessions, highlighted the strength of the transatlantic alliance. Concerted actions to stabilise financial markets, reduce inflation, and enable economic recovery showcased the capacity for collaborative action in times of hardship between the EU and the USA.

As a result of the development of Europe's trade relationships with the United States, the latter has been able to increase the volume of trade with Europe. Systematic policies combined with agreements have advanced trade. This equally strengthens the economic objectives of the two regions and reinforces their relationships.

Cultural and educational exchanges: Building soft power

Educational and cultural exchange programmes have become principal facilitators that enhance the relationships between Europe and the United States. They create understanding of national identities among citizens and help enhance the soft power of countries on an international level.

With the help of these programmes, there is a deep understanding of the United States from the European side and vice versa. Europe is able to gain soft power through these initiatives. Regarding their impact, we can say that the flow of information is not limited to these individuals. These programmes have greatly enhanced the perception in Europe and the United States. Almost everyone is able to understand the value of the arts, technology, and science. They feel the urge to create and help this nation flourish.

Collaborative educational activities and partnered research projects foster the development of skills and knowledge in important areas through mutual collaboration. Artistic exchanges, film festivals, and music festivals serve as examples of cultural outreach programmes that display the marvel of transatlantic creativity. Such programmes not only acknowledge and share common customs and values, but also amplify pluralistic views and narratives to foster appreciation of life's interconnectedness. Programmes focused on language instruction and multicultural training allow individuals to understand and interact in unfamiliar settings with sensitivity and appreciation, qualities essential for global citizenship. Cultural and educational relationships form soft power that increases the strength of transatlantic relations even in times of political strife or differing government policies. They go beyond the formal limits of diplomacy, providing a means for people to build lasting relationships that enhance constructive interactions. In today's world, the impact of cultural and educational relations as tools of soft power will continue rising. Acknowledging the diversity and dynamism of transatlantic societies reinforces their willingness to work towards a peaceful and prosperous global community.

Reunification and transformation: The challenges of the post-Cold War era

The post-World War period is characterised by the shift in focus of transatlantic linkages that accompanied the dynamic restructuring of the global power system following the collapse of the Soviet Union, which was a milestone event in international relations. The profound transformation Europe underwent after the 1990 German reunification, marked by the mobility of fusions in Europe, was for the best. This time also offered its fair share of challenges as the long-held East – West divide was replaced by new geopolitical sobering realities. The dissolution of the Warsaw Pact along with NATO's eastward expansion created security provisioning challenges, while the European Union's integration drive with Central and Eastern European states transformed the political economy of the region.

Throughout all of this, Europe and the United States had to manage a complicated and dynamic global system. With the conclusion of the Cold War, the possibilities of collaboration were more appealing than ever, but the strategic uncertainty it spawned was concerning. The Balkan Wars in the 1990s strained the resolve of the Western powers and highlighted the need for efficient peacekeeping and crisis response capabilities. The collapse of the Eastern bloc brought the former Soviet satellites in Eastern Europe transforming into new democracies that desperately needed assistance with institutional reform and democratic consolidation—including transcending the remnants of the communist framework towards integration with Western Europe.

The transatlantic agenda with its contradictory and bilateral approaches to intervention and nation-building reveals the cross-current tension regarding the expansion of democracy and protection of political stability. The post-Cold War blend of the liberal and realpolitik school of international relations promoted a set of challenges to the international system. Humanitarian interventions in the Balkans and, later, in the Middle East provide some evidence to the complexities of pursuing coherent policies informed by any principles within heavily networked societies.

The evolution of technology and the emergence of the digital era brought disruption and opportunity, transforming the economy and society of transatlantic countries. The development of information and communication technologies (ICT) has enabled more interconnection, but also created cybersecurity and privacy challenges. The growth of non-state actors and transnational risks required strong counter-terrorism and intelligence collaboration among Western allies, demonstrating the persistent post-Cold War security challenges.

In this context, the post-Cold War period advanced as a notable turning period in transatlantic relations. It created a shift through encouraging more active engagement and readiness to change and adopt in a transforming world. The need for the United States and Europe to change their partnership came as an outcome of grappling with new geopolitical changes and the overarching phenomena of globalisation.

Joint undertakings: Technological and Scientific Cooperation

After the Cold War, technological and scientific cooperation between the United States and the European Union has become central to their partnership strategy for both regions. Cooperation in the areas of technology, research, and innovation has not only deepened economic relationships, but has also facilitated advances which are beneficial to both parties and the global community. This collaboration has helped tackle very challenging societal and environmental problems while also gaining competitive advantage internationally.

For the innovation practitioners, joint ventures have led to milestone achievements in other fields including renewable energy, space exploration, information technology, biotechnology, and even beyond. Transatlantic partners have pooled their resources and expertise, which allowed the partners to push the boundaries of scientific knowledge and solve some of the most pressing global issues. These collaborations aided the transfer of best practices and standards toward the consolidation of regulatory frameworks, particularly with regard to the integration of advanced technology into the market.

The exchange of knowledge and resources enhanced the pace of advancements in medicine, environmental monitoring, and the implementation of green technologies. Through initiatives like multinational academic collaborations, joint research programmes, and collaborative projects, the US and the EU used their available human resources to foster innovation and effectively tackle mutual issues.

Collaborative endeavours for space exploration mark the peak of the synergy between the two entities. Their collaboration has yielded new boundaries of knowledge and astonishing missions, scientific discoveries, and other milestones pertaining to human understanding. These include the launching of joint spacecraft and the development of satellite systems for transatlantic partnerships which assist growth in engineering ways for the exploration and observation of space and promote the shared goal of unlocking the universe's mysteries.

Since technological and scientific cooperation remains one of the areas of relations between the US and European Union, it is important for us to leverage this synergy for the common good. To maintain the transatlantic partnership as the world's leader in innovation and progress, sustained investment, open discussions, and strategic alignment need to become the hallmarks of future efforts.

Historical legacy: Ensuring strategic alignment

When we think about the historical legacy of transatlantic relations, it becomes evident that ensuring strategic alignment has been one of the major undertakings of the US and its European partners. The emerging framework of cooperation based on scientific and technological synergies has been created and acts as a strong foundation for the strategic alignment today.

Transatlantic relations have not only emerged recently due to geopolitical factors, but also due to historical cooperative undertakings. The Collective Commitment to Peace, Stability, and Progress, which emerged after World War II, acted as an impetus for forming numerous alliances and partnerships that serve as the backbone for relations today. Collaborative efforts pertaining to space, scientific research, and technological advancements further strengthened the trust shared among nations, showcasing the impact of strategic alignment on history.

The alignment on strategy transcends past and future, requiring an assessment of shared goals against current global challenges. Whether it be the threat of security, economic imbalance, climate change, or fostering resilience, the commitment acts as a compass for policy alignment. Moreover, the commitment acts as a binding force alongside the transatlantic legacy that ensures respect for democratic ideals and the promotion of human rights, underscoring the strengthened partnership.

The impact of a historical legacy cannot be overlooked while managing times of divergence or discord. Even in circumstances of disagreement or changing focus, the integrated historical legacy serves as a backbone or anchor resource acting towards convergence and cooperation. The lessons which other people have attempted to use in the past through collective actions give these decisions a strong reservoir of wisdom.

For the future, the increasingly complex realities of the world warrant the requirement to revisit and remember the civilisational history as a source of inspiration and resilience. Understanding and appreciating the impact of joint avails in science and technology helps harness the profound historical legacy to align purposes for resisting emerging geopolitical and technological disruptions. Accepting this legacy inspires future generations, creating a foundation for mutual understanding, solidarity, strategic alignment.

3

Post-9/11 Dynamics: United in Counterterrorism Efforts

United in the fight against terrorism

Understanding the Post September 11 World

The attacks on September 11, 2001, remain one of the global defining events, marking a significant shift in the world's affairs, international relations as well as the geopolitical order. Attacks on the United States marked a new period of vigilance across the whole world. The impact of 9/11 was not only felt in America, but also across the globe in the systems of states, their unions and international organisations. This unfortunate event marked a new period of alert for various nations globally. There was a complete change in the way security was viewed as a concept because there was a shift from defending a nation in a physical sense, borders, and land to a more intricate issue based on terrorism which was more abstract. The entire landscape of policies, systems, and strategies of the nations had to rapidly evolve to adapt to the unconventional threats posed by terrorism.

These attempts are done post 9/11 era and try to explain the complexities around power, national interests, and collective action, in the framework of counter-terrorism and terrorism. The central question of this book is to comprehend how the changes taking place to the political structure marked by 9/11 is affecting the system of alliances and rivalries as well as the nature of inter-state relations in the modern: post-9/11 world. Through constructivism, this chapter explores the intersection of statecraft, diplomacy, and security to understand the dramatic changes that redefined the world order after September 11. As a result, in the environment of risks and uncertainties, states are forced to slide through the landscape riddled with moral and ethical dilemmas. All along, such factors prompted systematic structural changes in how diplomacy, military partnerships, intelligence cooperation, and legislative arms are woven together in defence of collective security. Sooner or later however, this collective architecture of security, dominates the way states engage with each other post 9/11. Essentially, the span period post September 11 acts as a lesson on how a single event with such profound shocks can reshape global relations for a very long time.

Responses and Reactions: Global shockwave

The aftermath of the 9/11 attacks threw the world into an extraordinary state of panic. The terrorist assault on the United States sparked a worldwide awareness to bolster their defences against evolving terrorism. The world was caught up in the chaos: governments, defence organisations and civilians tried to come to terms with the reality and scale of damage inflicted on global security. The shockwaves of the attacks were felt all over the globe, with media coverage and international discourse surging to alarming levels. Policymakers, military personnel, and intelligence bodies were placed on high alert and worked around the clock to develop a comprehensive assessment and plan of action. Along with the trauma brought upon citizens of Western countries, the attacks claimed thousands of lives which surfaced an outpouring of grief from everyone. The urgency of the matter emphasised the susceptibility of national and international security systems, therefore, there was an immediate overhaul of counter-terrorism policies and defence strategies.

The attacks served as an impetus for a shift in the mindset of the global community regarding the problem and threat of terrorism, as well as the need for international collaboration and greater sharing of intelligence. The shockwaves of 11 September also highlighted the necessity of a global multilateral response to the problem of terrorism since it was evident that no one nation could single-handedly fight the menace of extremism. The impact of the attacks internationally provoked a reconsideration of diplomatic relations, alliances, as well as domestic and international law due to the need for countries to recalibrate their policies and commitments to deal with the emerging realities of asymmetric warfare and non-state actors. This period of global shock, turmoil, and change provided the impetus for a profound adjustment of collective security needs, which defined the later development of counter-terrorism strategies at both national and international levels.

The development of counter-terrorism strategies

Following the initial reactions to the global shock of terrorism on 11 September, nations were left with the multi-faceted and urgent task of devising coherent counter-terrorism strategies. These strategies include a broad spectrum of actions related to the identification, deterrence, and response to terrorist threats, all within the framework of fundamental human rights and international law.

Counter-terrorism strategies focus on adapting to new potential threats from different sinister origins that require prompt actions to be taken. The need for intelligence services to collect and analyse enormous amounts of data to neutralise threats before they emerge is vividly essential in this case. When terrorists changed their strategies towards cross-border operations, enhanced sharing and collaboration between countries' intelligence services became pivotal towards a united global defence.

Equally, normalisation of relations between law enforcement, the armed forces, and security agencies also came into focus. These collaborations led to increased strengthening of the national response to foster resilience. Some of those measures include protecting critical national assets, reinforcing borders, and refining techniques for crisis management. The enactment of proper legal policies aimed at prosecuting those labelled as terrorists and dismantling their networks became pivotal.

Another equally important part of counter-terrorism strategies is to address the terrorism and extremist violent narratives. Various government and civil society organisations have sought to stem the tide of radicalisation and extremism through education and outreach programmes, as well as by fostering tolerant and inclusive societies. These programmes aimed at changing these societies have focused on reducing the number of terrorists by increasing the number of people who actively defend against terrorists' recruitment and indoctrination drives.

International diplomacy has also been crucial in the evolution of effective counter-terrorism strategies. There has been collaboration among these countries where sanctions have been placed, the illegal trafficking of funds used to finance terrorism has been cut off, and there are multilateral arrangements to deal with state-sponsored terrorism. Simultaneously, diplomatic efforts have been directed towards resolving the violent extremism defining conflicts and grievances in order to foster a more stable world that is less prone to terrorist activities.

The development of counter-terrorism strategies is a complex issue concentrating on one single area demanding a high degree of attention and creativity from many different people. There has to be an enduring change to the terrorism picture at hand and there needs to be a change of aggression to new dangers and modifying places without change in fundamental values that democratic societies are grounded on.

Definition and the Purpose of Intelligence Sharing in Counter-Terrorism

To effectively counter terrorism, intelligence sharing and collaboration have emerged as key components on a global scale. The need for cross-border cooperation in intelligence sharing came into sharp focus after the September 11, 2001 attacks. We analyse the aspects of intelligence sharing and collaboration with regard to the challenges, successes, and importance of these endeavours.

In simple terms, this is the sharing of classified information, including threat assessments, the identity of suspects, and even potential plans for attacks by allied countries and international organisations. Such cooperation enables security agencies to gather critical information concerning multinational terrorist groups and their activities, thus allowing for the initiation of steps to avert their operations. Intelligence is used to enhance the understanding of the situation and improve the likelihood of encountering terrorist attacks before they happen or are in the process of being executed.

Nonetheless, the practice of sharing intelligence has underlying challenges and problems that practitioners need to navigate. One of the most prominent problems is balancing varying national interests, jurisdictional legal systems, and the nature of intelligence "sensitivity" grey areas. Issues of safeguarding intelligence information frequently add an extra layer of complexity to the sharing process, which involves strict protocols and information protection measures.

Multilateral collaboration enables effective intelligence sharing alongside law enforcement and diplomatic channels. Agreements of an international nature, along with mutual assistance pacts, substantially provide the terms of cooperation and delineate the pathways for trustable sharing of information. The existence of joint task forces and liaison officers in foreign territories facilitates real-time information exchange and coordination of joint operational planning, which enhances the collective effort against terrorism.

The advent of data analysis, as well as digital communication technologies, aids in the rapid dissemination of information and synthesis, making real-time information sharing easier. With the help of advanced software tools and other databases, analysts are able to identify patterns, analyse trends, and link unrelated pieces of information, thereby increasing the collaborative power of intelligence efforts.

The scope of intelligence sharing goes beyond government to include private sector partners like banks, technology firms, and research universities. These partnerships deepen the understanding of the financial and digital activities of terrorist organisations and consequently help in curtailing their funding and propaganda activities online.

To sum up, sharing and colluding intelligence are crucial components in the battle against terror on the global stage. Balancing trustful relationships with the intricacies of international data sharing alongside modern technological innovation can allow countries to reinforce their coordination in forecasting, intercepting, and dismantling terrorist activities, reinforcing the need for enduring collaborative efforts towards the protection of international peace.

Legislative techniques: Issuing security policies

After 11 September 2001, most countries had to tackle the problem of enhancing their security policies and legislative systems to deal with the ongoing threat of terrorism. Their response contains several components designed to strengthen the protection of the country's national security, and at the same time preserve as much as possible the individual rights and freedoms of citizens. We are particularly concerned with the multitude of legislative responses in other countries, with particular emphasis on the enforcement of the US Patriot Act, which has provided law enforcement and intelligence agencies with the means to monitor and surveil civilians at great length in order to avert a perceived threat of terrorism. The emergence of specialised counter-terrorism branches in police and judicial structures, equipped with advanced legal and investigative technologies, marked a decisive shift in the legislative approach to terrorism. These policies sought to adequately allow law enforcement officials to take all necessary steps for dealing with terrorism while balancing compliance with constitutional guarantees of personal freedom.

Transnational terrorism has become rampant with the newest advances in technology. Constructive fencing and detection measures that attempt to pirate or control passive access over flight paths open waterways, strengthen constructed borders to cut off flows, and attempts to outsmart new technologies. Governance alternatives within pillars of terrorism-sponsored polygons provide frameworks influenced by non-state actors. Individual crimes or terror acts that are local in nature can incorporate and fuel into a larger conflict ultimately dependent on a state or a group that completes to tear down the existing map. Over time, learning entities have been bound with non-governmental transnational open border associations. In contrast with static approaches, the rise of abusive practices posited by regional social contexts has complicated the removal of the strengthened welfare of the most arbitrary sponsor-deficient intersection of state schemes. Collaboration of institutions has strengthened the legal cross-border fluidity of sponsor-maintained changes accompanying treaty motions on restorative forces. The region has opened states to the use of beggars.

Military alliances and counter-terrorism operations

The 11 September 2001 attacks reshaped the world for many countries as they shared a common goal of fighting terrorism. The formation of military alliances has greatly aided the joint efforts towards combating the activities of terrorist groups and dismantling their networks. For instance, NATO unprecedentedly employed Article 5 for mutual defence and solidarity after the attacks on America, thus showcasing its collective commitment to mutual defence. This invocation enabled member states to undertake joint military actions aimed at defeating the terrorist threat.

The establishment of coalition forces such as the International Security Assistance Force (ISAF) in Afghanistan illustrates a greater global effort toward fighting terrorism. Composed of soldiers from various countries, ISAF sought to stabilise Afghanistan and dismantle terrorist strongholds. Equally, the global war on terror has witnessed the establishment of several partnerships which demonstrates increased willingness to confront extremist violence and prevent further inhumane acts of violence.

In addition to traditional military actions, special forces and intelligence agencies have worked across borders to pinpoint and deal with high-value targets, counter insurgent activities, and gather critical information. The implementation of advanced technological capabilities facilitates greater emphasis on precise strikes with lesser collateral damage.

Terrorist groups often take advantage of no-man's lands and cross-border safe havens to carry out, and later escape, violent acts. In response, military coalitions have put into action strategies that include air and ground assaults, covert intelligence operations, and local force empowerment programmes, which focus on building the capabilities of local security forces. The formulation of counterinsurgency doctrines aimed at winning over civilian populations and rolling back extremist narratives while restoring order in severely conflict-ravaged areas.

Meeting the challenges posed by asymmetric warfare requires flexible approaches and strategies that integrate military action with diplomacy, economy, and development. The ever-changing nature of terror threats calls for more creativity and flexibility in military operations, such as the training and equipping of allied nations with robust counter-terrorism capabilities.

Although military action has been integral in curbing the activities of terrorists and shattering their operational systems, the geopolitical nuances, as well as the consequences of these moves, require continuous evaluation and adjustment. The balance of international humanitarian law and human rights will always take precedence in counter terrorism efforts, and by extending analysis factors of counter-terrorism dynamics after the 9/11 attacks, we can assess how military coalitions and counter-terror operations altered the international balance of power.

Civil liberties with security

The aftermath of 9/11 triggered a newfound concern for governments and societies across the globe; the delicate balance of preserving civil liberties while ensuring national security. In most cases, the focus of counter-terrorism shifts towards counter measures, which raises the questions of the level of control a government can have under the guise of protecting its citizens. There is a growing struggle to address terrorist threats while seeking to maintain democracy and the rule of law, blurring the lines of governance in many countries.

The discussion regarding finding the balance between security and civil liberties has used as a basis controversial matters such as surveillance, detention policies, and the use of force in the war on terrorism. Government agencies have balancing issues in collecting intelligence and preventing further attacks without infringing fundamental rights such as privacy, freedom of expression, and the right to a fair trial. With advances in technology, the possibility of mass tracking and data collection became available which brings forward the concern of erosion of the right to privacy and the misuse of information with the guise of national security.

Counter-terrorism strategies have frequently clashed with how legal and ethical lines are drawn treating suspects, enemy combatants, and the conduct of military and intelligence operations. For instance, disputes have emerged with the application of enhanced interrogation techniques, the existence of covert prisons, and preemptive strikes in the assassination of suspected perpetrators, which lead to fundamental legal and ethical questions about 'what level of violence is justifiable in achieving security?'

The security of citizens and preserving the freedoms integral to democracy create a delicate balance, which also poses a conflict that is vigorously debated. The examination of this balance is contested publicly and legally, resulting in historical decisions made by courts and reforms that seek to check the balance of power. Such power is bound to be abused when implemented through national security measures.

Moreover, as socio-political shifts take place, discriminatory profiling and the risk of alienation stemming from strict security governance prompt debates on social integration, pluralism, marginalised groups, backlashes from extremism, and the impact of terrorism. Many of these complex implications put extreme focus on how deeply rooted bias and stigma ensue. In addressing these issues, the discourse turns to the need for inclusive policy devoid of domination that fosters discrimination within marginalised communities.

These intricate issues pose an existential challenge for governments, compelling them to showcase the ability to absorb shocks and remain democracies that protect freedoms and individual rights in the long term. The current discussions regarding the controversy of security and civil liberties outline the complex problems associated with countering terrorism while still upholding fundamental principles of liberal democracy.

Building coalitions as a form of diplomatic initiative

The need for coordinated global action against terrorism sharpened after the September 11 attacks in 2001. Diplomacy has proven to be essential towards gaining worldwide support and facilitating relations between countries. However, coalition building has emerged as one of the most important approaches to increase the range and scale of counter-terrorism operations by harnessing the abilities and resources of various stakeholders. It is necessary to examine the wide-ranging diplomatic initiatives to build coalitions in order to fight terrorism. Diplomacy has sought to bring nations together as they face diverse political, cultural, and historical differences. Closing gaps in focus and priorities was also needed as it became clear that tackling terrorism required a united effort on a global scale.

The United Nations, NATO, and other regional organisations serve as multilateral forums that facilitate dialogue, coordination, and consensus-building. In these forums, states negotiate, engage in joint planning, and pool their skills and resources. Beyond formal institutions, there exists diplomacy through both unilateral and multilateral means at various tiers, including summits, working groups, and technical interchanges. Trust fostering, intelligence sharing, and mutual aid promotion are some objectives of this diplomacy.

The formation of coalitions required not only synchronising military and policing activities, but also tackling the elements enabling extremism. This meant working with the concerned communities to promote diverse ways of addressing grievances to avert radicalisation. Such diplomatic efforts aimed at garnering the support of non-state actors such as civil society organisations, religious figures, and business people, who are equally important in combating the narratives of hate and intolerance. Building these coalitions demanded continuous diplomacy, flexibility, and relentless resolve in dealing with the permanently shifting geopolitical priorities. With the emergence and evolution of new terrorist challenges, the underpinning diplomacy needed to be agile, anticipatory, and nimble. At the same time, however, some enduring problems remained, including differing national priorities, asymmetric resource distribution, and clashes over strategic goals. Those intricate relationships forming the alliances came with the need for navigation, bargaining, and the most important blend of many perspectives. Working around the clock, these diplomats laid the groundwork for enduring relationships, trust, and partnership built around shared values of upholding international peace and security. The effectiveness of coalition-forming strategies concerning terrorism relied greatly on the ability to galvanise collective action, foster trust, and exhibit unity against a common threat. This illustrates the role of diplomacy in shaping strong and flexible coalitions and underscores the need for collaboration in addressing multifaceted challenges.

Media and Social Perception

After the terrorist attacks on September 11, 2001, social perception and the media heavily influenced public discourse around the counter-terrorism narrative. The media portrayal of the global 'war on terror' has contributed to the complex and often ambiguous narrative surrounding it. Essentially, the media has played the role of a mediator, filtering information, ideologies, and policies from the benched audience to the wider public.

One of the principal reasons the media has had a great impact on society was how the threat of terrorism was portrayed. The graphic images and live broadcasting of terror attacks created fear and anxiety in people's collective memory, reinforcing an impression of helplessness and the need for action. In turn, people began to rally in favour of initiatives put forth by the government to fight terrorism, including military action and stricter security policies, which were adopted with little consideration.

Beyond the journalism of the day, there were also other features of the media that helped the public form an image of the nation on a global level. People began to shift their views on the policies of the state as a result of editorials, opinions, as well as political talk shows on television. The portrayal of some actors as enemies heavily shaped the public discourse and social cohesion in a way that raised national identity and rallied citizens to enhance patriotism.

The level of public trust in a government institution was greatly affected by the way counter-terrorism operations and policies were communicated. The information given needs to be transparent and accountable to prevent the spread of unsupported narratives while upholding democratic principles and values. Furthermore, the media's attention on the actions of the government has been crucial in holding the government accountable, as well as safeguarding civil liberties while pursuing security objectives.

With the advancement of social media, the relationship between media and public perception has intensified. The dissemination of information at the click of a button from various opposing views presents an opportunity but also obstacles in the development of public perception. The rise of extremist views, propaganda, and misinformation creates an argument for accurate and responsible journalism and critical media literacy in the public sphere to help the public make informed decisions.

Evaluating how the public perceives information as well as how the media shapes narratives reveals how the public is post 9/11. Thus, it becomes apparent how crucial it is for the public to be educated enough in dealing with modern security risks. For cohesive cooperation among nations and addressing common issues, there needs to be a multifaceted approach regarding how the media portrays events and how the public feels about policies introduced.

Evaluating success and lessons learned

The global attempts at curtailing terrorism following 9/11 put into scrutiny how effective these actions were. First and foremost, there is a need to evaluate the effectiveness of counter-terrorism efforts made by the US and allies. It would mean looking closely at isolating terrorist groups from the potential to mount attacks and general activities tagged as terrorism. Understanding the laws passed during the period is also vital for appreciating the steps that were taken to fortify national security and civil liberties. Equally important is how these policies provided a concrete approach towards integrating security and fundamental rights.

Studying the history of military partnerships and activities executed in the context of the so-called "war on terrorism" can shed light on the collective efforts and operational capacity of allied forces. There is a need to study the collaboration of different military structures and their joint activities towards reaching common goals. It is also important to examine the coalition-building diplomacy coalitions and their efforts against the global menace of terrorism. Within this framework, the analysis will emphasise the significance of diplomacy in fostering international collaboration against terrorism.

In measuring effectiveness, it is necessary to analyse public opinion and the role of the press in the context of counter-terrorism. Examining the influence of public opinion and media portrayals of counter-terrorism strategy and policies adds another dimension to understanding the impact these initiatives have on society. This analysis should capture the level of trust that the public has in the government, as well as the media's portrayal of counter-terrorism policy in relation to public accountability and transparency.

As much as documenting milestones is important, it is equally crucial to capture the lessons learned in this timeframe. This includes assessing deficiencies, operational difficulties, and areas that require additional focus. By observing these lessons, future strategies can be better tailored and formulated, thereby enhancing the response to lapses in dealing with evolving threats. To withstand contemporary as well as future security challenges and build resilience and agility, learning from mistakes and past experiences is essential.

Taking into account the counter-terrorism strategies employed after 9/11, analysing and evaluating the accomplishments alongside the lessons learned assists in understanding the best approaches to guide future strategies and policies. These policies and strategies can then inform governments and security personnel on how to tackle the complexities posed by modern-day security threats and enable them to construct better responses. This evaluation enables informed and timely decisions to protect both national and global security in an evolving geopolitical environment while proactively adjusting to the situations at hand.

4

The 2008 Financial Crisis
Economic Interdependence Revealed

Summary of the Crisis

The seismic shock of the global financial collapse in 2008 marked a notable moment in economic history, shaking the world's most advanced economies while simultaneously illustrating the tightly interwoven web of the international financial system. To understand this crisis's impact on transatlantic relations, international finance, and the rest of the world, one must follow the chain of events that led to it and its profound consequences. It can be attributed to a culmination of different factors, from an economic recession to the housing bubble and growing credit too readily accessible, to the chaos that ensued. In the years leading to the crisis, a combination of aggressive and reckless mortgage lending practices coupled with a sharp rise in mortgage financing in America created a sense of sustained optimism characteristic of an economic boom in the US housing market. The volatility of the housing market increased because reckless speculation drove up property prices, bankrupted financially strained institutions dependent on mortgage-backed securities, and heightened the risk to financial institutions that were heavily invested. In addition, risk exposure in global financial markets was made worse by the invention of complex financial instruments and derivatives. The backdrop of heightened tensions and concern due to the prevailing environment was welcoming of systemic shocks.

The collapse of the housing bubble caused defaults on mortgages to ripple through the economy. This resulted in a major loss of investor confidence and increased financial turmoil cutting across all levels of the economy. The collapse of asset prices and widespread foreclosures brought to light the vulnerability of supposedly advanced and self-sufficient financial systems and made clear the degree to which those systems depended on each other. The interrelationship between these factors is precisely what we are trying to explain disentangling the story behind one of the most devastating financial downturns of the modern era.

Origins of the crisis: housing bubble and credit expansion

Several factors contributed to the 2008 financial crisis, but the housing bubble, along with credit expansion, are the two primary factors that drove the crisis. The housing bubble, a speculative fueled rapid escalation of property prices during the early 2000s, posed a threat to the real-estate market from the demand side. Low stubborn housing demand, coupled with subprime mortgages, propelled speculations within financial markets as well. Moreover, mortgage lenders provided housing loans to people with poor credit scores and of unsteady employment, which fuelled the real estate price inflation even further. Also, the issuance of sophisticated banking instruments, such as securities backed by mortgages and collateralised obligations of debt, made the extension of credit easier than before. These complex vehicles exacerbated the interconnectedness of the financial system by increasing default risk and deepening systemic crises.

These instruments' associated diversification benefits led to enhanced investor participation in further mortgage-backed assets. These dynamics resulted in an environment with leverage and exposure being fundamentally unsustainable. Claiming that property prices would perpetually appreciate led to an illusion of security overwhelmingly favouring abdication of a risk management discipline. Consequently, market participants operated under the expectation that any possible slowdown would be counterbalanced by incessant value appreciation of the assets. However, this assumption, as is commonly known, turned out to be overshooting the mark, as the US housing market had to, at some stage, collapse on its self-inflicted weaknesses that set off a chain reaction across the entire globe's financial system. The underpinning implications of the property bubble and the credit expansion highlight how the 2008 financial crisis scenario was constructed as an intersection of reckless exuberance and creative finance without proper analysis of risk control measures.

Inadequate Risk Management and Regulatory Frameworks

The transatlantic region's risk management measures and regulatory policies in place prior to the 2008 financial crisis were all deeply flawed. The decade preceding the crisis was characterised by a lack of regulation on the part of financial institutions who, for example, partook in mark-to-market accounting practices well out of the view of regulatory authorities, engaging in derivative trading, stock buyback, and share sales without due diligence. The absence of sufficient market oversight led to perilous lending strategies and the uncontrolled growth of the derivatives market, which considerably weakened the international financial ecosystem. The underlying risk management structures in place at these institutions only made things worse. The risk models developed by banking and financial services were fundamentally incapable of estimating the maximum possible economic loss that could be accrued during a recession, and as a result always undercalibrated systemic risks. Relying heavily on credit rating agencies' evaluations led to the fundamental miscalculation of risk and market vulnerability. Forget about the viability of particular financial institutions—their failure on a broader, systemic scale becomes impossible to ignore. The vulnerable state of the world's financial systems makes their interdependence all the more potent.

The links between banks, securities, and other financial institutions in different regions of the world intensified the negative effects of shocks, accentuating the impact and severity of the crisis. Cross-border financial activities demonstrated the gaps existing in the national regulatory mechanisms when confronted with complex modern finance, creating the need for a coordinated solution aimed at restoring order. The crisis aftermath stimulated a rethink of the approach taken towards regulation and supervision and, in general, increased the focus on strengthening transparency, accountability, and risk control in the financial system. Reforms of the financial regulation included the introduction of more stringent capital requirements, improved standards for liquidity, as well as greater secrecy and control over transactions involving derivatives. These measures were implemented through cooperation between the United States and the European Union aimed at aligning the regulations to reduce regulatory arbitrage and diminish gaps in cross-border supervision. Despite the regulatory changes made to improve the resilience of the financial systems, adapting to rapidly changing financial innovations and emerging systemic risks remain challenges. The need to protect from crises while sustaining long-term economic development in the transatlantic region highlights the need for flexible and effective regulatory policies.

Effect on the primary transatlantic economies

The financial crises in Europe in 2008 profoundly altered the primary transatlantic economies. It began a new era of uncertainty for Europe and the United States with the integration of their financial systems, as countries became more connected. Economically desperate nations such as Greece and an intricate network of ailing banks were difficult in Phase 1 and 2. Allogenic with the American economy to the point their interdependence merged geographical borders posed serious risks to their economic stability. The drying up of various financial fluids post the economic crisis became detrimental to Phase 4 or transatlantic growth. At the epicentre of the faulty bubble, the economy propelled growth by deeply encouraging spending through credit expansion and sub-prime loans secured by inflated property, with devastating repercussions on the lending and housing markets. The Fed induced consumption by reducing interest rates which led to home construction, pushing spending through a multivariate shifts matrix of diverse productive systems policy tools that induced growth across the Pacific, coming with heavy costs. The loss increases started in late 2007 to rise at an annual rate of 12%, adding fuel to the fire of the economy's collapse globally, sending shockwaves resulting in mass losses federally with a violent impact on worlds interconnected through shared borders. This drove blocks of constructively American integration to collapse globally at a rotating pace. This increased unemployment transatlantically, leading to American automation and began European dependencies in turmoil serviced off inflation, which became a desperate realm. The euro disintegrated post warrant. Extremely sophisticated multinational aid further combined to increase spending markets imbalance, as predicted by decreases in taxes. The paradigm shift towards the other collapse sheds light on a Europe of two rapidly hyperactive inter-trans predominantly networked finances intensely driven by unrestrained convergence at the core while a plethora of fed interventions stimulated the entire Pacific with amicable redirection of euro financial flows. The contracting progress accumulated as loans, central competitiveness, and withdraws shed commiserate scaling by sustaining equities under comprehensive go-arounds shaking the gulf. Euro boosts have in turn steadily imploded the supply inter-consumption enormously as advanced systems faced hyperinertia. Scope was awarded on orienting the trend triggered by technocratic infused set expansionists remaining on the graph as the value shed declining originated in America.

The impact of the 2008 shocks, with inflation and European unemployment rates inversely driven by greedy retrenchment, are directly reflected in the reports allied with international depths colliding reserves disassociated from the single global bottom formed system across Europe, which seemed set to sink the region. Power per capita integrated most while everlasting welfare across borders posed available sales collapse expectations, disrupting cooperation over borders with devalued bailouts atomising stares across totals. The shift significantly allied with dysfunctional inflation resulted in a euro demand collapse, parasitic on global financial transformation and non-responsive results of the American cooperative alliance, reflecting their flow in interconnected output free quantity credit decreases, utilising gears on logistical integrated financing bound by the crisis of dejected basarmed bull shifts.

The parallel is seen in panning interconnected staggering emerging reliance that underwent surge pooling investments, fundamentally anchoring the euro while spending continued to decline to an extent that propelled intensified support to transformation of the European system. Steady exports and intricate technological enhancements net spiralling Europe drastically decrease the drain on core without sustaining collapse of hyper ratios, with fluid stagnation shedding transgressively across a universal void. Mapping enhanced complete capitalist combats results in acute divisions instead of producing seamless modern controls along borderless structures, with the export defaults of the continent acting as deep proactive systems unintegrated rapidly.

Likewise, the economic turbulence throughout Europe cascaded into the United States, jeopardising the financial stability of American institutions deeply intertwined with European debt. As the crisis deepened, policymakers on both sides of the ocean had to deal with the chaotic tangle of dependencies, looking for cooperative ways to equilibrate the market, restore dormant investor sentiment, and minimise damage to economic activity. This underscores the robust and acute reality of the interplay of economies within and beyond Europe and the United States, as leaders were compelled to adopt cooperative frameworks to contain the dynamics of financial turbulence and coordinate unified policy action. With the help of combined efforts, the transatlantic economies endured the turbulence but the consequences of the crisis remained, altering the economic relations and reinforcing the need to address mutual economic vulnerabilities.

From bank rescues to coordinated policy responses: Recovery plans after the bailouts

Following the 2008 financial crisis, the largest transatlantic economies were in a hurry to create coordinated policies to address the strained financial systems of their economies and set a path for economic growth. This is the context in which it is useful to evaluate the countermeasures and put into practice the provisions constituted by government and central banks - from the financial bailouts of troubled banks to the implementation of broad-based stimulus programmes aimed at rebuilding demand and confidence in the economy and its markets.

One of the immediate challenges for policymakers was avoiding a total meltdown of the banking system. Governments on both sides of the Atlantic poured enormous amounts of taxpayer money into failing banks, effectively nationalising some and providing liquidity to others. The controversial nature of these bailouts sparked debates on moral hazard and state intervention in free market economies.

Simultaneously, monetary authorities took extraordinary steps to liberally provide access to credit and liquidity required by the system, while easing stress levels. Central banks embarked on quantitative easing programmes, widening their balance sheets by acquiring government bonds and mortgage securities. These audacious steps were intended to stimulate credit availability and lower borrowing rates for firms and households.

Concurrently, fiscal policymakers initiated aggressive stimulus spending by directing money towards infrastructure, tax relief, and welfare spending. The goal was threefold: generate new employment to encourage consumer spending and provide relief to industries worst impacted by the recession. The magnitude of these measures underscored the intensity of the crisis, as these sought to curtail stagnation in economic activity.

But, the impact of these policies is still being evaluated. Some contend that the bailouts and stimulus policies exacerbate moral hazard and do little to mitigate the system's foundational weaknesses. Others counter that the action was crucial to avoiding a more severe and prolonged recession, and that this experience should shape future policy frameworks.

The collaboration between the United States and the European Union, while having shared interests and goals, faced challenges because of divergent institutional frameworks and political factors. Still, the experience during this crisis has created a debate on the necessity to enhance international collaboration for regulating and developing strategies for dealing with systemic dangers in global finance.

The function of global monetary institutions

The global financial institutions like the International Monetary Fund (IMF) and the World Bank have provided necessary guidance and management in the aftermath of the 2008 financial crisis. These institutions served as chief conduits of funds, information, and guidance towards the affected countries, especially those in the transatlantic region. For instance, the IMF opened numerous loan facilities for nations that were experiencing balance of payments problems as well as currency crises. The IMF also collaborated with national governments to develop comprehensive economic reform strategies for the recovery of their economies and rehabilitation of markets.

Also, the World Bank has concentrated on systems of economic recovery stemming from long-term infrastructural projects as well as other development activities targeting the countries that were hit by the crisis. The Bank had, through concessional loans and grants, catalysed positive investment in the critical economic sectors like healthcare, education, and even sustainable energy which also sidestep chronic economic issues of the region.

The international financial institutions enabled multilateral collaboration among countries and global regulatory entities in establishing unified benchmarks for the supervision of finance and the management of associated risks. This included the convergence of prudential conflict resolution regulations, banking supervision frameworks, and transparency protocols aimed at reinforcing the global financial system's stability and integrity. These institutions conducted significant scholarly work and policy research to unmask systemic vulnerabilities and propose strategic solutions to avert systemic risks in the future.

Post-crisis, the evolving international financial institutions' complexities intensified, alongside these institutions being asked to demonstrate greater responsibility to both developed and developing economies. The discourse on the governance and operational frameworks of these institutions has sharpened in response to the reality of the global economy's evolving state and the need for greater inclusivity of addressing voice and participation.

Looking forward, the contribution of international financial institutions regarding the design of a post-crisis financial architecture is very important by utilising per existing and emerging gaps. With the continued economic interdependence of transatlantic economies experiencing new challenges, these institutions are poised to aid in the development of creative policy solutions as well as additional sustainable growth and development strategies while alleviating rising financial vulnerabilities. The adaptability to complex and ever-changing economies and geopolitical realities is important in ensuring the stability as well as the resilience of the transatlantic financial system.

Recovery strategy assessment: which ones work, which ones do not, and why

Following the 2008 crisis, transatlantic economies undertook different strategies to recover, revealing a blend of convergence and divergence in policies used. In the United States, the Obama administration sought to stabilise the financial sector and boost economic growth through a combination of fiscal spending and regulatory reforms in the form of a stimulus package. In Europe, countries simultaneously focused on austerity and structural reform in the context of a sovereign debt crisis, which resulted in a more divergent path to recovery. Detailed analysis of the response strategies of the economies is essential to understanding the implications and creating frameworks for future crisis responses.

One core analytic takeaway is the need for coordinated action alongside coherent cross-border policies. While the United States focused on recovery, Europe was concerned with consolidation, thus underscoring the challenge of integrating diverse national priorities within a single integrated market. In addition, the differing implementation of quantitative easing in the United States versus the more conservative approach by the European Central Bank reflects different views on the effectiveness of monetary policy. Another important facet affects social protection systems and inequalities. The recession has intensified the marginalisation of certain social groups, which has amplified calls for more comprehensive stimulus and social safety net policies aimed at social inclusion. Simultaneously, global economic interdependence has required a reassessment of the approaches to trade and investment. The crisis spurred a shift toward more protectionist policies and bilateral conflicts, leading to confrontations over trade deficits and currency value disputes. It underscored the need to construct more resilient supply chains as well as address the gaps in border-crossing investment flows. Apart from the above, another pointed area of concern was the strength of financial institutions and the recovery's sustainability over time.

With the aid of extensive stress tests and capital infusions, the banking sector in the United States recovered much more rapidly compared to European banks, which underwent prolonged restructuring and deleveraging processes. In the end, the varying patterns of recovery deepened the interdependence of economies across the Atlantic while underlining the need to formulate integrated approaches that consider specific individual country conditions. Transatlantic policy frameworks are better positioned to withstand and anticipate future financial crises by analysing the divergences and recoveries of past financial recoveries, thereby fostering deeper economic cooperation.

Transatlantic Trade and Investment Long-Term Effects

The 2008 financial crisis had a profound and long-lasting impact on transatlantic trade and investment as it transformed the economic structure of the US and Europe. Within the global economy, the disruption of supply chains along with changing consumer behaviour due to recession heavily impacted the finances of various companies. Subsequently, available trade in goods was deeply influenced. The US and the European Union went through variations in their exports and imports, as there was an on-demand shift with manufacturing production adjusting to new market conditions. Additionally, foreign direct investment (FDI) flows, although altered, still showcased resilience. The crisis exposed the US and EU economies' interdependence to a much greater extent than previously known, which necessitated changes in trade and investment policies. In the aftermath of the crisis, the transatlantic partnership struggled but stabilised itself, remaining as the fundamental source of strength in the post-crisis period. Trade negotiations and regulatory compatibility became pivotal to the transatlantic discourse as policymakers shifted their focus to economic relations to mitigate risks. It was concluded that enhancing regulatory frameworks and increasing market transparency would assist in tapping investor confidence while ensuring economic growth. Reviving transatlantic trade partnerships and pursuing more complex new investment strategies is becoming vital for both economies.

The Transatlantic Trade and Investment Partnership (TTIP) and other discussions regarding a bilateral investment policy showcase the efforts made to advance economic relations and engender growth benefits for partners involved. The crisis resulted in the scrutiny of the cross-border transactions and financial services' governance system which led to reforms aimed at bolstering institutional oversight and risk management frameworks. The narrowing of the parent approaches of US and EU regulations was crucial to eliminate regulatory arbitrage and level the competitive landscape for businesses on both sides of the Atlantic Ocean. Advanced initiatives include the alignment of banking policies, capital ratio frameworks, and monitoring of international investment lodges in signatory nations, which denotes an effort towards curtailing systemic risks and strengthening financial equilibrium. After the resurgence of transatlantic trade and investments, the emphasis shifted towards fostering innovation and entrepreneurship in order to encourage inclusive economic growth that is sustainable. Joint activities in new areas like advanced manufacturing, renewables and digital commerce showed active efforts towards economic diversification and progress in technology. A strong and responsive transatlantic market that is adaptable to the shifting global landscape emerged due to the increased focus on investing in infrastructure and digital connectivity projects.

The impact of the 2008 financial crisis on transatlantic trade and investment serves as a reminder of the enduring impact on the resilience of the partnership while at the same time enhancing strategic rebalancing in order to accommodate the 21st century global economy.

Reevaluation of financial governance and regulation

Post the financial crisis of 2008, transatlantic economies required an immediate reevaluation and restructuring of financial governance and regulation. The systemic weaknesses that were exposed with the crisis underscored the need for deep reforms in order to lower the risk of systemic crises in the future.

Policymakers and regulators focused on building frameworks to enhance control over financial systems and mitigate risks. These approaches targeted, in particular, the dampening of the consequences of adverse developments and included compensatory adjustments. Balanced reforms addressing governance and regulation combined with the allocation of appropriate resources have been aimed at sufficient, if not optimal, strategic efficiency.

As a result, transatlantic regulators and policymakers set out to change the landscape of the economy. Among those was the recalibration of capital requirements of financial institutions to bolster their defences against potential shocks. In addition, severely constraining the ability of banks to lend, market-pruned liquidity standards were set forth to restrain market-induced turbulence, thus enhancing system-wide stability.

Reform of regulations did not stop at the banking industry and included important fields like trading in derivatives, consumer protection and the shadow banking system. Regulators have tried to establish confidence and good faith in the financial markets by redefining the rules of understanding intricate financial instruments and tightening the safeguards for consumer protection from abuse. Along with this, there has been an increased alertness and scrutiny toward nonbanking institutions performing functions that are akin to commercial banking, which has helped to address the regulatory voids that led to the crisis.

There is an increase in discussions focusing on whether regulations should be aligned or not, revealing the different positions taken by the US and the European Union. The debate for some level of uniformity gained traction as supporters started citing cross-border trade and global competitiveness as reasons, which led to some proponents advocating for harmonised standards. On the opposite end, some insisted on regulations tailored to different market structures and risk profiles. This debate showed the difficulty of bridging different regulations within a single interrelated and interdependent financial system.

The disruption of traditional regulatory frameworks due to the advancement in technologies and innovations within the fintech sector needs timely action in order to gain the most benefits while reducing risks. The rapid growth of cryptocurrencies, distributed ledger technologies, and algorithmic trading has created additional challenges to the existing regulations within both the European Union and United States. These developments forced regulators into the balancing act of supporting innovation while exercising extensive oversight.

The ongoing transformation, along with the need to create new and enduring structures for resilient governance and dynamic regulation, is foundational for collaboration between the EU and United States. It is important to adopt a fluid, future-facing mindset to effectively manage emerging risks while also fostering policies that encourage strong transatlantic financial integration in the 21st century.

The legacy of the crisis: Future economic interdependence

Understanding the consequences of the 2008 financial crisis, alongside its unprecedented impact on the relationship of economic interdependence between the United States and European Union, has been a significant and challenging task. It becomes more and more evident with passing time that the aftermath of the crisis is multi-dimensional; economists note the more transatlantic partners' splintering is tragic and fuelled by market disorder, regulatory changes add fuel to the fire.

The first key component of the legacy of the crisis encompasses the shifting balance of the power relations within the world financial system. Since the crisis, most emerging economies, particularly in Asia, have seemed to surge in importance within the world economy. This emerging reality adds new forms of competition and economic cooperation, which reconsider the previously held views of transatlantic trade and investment. Another important feature of the legacy of the crisis is the increased focus on risk management and maintaining system stability. The 2008 events stressed the degree to which financial markets across the world are interrelated and how costly system breakdowns are. Therefore, the US and the European Union have sought to enhance regulatory control, build better supervision structures and increase openness to reduce risks.

The crisis legacy has shaped the re-assessment of the trans-Atlantic economic partnership. The alliance's historical bonds and shared values remain crucial; however, their post-crisis reality compels both sides to prioritise different aspects of engagement and strategise to advance economic integration. Adaptation to new patterns of trade, technological shifts, geopolitical factors, and international relations will be essential for stronger economic interdependence moving forward. The paradigm shift on economic policy during the crisis has accelerated with emerging US-EU competitive imperatives in climate change, the digital economy, and demographics. Collaborative measures on sustainable development, innovation, and equitable social policies will be fundamental for the future of transatlantic economic interdependence. To summarise, the operational legacy of the 2008 financial crisis has profoundly influenced the direction of economic interdependence between the US and the EU. While the crisis was a stress test of vulnerabilities and resilience, it catalysed transformative policies that rebalanced the dynamics of transatlantic relations. Both partners need to be responsive, creative, and cooperate to address the challenges of an interconnected economy and unified global imperatives.

5
Obama's Diplomacy
Multilateralism and Smart Power

The idea of smart power: Its meaning and context

Smart power is gaining attention as a means of understanding and managing world affairs by combining both hard and soft approaches to international relations influence. The concept of "smart power," put forth by political scientists Joseph S. Nye Jr. and Richard Armitage, understands that modern challenges require more than the application of military force. It rather seeks to advance using diplomacy, culture, values, and military power. This approach attempts to accomplish strategic objectives through violence, but not without prior attempts to build alliances and foster dialogue. It seeks to navigate a world in which authority and influence intersect between the two extremes of coercion and appeal. Soft power is the ability to appeal to the culture, political ideals, and policies of a nation and is also highly important in winning the favour of global actors. At the same time, hard power, which is mostly understood in terms of military might and economic power, provides the trust and assurance to protect national interests.

Power presumes the use of all available instruments, ranging from diplomacy to economy and even military, which helps navigate the pre-existing international relations and their complexities. In practice, the application of smart power means forming strong alliances, having worthwhile diplomatic discussions, promoting common interests, and, when necessary, applying focused military actions. This approach recognises attunes unilateral frameworks and approaches that simply aim to put out fires, responding instead to complex problems in tailored, systemic ways. Consequently, grasping these approaches makes sense for modern decision-makers, diplomats, and strategists dealing with today's geopolitical puzzles.

Restoring America's Reputation in Foreign Relations

The Obama administration understood that America's image in world affairs had been greatly diminished by the previous administration's policies, especially with the Iraq and Afghanistan wars, and sought to change this. In response, President Obama, along with his diplomatic team, formulated a restorative strategy aimed at countering the negative perception and restoring America's global respect and leadership. To achieve this, they shifted from unilateralism to a more cooperative and consultative posture with international counterparts. Crucial to this approach was honouring international relations by promoting democracy, human rights, and respect for international law as the foundation of US power engagement and participation in global affairs. The intent behind many of Obama's policies was for the US to be regarded as a nation that advocates for positive global change while adhering to laws and collaboration amongst countries. Further, the Obama administration made it a point to incorporate accountability and transparency into foreign policy decisions to rebuild trust and credibility in American leadership. Deliberate efforts were taken to reach out to people around the world through traditional and digital media to highlight the American perception of diversity and inclusion as strategic advantages.

The administration has tried to redefine the nation's image by striving to redefine its identity as a sponsor of progress and achievement by adopting a caring and progressive vision of America. The encouragement of cultural understanding through strategic outreach to the Muslim world, which included the monumental presidential speech delivered in Cairo, served to foster understanding and cultural diplomacy. In addition, the administration fostered relationships with other peoples and communities through cultural exchange programmes, educational initiatives, and people-to-people diplomacy. In summary, the Obama Administration's efforts to restore America's place in global relations were marked by a mix of political reform, diplomatic engagement, and domestic outreach to reaffirm the ethical stance of America's leadership in international affairs and relations.

With Regard to Reengaging with International Institutions

How former President Barack Obama decided to reconnect the United States to international institutions significantly altered the way the United States interacted with the global world at the time. Understanding the value of multilateralism, President Obama sought to work with the leading international bodies and show willingness in participating in decision making and international diplomacy. This approach is different from the one-sided views offered by his predecessor and instead illustrates an interest in working with others on international challenges. The reengagement with international institutions stems from the belief that there is definitional international cooperation required to protect American interests and safeguard stability and prosperity all over the world. This policy initiative has especially focused on the revival of the United Nations, the World Bank, the International Monetary Fund, the European Union, and even the African Union. While participating in international debates and supporting joint action, the United States has tried to assume responsibility on important issues like security and development alongside human rights and environmental issues.

The cited passage illustrates how the Obama Administration advanced foreign relations. By reengaging with global commitments, the United States was able to restore its credibility and moral standing internationally while also being able to demonstrate its willingness to honour international obligations. The long-term commitment sought to build trust and cooperation with other nations. His Administration's willingness to endorse US values led to the US having a say in developing international policies aligned with American interests. Operating multilaterally, President Obama made efforts to advocate for shared objectives that advanced American strategic interests while emphasising international cooperation. In this regard, the authors highlight US international policies during the Obama administration and focus on international policies pertaining to international institutions.

Diplomacy concerning Iran's nuclear non-proliferation.

Of paramount concern to the Obama administration was the issue of nuclear non-proliferation particularly when it came to Iran, which was also an issue in international diplomacy. The issue of nuclear capabilities of Iran has remained an international challenge and hence the Obama Administration attempted to solve it through diplomatic outreach and multilateral interventions. The signing and the subsequent implementation of the Joint Comprehensive Plan of Action (JCPOA) in 2015 better known as the Iran nuclear deal is viewed as the centerpiece of this approach. The goals of the JCPOA were to control Iran's nuclear program in return for the lifting of economic sanctions, thus Iran was sought to be prevented from the possible proliferation of nuclear weapons in the region. The diplomatic negotiations which resulted in the JCPOA were not a simple affair because it involved deep and intricate diplomacy not only with Iran and the United States but also with other dominant countries like Russia, China, France, the UK, and Germany. It took this long because the negotiations illustrate the deep complexities and sensitivities of the questions of nuclear non-proliferation and prove the necessity for persistent diplomacy.

The JCPOA highlighted the possible success of using multilateralism in resolving global security issues, particularly in uniting forces to counter the dangers posed by nuclear weapons proliferation. However, the U.S. withdrawal from the JCPOA in 2018 along with the reinstated sanctions renewed discussions on the effectiveness and viability of diplomacy for non-proliferation of nuclear weapons. This development showcased the fragility of international agreements and the reality of domestic politics interwoven with global statecraft. Therefore, this example of non-proliferation and diplomacy with Iran serves as striking evidence of the balance and interplay in attempting to achieve international peace and security through diplomacy.

Multilateral approach to the fight against terrorism

Global security in the 21st century would be incomplete without the fight against terrorism. The United States, under President Obama, adopted a multilateral strategy in the fight against terrorism, recognising that it is a transnational threat that needs coordinated action at the international level. This shift signified a departure from the unilateral approach taken after the 9/11 terrorist attacks that focused on using unilateral force against the "axis of evil" and emphasised working with allies and partners around the world.

At the core of this approach was the adaptation of not only military action, but also political, humanitarian, and diplomatic efforts to resolve issues such as economic alienation, political aspirations, and even ideological extremism. There has been a wide array of proactive engagement efforts by the administration with different states and international bodies to form a common strategy on how to tackle the shared problem of terrorism.

One of the more important elements of the approach taken by the different countries is the enhancement of the sharing of information and intelligence between the nations. Knowing how interlinked terrorist organisations are, the Obama Administration worked towards better on-site intelligence sharing and cooperation in the neutralisation of terrorist schemes. This framework also aids in the formulation and implementation of joint laws and other governance activities aimed at dealing with international terrorism.

The authorities have sought to manage the factors that encourage the radicalisation and the extremist recruitment processes. Together with partner countries and other stakeholders, including civil society and faith leaders, violent extremism has been countered through programmes aimed at tolerance, inclusion, and socio-economic opportunity. This approach emphasises addressing radicalisation with proactive preventive measures towards the development of strong, protective societies as opposed to reactive measures to the consequences of violent extremism.

The US has been active within the context of the UN and its regional bodies as a participant of international fora to formulate and execute integrated counterterrorism actions at the multilateral level. This also included the promotion of respect for international legal instruments and norms relevant to the fight against terrorism, human rights, and the rule of law. Through these channels, Obama's administration attempted to foster agreement on actions to curb terrorist financing, the recruitment and transport of foreign militants, and the counter-message and recruitment activities of terrorist groups on the internet.

Certainly, the multilateral counterterrorism strategy diplomacy during President Obama's term exhibited a deeper appreciation of the holistic multifaceted global security issues and the need for a collective response. Throughout diplomacy, the United States constructed partnership and alliance frameworks which enabled the US to confront terrorism while preserving its core values and improving international cooperation against common challenges.

Relations between the United States and Russia and the reset policies

Following the difficult relations that the former President Bush had with Russia, President Obama sought to reset relations between Russia and the United States. The reset policy sought to enhance cooperation and address the concerns of both nations since its announcement in 2009, which marked a key shift in diplomatic approach. Finding common ground on issues such as nuclear disarmament, non-proliferation, and regional stability forms the essence of this reset.

An important aspect of the reset policy was the negotiation and signing of the New START treaty, which planned to limit the amount of strategic nuclear weapons each of the two countries has. The nuclear arms control treaty marked a significant achievement as it demonstrated the willingness of the Obama administration to deal constructively with Russia regarding essential security concerns. The policy led to increased cooperation between the two countries on global nuclear non-proliferation efforts, underlining a shared responsibility towards global stability.

As part of the reset policy, economic relations between the two countries were expected to expand alongside controls on arms. Trade and investment relations have made considerable progress, which was marked by Russia joining the World Trade Organisation in 2012. Like other initiatives aimed at increasing cooperation and integration, these also confronted obstacles stemming from the disparity of systems, human rights issues, and geopolitical conflicts.

However, even with the promising signs linked to the reset policy, US relations with Russia worsened after the annexation of Crimea and the military intervention in eastern Ukraine in 2014. The alliance sanctions from the US and other allies worsened the situation and were a major blow to reset efforts. The decline in relations illustrates the depth and extent of the multi-faceted character of the two countries' relationship, discernible through the lens of global power rivalry, differing strategic priorities, and deeply rooted historical hostilities.

Disputes regarding defence policies, suspected meddling in elections, and wars in places like Syria have further complicated the already tense bilateral relations. These disputes have resulted in an ongoing cycle of confrontation and minimal cooperation, defining the current state of relations between the US and Russia and moving away from the intentions of the reset policy.

The legacy of the reset policy, particularly its antagonistic or conciliatory impact on Russia, continues to be evaluated in the context of contention between us, looking at its more immediate and far-reaching consequences on the relations between the two countries. Yet, it is an important episode in the history of the relationship of rivalry and conflict between the two powers and demonstrates the intertwining diplomacy, security, geopolitics, and international relations, on which the evolution of international relations is based.

Pivot to Asia: Strategic Rebalancing

Following reset diplomacy focused on Russia, the Obama administration marked a shift of attention to Asia, which was, in fact, a strategic rebalancing, trying to achieve equilibrium in foreign policy. The move to capture the attention of the United States was purported to address the emerging power scenarios and economic opportunities in Asia, recognising the region's importance in global affairs. This shift was aimed at increasing U.S. interactions with Asian countries in order to foster alliances, bolster their security, and ensure stability in the region. Key to this was acknowledging continental America's increasing power and the balancing approach needed to cope with the intricacies of US-China relations.

In regard to the pivot to Asia policy, one of the most emphasised factors was the strengthening of alliances alongside the formation of new partnerships. The US had also renewed its commitments to long-time allies such as Japan and South Korea by increasing cooperation through enhanced bilateral defence cooperation and modernised security arrangements. Emerging powers like India and Indonesia have also been acknowledged, and efforts made to consolidate their regional power recognition in the context of sustaining the regional balance. The US, with diplomatic initiatives combined with military alliances, has worked hard to ensure support for their allied nations and to forge a web of partnerships which cater to collective goals.

The growing intertwining reliance of the American economy with its Asian counterparts can be clearly seen in the pivot to Asia strategies highlighting changes in economic considerations. The administration was keen on completing trade deals as well as establishing other forms of international economic collaborations focusing on the transpacific region. The United States, attempting to sustain its economic dominance in the market, had looked forward to the inception of the Transpacific Partnership (TPP) programme which underwent great lengths to form an economic collaboration zone and instate high standards for commerce within the territories.

Apex policy captures the shift in allocation of American attention where Asia as a region is given higher priority in addressing multi-faceted security concerns and instilling order. While working on diplomacy, issues of sovereignty and jurisdiction relating to securing and maintaining freedom of navigation, peaceful resolution of conflicts among others were primary concerns. Support for measures that advance the rule and the peaceful order in the governance and security of the Asia-Pacific was also underscored. To these ends, the administration through various forums and dialogues sought to consolidate regional institutions in order to enhance the systems of collective security.

Despite the attempt at integration, the pivot strategy has been subject to misgivings and problems with balancing interests along with commitments in other regions. Disallowing and openly confronting China alongside questioning long-term commitment suffices the discourse. The realisation of the pivot goals has been further compounded by advancing geopolitical changes and some uncertain situational requirements. Regardless, this is less of a concern when looking at the shift towards Asia, especially in the case of Obama's administration as it adds to the chronicle of US foreign engagement "shifts" policies straddling the realities of changing global geopolitics.

In the context of environmental protection and green initiatives

Alongside the international community, the Obama administration crafted powerful policies to spearhead initiatives focused on tackling climate change. It employed a multi-pronged strategy incorporating diplomacy, domestic policies, international collaboration, and cooperation to achieve sustainable development. The US joining the Paris Agreement is a testament to President Obama's commitments towards combating climate change sustainably. The country actively participated in negotiations to establish this international agreement aimed at curtailing global temperature rise and climate change impacts, marking a profound development in the international approach toward climate change policy. Domestically, the administration is also taking steps at a national level, which include system-wide reductions in greenhouse gas emissions, expansion of clean energy and technology adoption, and building greater environmental resilience. Investment in renewable power proves commitment towards a low-carbon economy while the clean power plan seeks to cap emissions from power plants. Obama's implementation of the Climate Action Plan signalled the US is ready to tackle fundamental issues and balance fostering economic activity with environmental action.

Outside of the United States, the administration has worked towards developing collaborative efforts to increase access to climate finance and technology for developing nations, demonstrating their recognition of shared responsibilities in combating climate change. Parallel to these efforts, Mr. Obama's interactions with some of the world's major economies like China resulted in landmark agreements that furthered the already existing international progress towards sustainable development. The administration applied climate change as an element within foreign affairs as well as in national security policies, which indicates the degree of their integration with regard to environmental sustainability as well as the political order of the world. The intention of the Obama administration was to shift the focus of international policy debates to America's efforts in resolving climate change issues so as to showcase US leadership on achieving a sustainable future. While the political climate in the US was not particularly supportive and the world was of diverse opinions, the administration's attempts for directed climate leadership as well as other environmental initiatives showed decisive movement towards framing a collective approach to what is arguably the most important challenge facing humanity.

The importance of soft power and social diplomacy

Public diplomacy, complemented by soft power, was an essential part of President Obama's diplomacy. It was incorporated into the comprehensive strategy seeking to restore the standing of the United States in the world. In relation to other countries, the US had not placed adequate emphasis on the perception and public opinion. Therefore, the Obama administration devoted numerous initiatives to attract foreign audiences and fulfil American objectives. This was done to improve the standing of the United States, and aid in restoring the credibility required to forge goodwill to other nations. One of the notable components of this effort was the focus on cultural exchange programmes and educational relations, and people-to-people contacts. These programmes not only helped foster relationships, but also encouraged cooperation between nations. The administration harnessed the power of modern technology, which included social media, to spread its policies and values beyond traditional diplomatic communication and directly to the people. Such advancements in technology and new media have radically transformed how American ideals and narratives are disseminated across the globe.

The defence of fundamental human rights and the promotion of democratic values serves as the anchor of public diplomacy and advances universal principles and support for common objectives. Activities like the Global Entrepreneurship Summit and the Young Leaders of the Americas Initiative helped the administration to leverage emerging leaders and foster innovation and collaboration, which strengthened American influence from the ground up. The projection of American values and narratives is achieved through the implementation of soft power assets such as cultural exports, entertainment, and academic exchange programmes which shape perceptions and attitudes towards the United States. In this context, increasing investments in cultural diplomacy is a strategy to promote conflict resolution that enables dialogue and cooperation, thus creating partnerships that transcend political considerations. The combination of public diplomacy and soft power served as the framework for Obama's multifaceted global engagement strategy, enabling him to advance American interests while fostering international cooperation. Regardless of the significant results attained, these strategies have faced critical assessment regarding their effectiveness and impact on foreign policy outcomes.

Evaluating the soft power diplomacy during the Obama era, it is important both to tackle the pros and cons of public diplomacy in order to prepare for other more complex advanced engagements in international relations.

Evaluation and critique of the Soft Power Diplomacy of Obama

Like other presidents before and after him, Obama has had both defenders and critics of his diplomacy. They all received a distinct mark of formulating a multilateral approach coupled with the employment of soft power in foreign relations. These attempts to assess the performance encapsulate the dire need to establish if the intended foreign policy or policy goals were met.

The Middle East and North Africa region is one of the focal areas where the administration had to grapple with multifaceted issues such as the Arab Spring upheavals, the Syrian civil conflict, and the ascendance of ISIS. Critics contend that America's influence in the region has been undermined by a half-hearted approach to resolving conflicts in Syria and Libya, only to be worsened by the American failure to broker a meaningful peace deal between Israel and Palestine. Obama's loyalists defend his approach by arguing that there was a calculated, deliberate attempt to grasp the intricacies involved and circumvent aggravating already precarious situations.

Another significant hallmark of Obama's diplomacy, which is also referred to as pivoting towards an Asia-focused strategy, is a move aimed at reinforcing the United States' focus on the Asia-Pacific region as an area of American influence. While lauded for exhibiting concern towards the role of Asia in global affairs, the approach has drawn criticism for neglecting other regions, particularly the Middle East and Europe.

Considered from the perspective of international relations, the focus remains on the Iran nuclear deal and its implications for the global non-proliferation regime. Advocates of the agreement regard it as a landmark diplomatic accomplishment since it significantly curtails Iran's nuclear aspirations through peaceful negotiations. On the other hand, critics have questioned the effectiveness of the agreement over time, along with its repercussions for the balance of power in the region, especially the Middle East.

The proactive stance of President Obama dealing with climate change, as one of the primary diplomatic objectives, came with the signing of the Paris Agreement, which framed yet another pledge for global cooperation towards dealing with environmental challenges. The fact that the United States withdrew from the agreement during the Trump presidency underscores the difficulty of maintaining such diplomatic windows of opportunity across administrations.

As a whole, the analysis of Obama's foreign policy legacy focuses on his leadership style, the perception of American power in the world, institutional reforms, and where Obama advanced or altered profoundly American diplomacy. In any case, there exists criticism, especially in terms of perceived passivity in some crisis situations; what remains is that during Mr. Obama's presidency, his diplomacy was marked by a profound commitment to the international community and the adoption of sophisticated means to address challenges of global importance.

6

Trump's Era
Unilateralism and 'America First' Policies

The foreign policies of Trump

The assumption of office by Donald J. Trump as the 45th President of the United States marked a departure from the foreign policy doctrines of his predecessors. The 'America First' doctrine under which Trump operated essentially mirrored the way he conducted business. It shifted towards a more unilateral and nationalistic approach to global affairs. Unlike the multilateral efforts of his predecessors, the Trump administration focused on prioritising the interests of the United States. There is little doubt that the intention was to fundamentally curtail the United States' established role as world leader and promoter of international cooperation and collective security. In attempting to reshape the relations of the US with the world, the Trump administration sought to redefine the role of the US in global affairs by changing trade deals, reviewing alliances, and contesting international systems of governance. The main features of Trump's foreign policy are characterised by an emphasis on the defence of American sovereignty, economic fiscal nationalism, and a retreat from internationalist policies.

It is well documented how a strident Trump campaign rhetoric, one which resonated with his electoral base, fundamentally changed how international relations are conducted from the perspective of an international public good to one heavily focused on advancing national self-interest. Indeed, consequently, it is argued that it is due to emerging world powers that the United States has adopted this stance on foreign relations. Not only does such an approach challenge established diplomatic customs, seeking to enhance international institutions and agreements, but it also optimistically puts them to the test. Therefore, the ideology that underpinned Trump's foreign policy doctrine has without a doubt propagated one of the most peculiar and controversial approaches a nation has ever undertaken in engaging with the rest of the world. With such an unconditionally nationalist programme, the administration set a paradigm that no American president had previously sought to adopt, turning global diplomacy into regional vicious political competition. This, without a doubt, has changed the trajectory of US foreign policy for many years to come.

Historical context: From campaign promises to presidential actions

To better comprehend the radical 'America First' step of the programme within the broader context of Trump's foreign policy doctrine, which alters the scope of his 2016 campaign promises, one must take reference during his presidency. While many candidate manifestos during presidential campaigns are often riddled with dramatization beyond what is deemed realistically plausible, they made international relations appear as a ONE to many relationship, a public good not focused on broadcasted unlimited offers.

President Trump was quick to act on his campaign promises as soon as he took office. In his inaugural speech, he underscored the importance of 'America First'—a dramatic pivot from the globalist worldview that characterised U.S. foreign policy since the Second World War. Soon thereafter, executive steps were taken to withdraw from and renegotiate several international agreements, including the Trans-Pacific Partnership (TPP) and the Paris Climate Agreement. All of these actions signalled a stark shift toward a political paradigm that focuses on retreating from international commitments to accentuate US sovereignty and competitiveness.

The roots of this change date back to the surge of populism and nationalism that has taken over the United States and many of its Western counterparts. Growing concerns around globalisation and its repercussions on domestic industries, coupled with the public's wariness of ongoing military campaigns abroad, created the backdrop for Mr. Trump's political endeavours. Moving forward, the boundless public distrust of political elites and institutions, symptomatic of the uncontrollable spread of populism, created fertile ground for Trump's anti-establishment narrative.

The growth and strengthening of China's economy, alongside the assertiveness of its foreign policy, has reinforced Mr Trump's belief that international affairs are a zero-sum game requiring a combative stance to protect American interests. Simultaneously, the revival of Russia as a geopolitical player has intensified the debate over the need to reassess US global obligations, encouraging the administration to pursue a rebalancing strategy that shifts the traditional balance of power towards more aggressive unilateral tendencies.

This account of events demonstrates the interplay of external and internal elements that have culminated in Trump's policy decisions aimed at America's foreign relations. The relationship between the dominating economic interests, the pessimistic view of international relations, and the prevailing order of the world is what the former president exploited to justify the decision to disengage from international commitments and redefine the parameters of America's international activities during his presidency.

America First and its impact on traditional alliances

The policy of "America First" turned out to be disruptive for the relationships that have been international allies and frameworks, which have operated as the foundation for the world order since the end of World War II. The polemic of prioritising self-interest and sovereignty was inward looking and appealing to diverse audiences, but was met by diplomatic shockwaves from partners across the globe. The current US administration marks a critical turning point in the historical trajectory of US foreign policy by questioning the value multilateral institutions provide, for example NATO and the UN. By doing this, the traditional allies, who heavily depended on the leadership of the US, became plagued by the notion of uncertainty. These partner nations no longer felt secure regarding US commitment to collective security. The focus placed on burden sharing in combination with the re-evaluation of defence spending placed additional strain on key allies, suffering from a lack of cohesion and partnership effectiveness. The withdrawal from the Paris Climate Agreement and the Iran Nuclear Deal not only raises questions of trust regarding international agreements, but also and most critically turns a dramatic shade on US credibility as a negotiating partner.

Consequently, perceptions of US credibility and reliability came under scrutiny, making some allies rethink their strategies and diversify their foreign relations. In response to the 'America First' policies, traditional allies used to supporting the US propelled them to reinforce intra-regional alliances while creating new partnerships in order to alleviate the impact of an unpredictably aggressive US foreign policy. The restructuring of trade relations, alongside the imposition of tariffs on key allies, is escalating economic tensions and initiating counteractive policies, which undermine the cooperation and the basis of longstanding trade relations. The 'America First' doctrine shaped an unprecedented challenge for longstanding alliances as these nations reevaluate their reliance on American global leadership and their geopolitical strategies in the face of an evolving world actively.

Economic nationalism and trade wars

The doctrine of 'America First', which was supported by Trump's administration, signified a new development in trade policy towards aggressive protectionism and trade wars. America has, over the last decade, increasingly adopted a 'trade for profit' stance that has resulted in a blistering sequence of tariffs and trade obstructionism dubbed "the Trade War". There is a faction within every country that supports domestic trade at the expense of international trade, but few pay attention to the larger turmoil that this causes in international trade.

Tariffs on imports from other traditionally allied countries such as China and the European Union have led to further division on these issues, and the subsequent retaliatory actions have stagnated the trade wars. The international relations associated with trade have integrated nations' economies more than ever before, so the outcomes are not only suffered by the involved party, but every nation that relies on the dynamic global economy.

The principles of free trade radiating from the world's most powerful economy, America, are now being challenged by the fundamentals of economic nationalism that underscore self-sufficiency and bringing all the necessary components of production within the borders. Such developments create an intense discussion on whether shielding the domestic market is better than losing control of fundamentally interdependent global supply chains and subsequently triggering a global recession.

In this regard, businesses engaged in foreign trade have encountered greater risks and difficulties due to a shifting trade milieu. Heightened competition for resources, increased cost of doing business, volatility in the economy, and recession remain striking challenges to these firms' processes and pose fundamental risks regarding their sustainability and competitiveness vis-à-vis international markets.

The impacts of trade wars are not only confined within borders; waning economic activity also contributes to the cooling of diplomatic relationships and testing alliance solidarity. The conflicts spawned by these policies identify the nuances of geopolitical economy, underscoring the pursuit of sovereign objectives and fostering multilateralism.

The overall framework of neo-mercantilism operating on the domestically-oriented policies with an emphasis on the achievement of self-sufficiency sums up these developments quite lucidly. It encapsulates how governments restrain the flow of resources into their countries and redirect investment to appropriate economic sectors. Global investors and policy-makers were acutely concerned during these developments, pondering the implications for international investment, economic growth, and stability as outcomes of extended trade interruptions.

While the US was simultaneously negotiating and re-negotiating trade agreements during this protectionist period, the impact of its policies was felt beyond its borders. The resulting narrative of trade wars and economic nationalism encapsulates the defining features of a remarkable moment in international economic relations and profoundly influenced debates on international trade and the prospects of globalisation.

Diplomatic relations in limbo

Apart from affecting the global economy, the trade confrontations and 'America First' policies of the Trump administration had far-reaching consequences on diplomacy with traditional allies and global partners alike. The combination of volatile policies and sharply nationalistic rhetoric blended with an emphasis on bilateral relations had attendant risks for established diplomatic frameworks and relations. This disorderly phase of international relations has challenged the endurance of multilateral frameworks while simultaneously casting doubts on the extent of global cooperative efforts in the world. In this geopolitical fog, there is a greater likelihood of disruption to predictable diplomatic relationships that have been traditionally cultivated on principles of collaboration, civility, and mutual goodwill. America's closest allies, accustomed to bearing the burden of international leadership and participating in collective defence, found relations strained when the administration shifted towards transactional diplomacy seeking to re-establish US international primacy. The diplomatic shock from tariffs, sanctions, and withdrawal from international treaties was a clarion call for the world's democracies about the impending breakdown of trust and the destabilisation of partnerships built on decades of collaboration.

As the US has shifted gears with diplomatic strategies, foreign diplomats encountered new challenges when interacting with an administration keen on finalising bilateral deals and revising existing treaties. The solo conduct of foreign policy and lack of recognition of existing structures of international governance worsens the problem of already strained diplomatic relations. These disputes, alongside key differences over climate change, the Iran nuclear deal, and the Israeli-Palestinian conflict, make it more challenging to project a common alliance for international diplomacy. Taking part in direct and indirect confrontations of diplomacy with increased confrontation and changing priorities requires working through different spaces for collaboration and coalition-building without conventional standards. Maintaining track of some common principles helps construct flexible approaches toward joint diplomatic initiatives during times dominated by turbulence. The thorough and rapid consequences of this period triggered significant change in the balance of existing dialogues claiming the attention of the public and academic world, diplomatic circles, politics, and setting direction for further reconsiderations of diplomacy abroad.

Lifted from global treaties

President Trump's term of office featured a noteworthy shift with regard to international agreements as his administration approached them from a fundamentally different angle compared to traditional U.S. policies. Under his presidency, the United States' international policy is focused on unilateral multilateral agreements, which is why the U.S. withdrew from key agreements such as the Paris Climate Agreement and the Iran Nuclear Deal. The rationale was to place America's interests first, which he championed during his election campaign. This was a shift from foreordained agreements to "America First" policies.

Withdrawal from certain agreements brought both domestic and global challenges. Debates around these policies tended to focus on the political and economic implications of the decision. Multiple opponents argued that removing leadership guarantees would create a significant gap in globally accepted governance frameworks while the issues agreed upon were pressing. Most of the debates focused around the existing imbalance within global governance frameworks and whether rising powers would fill those gaps.

Proponents of these agreements justifications claimed prior agreements were unfavorable to America and did not advance America's self-interest. Claiming modifying existing agreements revised would better serve Americans interests, they justified their beliefs through claiming American autonomy and economic growth was restricted.

The reason why the outcomes of pulling out from international treaties is broadly more pronounced than just diplomatically is multifaceted. Such a decision absolutely has consequences for other globalitarian efforts like non-proliferation, militancy initiatives, warfare endeavors, humanity, world climate Wars, global governance and even governance at large. These withdrawals did not only affect the reputation of the United States, but also shifted the reliability and credibility among allies, influencing, in a wide sense, diplomatic relations.

As far as foreign policy goes, any shifts made would result to added consequences pertaining to the existing world order and this leads to redefining of partners and allies. States needed to re-evaluate their strategic partnerships and attempt to bridge the possible voids that surfaced due to American absence and lack of leadership these treaties created.

This raises concern around the role of the United States in the sustenance of international relations and treaties within a rule bound system. After accepting it as an deemed cornerstone of US foreign policy initiative, the question now becomes how can one reconcile theem withdrawal from global treaties without raising a doubt pertaining to citizenship and governance in question.

His withdrawal from international treaties marked the at the international stage the culmination of the break in the stream of US global engagement diplomacy. It sparked discussion on the nature of US global leadership, the importance of multilateral actions, and the degree of cooperation with the other countries.

Strategic military policies alongside spending on arms and defence

Trump's strategies on funding the military, allocating, and even cutting expenses shows the striking change on focus that was previously placed on other areas. Under 'America First' policy, President Trump has made it clear that he plans to build up the US Armed Forces while scaling back foreign military interventions. The shift in military policy has been accompanied by an emphasis on building national defence programmes and modernization of the armed forces to ensure the US preserves its technological edge in its global competition.

Among the notable policies adopted by Trump include the increases of the military budget aimed at strengthening and modernizing the capacities of the US armed forces. The administration made efforts to restore the country's military defence through high spending on modern arms, military, cyber warfare, and technology. There were other efforts directed at the sharpening of military readiness and the improvement of the projection of US interests around the globe.

While emphasizing national defence, the Trump administration intended to redefine the global military structure of the United States. This strategy involved reviewing the existing international security agreements and alliances, which tended to spiral towards a more unilateral approach in addressing geopolitical challenges. By shifting to self-strategic sufficiency and pulling back from forceful conflict engagements, the administration aimed to redirect resources towards domestic-security-related issues.

The military strategies were rationalised with systematic planning to optimise defences and streamline procurement processes. President Trump endorsed competitive bidding and negotiating practices to maximise contract optimisation and control spending on the defence industry. This is designed to ensure efficiency and further optimal returns on taxpayer investment through defence spending.

As the administration coped with the changing global security environment, it garnered both backing and criticism concerning its defence policies. Advocates highlighted the focus on modernisation as well as the restructuring of defence spending towards more contemporary issues, while critics contended the impact of reduced engagement with traditional allies and increased unilateralism.

To summarise, analyses of the strategies and spending on defence in the Trump era highlight the intersection of security concerns, global responsibilities, and financial considerations. The consequences—intended and otherwise—of such approaches on the US military architecture and the world's geopolitical configuration still inform contemporary debates and discussions regarding advancing strategies for future defence and foreign policy.

The rest of the world's view of the US during the Trump presidency

The 'America First' agenda adopted by President Trump greatly altered the global view of American leadership. The administration's foreign policy was monitored by numerous countries alongside global observers for its repercussions on the shifts in international power dynamics. The treatment given to traditional allies and their international pacts has raised alarm and debate in equal measure among the allied countries and strategic partners of the US. The reconsideration of longstanding alliances and security partnerships alongside a focus on quid pro quo relations brought doubt on the dependability of the US as a global leader. A great number of nations had mixed responses during the period of the Trump administration, which caused diplomatic rhetoric and attitude to diverge from established diplomatic standards. A good number of people considered the aggressive and straightforward attitude embraced by the administration to simply be a form of strength, whereas numerous others viewed it as a marked departure from cooperative principled diplomacy as well as an attack on multilateralism. These kinds of perceptions had different transformational effects in various geopolitical areas. Economically global leaders were adversely affected and as a result, the imposition of tariffs along with the changed trade policies led to fierce confrontations among key commercial allies and reshaped the very core of international trade dynamics.

The administration's exit from the Paris Climate Agreement and the Iran Nuclear Deal marked a departure from previously held global commitments and frameworks. It sparked numerous discussions on America's role in addressing international issues and sustaining the common good on a global scale. The response of superpower states to issues and conflicts around the world during this period has drawn particular attention. Some observers have pointed out the discrepancies and contradictions in terms of American foreign policy action and its wartime decisions. Soft power embraced cultural factors, education, and even innovation emerging from the US underwent radical shifts across the globe, affecting previously set standards of international interaction. In sum, global expressions of US leadership during Trump's presidency drew attention to the 'America First' strategy and its effects on the world. Discussions and debates concerning US leadership are bound to have a broader impact across the world.

Analysis of remarks of derogation and endorsement of Trump's policy policies

Materials Trump's policies have received copious reactions across the globe. A common criticism of Trump's policies tends to focus on its isolationist undertones, its short-term thinking, and the damage cast on pre-existing partnerships. Critics often defend that his slogan 'America First' does indeed strike down the world order and tarnish America's credibility and image as a partner on the international stage. Detractors have condemned the administration's application of tariffs and trade wars with some of the world's economically viable powers, contestants and allies as reckless for the states economic stability. Furthermore, Mr. Trump's unorthodox style of diplomacy and vocal confrontation with a number of foreign dignitaries has drawn ire for what is perceived as a departure from established international diplomatic etiquette. In regard to Mr Trump's policies, his opponents in America have feared the social and economic impact of such policies are bound to widen any existing inequity gaps. Alternatively, defenders of Mr Trump's policies argued that his emphasis on American priorities, especially in regards to trade agreements, was helpful for the United States. They praised the administration's hardline approach towards immigration and national security as fundamentally important policies for the defence of America and their people against threats abroad.

Some supporters applauded Mr Trump's readiness to challenge international treaties and entities. They have interpreted this as a sign of an effort to recalibrate American dominance and foster more justice around the world. Also, supporters of Mr Trump's foreign policy have praised his attempts to resolve China's alleged trade abuses and other perceived advantages, considering such actions as vital to defending American industries and employment. The differing views on Trump's policies demonstrates the worrying degree of fragmentation in political thought today while showing the wide-ranging effects, both positive and negative, of his administration's foreign policy.

The foreboding presence of Trump's foreign policy "America First" slogan still persists in the agenda of his successors, as well as in international relations. America's global diplomacy was turned upside down during Trump's term, and the consequences have resonated throughout the world, undermining long-standing diplomatic practices and altering the way international systems view US dominance.

While there are many negative impacts of the 'America First' regimes, one of the most critical is the subversion of trust placed on traditional partners, alliances, and multilateral institutions. As a result of the US pulling out from international treaties and adopting a business-like approach to diplomacy, there is strained trust from US allies. Previously, there was assurance provided that there would be international cooperation exercised and that global governance institutions provided would be maintained. Other countries have now lost hope that America is ready for being relied upon for joining coalitions to defend international security or provide necessary governance in various global regions facing deep-seated issues which need multifaceted resolution efforts. America is on a path to divide and rule approach which is a huge detriment towards international stability. This puts severe strain on future presidents as they are now bound to undertake the arduous task of rebuilding robust collaborations and enduring constant distrust from their international colleagues.

The abandonment of the US as an active participator in global concerns such as climate change, trade, and human rights redefines the role America aims to play, establishing 'America First' as an opportunity for debate so the nation solely focuses on domestic interests. Narrowly focusing on issues within the country's borders does not change the fact that international relationships exist. The harsher measures led by the Trump administration, such as price raises on imports from specific countries and the aggressive foreign policy of the USSR called 'Tarifite Ideology,' further propagate issues faced by America First supporters: never-ending walls and vicious disrespect of global integration systems. Any upcoming US policy maker will have the challenge of crafting a solid approach for international collaboration.

The strategic spending discrepancies the Trump administration placed on the military stem from discussions on America's international military commitments and interventions. The approach taken towards amping the military showed an undertone of skepticism towards current pacts affording cooperation bases arguably undercuts any prospective America's role as a unilateral source of security in the world. Subsequent aides are expected to redefine their priorities on defence policies and obligations towards allies in relation to the borders of that country sufficiency threshold for national security on one side and global equilibrium on the other.

The security paranoia triad under the previous administration deeply impacts the popular perception of America's position in the world. The divisive framework of 'America First' serves as useful shorthand labelling debates over the American role in the world. This sets the stage for coherent strategy that the US government's successors will have to forge within the contours of defining and portraying American statehood internationally.

To conclude, the consequences left by the 'America First' policies during Trump's era offer both struggles and prospects for succeeding US administrations. Fostering diplomacy on a global scale, mending broken relationships, and regaining trust in America's position as a leader will be an intricate puzzle needing careful planning and adept political navigation. This enduring legacy underscores the need for a focused foreign policy designed around the United States' goals of fostering peace and prosperity throughout the world.

7

The Biden Administration:
Rebuilding Bridges Amid Challenges

Diplomatic catering: Renewing transatlantic alliances

Restoring diplomatic relations with European nations and strengthening their historic alliances are crucial goals for the Biden administration, and one on which they have placed great focus. With the renewed emphasis on the Atlantic, the Biden administration is focused on diplomatic deepening with European countries and recognises the need for multilateral cooperation around global problems. The administration's plan builds on the premise that something transatlantic partners need to fashion is galvanising unity around the world's most important challenges like climate change, economic recovery, international security, or humanitarian crises. Affirmatively, Biden's international relations strategies serve towards creating effective conflict resolution frameworks in which consensus, cooperation, and collective action would even out the political divides posed by shared priorities. These aim towards marking the return of US commitment in multilateral and international coalitions, shifting the previously adopted isolation policies from the prior administration. The newly witnessed positive culture of collaboration and synergy reflects the changes of attitude on strategic dialogues and joint political initiatives at the highest levels, which are shifting across numerous bilateral and multilateral settings. These efforts have restored the United States' standing in democratic alliances. The constructive and regular engagement with allies has been reworked, which in turn restores unwavering trust that is necessary to shoulder consistent engagement towards working through complex global challenges.

The rebuilding of transatlantic ties required not only the restoration of bilateral ties but also the rehabilitation of the United States as a dependable partner under important international commitments and institutions. The administration showed willingness to cooperate with allies in determining the contours of global governance and addressing shared challenges by joining international bodies such as the United Nations, the G7, and the European Union. Such commitment has been critical for the effective coordination of responses to issues of varying complexity, including peacekeeping and humanitarian assistance, trade diplomacy, and global health emergencies. Thanks to extensive diplomacy and outreach, a common strategic vision for transatlantic cooperation was developed to more effectively respond to the increasingly complex global challenges. In essence, the diplomatic restoration in Biden's term positioned the United States and Europe for renewed cooperation while providing a clearer structure to tackle the challenges of an interdependent world.

The Reinforcement of Multilateralism: Global Institutions and Their Responsibilities

"To reaffirm multilateralism", committing to multilateralism and global governance priorities has shifted affairs within the Biden Administration seeking to actively renew America's engagement within global institutions. "To strengthen diplomatic relations with allied countries" reaffirms the need to work through the United Nations, World Bank, International Monetary Fund, and World Trade organisation engaging them to strengthen relations towards achieving mutual objectives. World diplomacy along these lines demonstrates an understanding of the complexity of world problems and their global character and the fundamental need for cooperation through these institutions. Along these lines, attention has to be paid to the administration policies aimed at the strong deepening of international commitments toward multilateralism and complex geopolitical power relations.

Strengthening multilateralism is rooted in the set of problems recognising the need for collective actions to work through the most critical international issues stated administratively. Together with a systemic approach to these challenges, the Administration plans to galvanise with allies on the recommitment to international agreements to face climate change, public health crises, and the economic development issue, fostering alliances on the international front to advocate diplomacy. Cooperative and consensus building through multilateralism captures the essence and multidisciplinary fusion toward a solution at the policy level.

With regard to key global institutions, the Administration's efforts go towards their revitalisation, where they advocate for necessary reforms and enable these institutions to respond to contemporary global issues. Here, the proactive approach involves the utilisation of the leverage the United States has to enhance the function and efficacy of these institutions and improve their capabilities to effect change globally. The administration has also made it a priority to support inclusion and diversity in these institutions to help incorporate a wide range of perspectives and input that is critical for informed decisions.

The administration, alongside the revitalisation of global institutions, is in active collaboration with partners from allied countries to achieve common goals. Under this type of approach, the administration concentrates on building a consensus around global issues and aligning policies towards achieving the agreed objectives. The administration aims to strengthen the spirit of cooperation and consultation to solve problems in complex geopolitical terrains that withstand time and promote stability and prosperity in all regions.

The government's strategy of implementing multilateralism goes deeper than mere diplomacy; it attempts to actively engage civil society, NGOs, and other relevant actors outside of formal structures. These kinds of engagements capture a more fundamental manner of changing global issues whereby many stakeholders appreciate why such issues are tackled and how various sectors are engaged with regards to building appropriate responses. Such engagement encourages dialogue and fosters new ways of building a system that is adaptive to the new global standards and flexible to meet the needs of the current situation.

As observed, the government's move to strengthen multilateralism can be seen as an essential element of the foreign policy agenda which demonstrates a shift to multilateral diplomacy and integrated global governance. While facing a myriad of increasingly global issues, the administration's commitment to multilateral approaches helps support the intention of achieving balance and stability in international relations.

Developing Transatlantic Strategies for Economic Recovery in the Post-COVID-19 Era

The unrelenting COVID-19 pandemic has posed a myriad of challenges, with the most prominent one being economic, requiring multi-faceted strategic approaches aimed at promoting recovery. It is no secret that transatlantic partners, namely the US and the European Union (EU), are focused on recovering their economies post-COVID-19, and are doing everything in their power to coordinate efforts towards that end. Both blocs have acknowledged that there needs to be a coordinated and comprehensive strategy to effectively mitigate the damage the pandemic has caused to trade and economic relations globally.

The strategies for transatlantic cooperation for post-COVID economic recovery come with a number of important components. First and foremost, it is very critical to foster a sustainable expansion of the economy through appropriately tailored recovery packages and investments in certain industries, including, but not limited to, healthcare, information technology, and renewable energy. The EU and the US need to synchronise their plans, as the combination of their resources and expertise will be much more effective in recovering economies.

More importantly, it is necessary to solve the problems brought about by the change of the international shock and recover from the global shocks. Active measures for the reduction and increase of redundancy in crucial supply chains, including in the fields of medicine and semiconductor devices, are intended to eliminate the risks and contribute to the system's long-term resilience.

It is important to work towards the integration of international trade and the elimination of impediments to access markets. This means removing existing tariff and non-tariff barriers; custom benchmarks for corporate governance ethical policies relative to competition, inclusiveness, and equal treatment are important as well.

Trade encouragement programmes, along with new financial instruments, should be created. Joint action approaches for advancing the economic stimulus under obligation, sponsoring trade and export will sustain the businesses on both sides of the Atlantic and bolster economic momentum.

Along with these policies, the programme for economic recovery would focus on actively shifting to ecological transition towards supporting sustainable development. The US and the EU can lead the changes by merging climate action policies with green technology investments; these moves proactively create a more sustainable and resilient economy.

Last but not least, to enrich the resilience of the economy and competitiveness over time, directing training initiatives and fostering digitalisation and innovation will promote collaborative skill development. Shifting towards emerging digital economy trends such as AI and cybersecurity will strategically make transatlantic partners spearhead in the future of work and industry.

With these collaborative approaches, transatlantic partners will not only be able to accelerate their economic recovery, but will also become an international case study on the effectiveness of cooperation during a period of crisis.

Trade Relations: Solving Problems Associated With Tariffs and Market Access

For a long time now, relations regarding trade between the two sides of the Atlantic have remained an integral part of the world trade system and have influenced the economies of the two regions. In the last few years, a number of geopolitical and economic factors have affected these relations, which have resulted in tariffs being levied and conflicts arising over access to markets. These trade issues, however, must be dealt with by the Biden administration as the war in Ukraine has worsened the fallout from COVID-19.

One of the priorities in these relations is to settle the current disputes over tariffs and prevent them from rising further. This means that there must be some form of cooperation with the Europeans to negotiate agreements on the reduction of tariffs and possibly the elimination of some trade impediments. By seeking to enter into favourable agreements, the US and EU stand to enhance economic growth and increase employment while reducing the negative effects of tariffs on businesses and consumers.

Access to markets is still one of the most crucial aspects of enhancing trade relations across the Atlantic. As part of the strategy, it is now critical to identify and eliminate non-tariff trade barriers. Changing regulatory frameworks and harmonisation of practices pave the way for greater access to markets for goods and services which would be conducive to transatlantic trade. This joint effort requires that both parties strive towards equitable market opportunities while providing balanced access to goods and services, protection of quality and consumer protection standards.

Aside from addressing the current trade disputes, the Biden government plans to establish a new strategically holistic model of transatlantic trade that incorporates new challenges and opportunities. This includes looking into joint cooperation on issues like digital trade, commerce relating to intellectual property rights, and sustainable development. Updating the strategy will enable the US and EU to respond to new global developments and retain economic relevance in the context of growing geopolitical interdependence.

To conclude, it is critical that both parties once again commit themselves to the ideals of free and fair trade, as well as the importance of an open market and honest business conduct. Governance of international trade through rules will enhance stability and predictability which boosts business confidence to invest and innovate on both sides of the Atlantic. With continuous efforts, the United States and the European Union can not only resolve pressing trade issues, but also create an enduring system for long-term trade engagements, diminishing economic threats while advancing a prosperous transatlantic collaboration.

Reinvigorating Climate Policy: Net-Zero Aspirations and the Paris Accord

The renewed U.S.-EU climate policy collaboration under President Biden signifies a remarkable shift towards addressing climate change as a transatlantic challenge. Following the EU's decision to formulate the US joined the Paris Agreement, there are talks among the United States and the European Union to set bold net zero emission targets. This partnership aims to foster global leadership in combating climate change by increasing the efforts to deploy renewable energy, reduce emissions, and promote sustainable development.

This transition aims to encourage clean economic exploitation alongside eco-friendly growth in the economy. Both sides wish to reap the benefits of technological innovation and "green" investments by pursuing economy-wide decarbonisation to gain competitiveness in the emerging international market for low-carbon energy. The United States and the

European Union intend to align their policies and regulations in order to formulate an agreement that fosters green finance, and empowers the private sector to undertake sustainable initiatives, thereby helping them to lead in the transition to a greener and sustainable future.

The initiatives focus on and transcend the framework of individual national strategies and create a "whole of government" effort to catalyse international actions. Transatlantic partners uniquely position themselves to gather and amalgamate with the rest of the international partners, including those from emerging economies, in a bottom-up approach to engaging the high emitters in the global climate movement to build international coalitions and campaigns for action on climate change. The dynamics of climate change policies, which focus on increasing openness, implementing accountability, and taking concrete actions to aid struggling constituents in the developing world, underscore the need not just for climate change measures, but for collective action that binds the world together in tackling the common problem of climate change.

Attention on climate policy comes with new collaborative initiatives in research and development, aiding in knowledge exchange and the transfer of technology, which bolster resilience and adaptation strategies in the context of climate change. The United States and the EU, by investing together in climate-related research, innovation, and green infrastructure developments, aim to cultivate an ecosystem of collaborative learning and development where newly devised solutions will be relevant and impactful internationally.

Along with supplementary policy approaches to unlock the adoption of climate-friendly technologies, advanced energy efficiency, and cross-sectoral climate mainstreaming, the partners aim to achieve net-zero emissions targets. This fosters optimal social welfare under a sustainable paradigm. The effort intends to go beyond merely achieving net-zero emission targets and focus on delivering substantial environmental benefits, boosting the economy, and improving societal welfare.

Security Collaboration: Modernising NATO and Defence Strategies

As new threats to security emerge, transatlantic security collaboration requires urgent refinement of NATO and related defence strategies. Recently, the Biden administration has focused on NATO and the need to address new state and non-state actor threats. Developing modernisation plans is a priority and one of the priorities is to enhance NATO's flexibility to ward off hybrid warfare, cyber-attacks, and disinformation campaigns that seek to subvert democratic systems and institutions. The thrust now is towards enhanced collective defence and stronger deterrence of member-state protection. NATO is working to streamline the procedures for decision-making and improve the degree of military interoperability among member countries. A unique feature of NATO's modernisation and defence strategies is the increased sharing burden on the alliance, appearing to emphasise proportional contributions towards alliance capability and operations. This means going beyond the prescribed political and military expenditure targets to include funding advanced technologies and innovative defence solutions. In order to respond to 21st century security issues, NATO's strategy and operational plans are fundamentally restructuring and require drastic changes to its strategic concept.

The form of cooperative activities like the joint combat concept and the European Defence Fund demonstrate the attempts that have been made to modernise defence capabilities and improve interoperability in the transatlantic community. Simultaneously, the provision of resources for emerging challenges, including those from hostile state actors, requires advanced levels of coordination and collaboration among NATO allies. That also involves dealing with asymmetric challenges, like cyber and hybrid warfare, through joint training, information and resource sharing, and building collective capacity. NATO's modernisation processes and defence strategies also incorporate the new domains of conflict, such as space and cyberspace, with collective defence planning and preparation. Modernisation of NATO and defence strategies serves as a focal point for deepening transatlantic unity, increasing resilience, and enhancing effectiveness amid the evolving dynamic threat environment.

Combating cyber threats: Digital security and resilience initiatives

Cybersecurity is one of the biggest issues on the agenda of the US and the European Union in this globalised world. Rising tensions with cyberattacks pose serious risks to national security, economic health, and even personal privacy. These difficult problems demand an equally complex and comprehensive response to ensure all-encompassing security and resilience initiatives. During the last two years, the Biden administration adopted policies to strengthen cyberdefences as well as foster international partnerships, which are important for the transatlantic alliance. This part of the paper will analyse the ecosystem strategies to mitigate cyberthreats and bolster cyberspace infrastructure on both sides of the Atlantic. Foremost among these is the growing recognition of cyberspace as a theatre where critical infrastructure, sensitive information, and democratic systems require proactive protection. Comprehensive policies adjacent to the development of cybersecurity standards, incident response policies, and information sharing mechanisms need to be tempered with cyber deterrence and active responses to inadvertent attacks. Alongside active policy development, stronger public-private partnerships and closer work with tech companies will allow an exchange of advanced practices to counter already existing solutions to modern cyber risks.

By advocating for responsible conduct and accountability in cyberspace by states, the United States and the European Union are attempting to set an exemplary precedent, highlighting the need for international norms and a structured approach to order in cyberspace. Initiatives to enhance cyber resilience will include creating awareness, establishing technical capability, and cultivating a culture of cyber hygiene and self-care among individuals, companies, and government agencies. Both partners can maintain a proactive stance against emerging cyber threats and vulnerabilities by utilising advanced technologies such as artificial intelligence, machine learning, and quantum computing. Coordinated responses to cyber incidents, including attribution and proportional counter-measures, enhance the overall deterrent posture against malign actors. The transatlantic community needs to remain proactive, in light of the fact that adversaries continue to pursue geopolitical and ideological agendas through cyber warfare, framing them with a need to adapt some approaches to cybersecurity. At the end of the day, the United States and the European Union are able to turn to shared values and resources to efficiently tackle cyber challenges and sustain the ideals of an open, secure, and resilient cyberspace.

Human Rights and Democratic Values: A Unified Position

As the United States and the European Union are balancing the wheel of global geopolitics, the promotion and safeguarding of human rights and democratic values is at the forefront. With the rise of authoritarianism and political repression, the transatlantic partnership is a shield against the decline of democratic freedoms and principles. Together, the two bodies can pose a global stance on human rights by coordinating their actions, combining their power, and harmonising their interests.

Human rights are multi-dimensional, and they include civil and political freedoms as well as economic, social, and cultural rights. The United States and the European Union, through collaboration, have the capacity to defend the rights of oppressed people, support freedom of expression and assembly, and combat discrimination and inequality while upholding the rule of law. It is increasingly important to unite in the pursuit of these fundamental rights. This is important to give a powerful retreat to violators of individual freedoms and very powerful dissent-curtailing regimes.

The belief in democracy and its values is the foundation upon which rests the transatlantic alliance. Joint commitments to democratic governance, including competitive and free elections, an autonomous judiciary, checks on power, and a functional government, serve as essential criteria for democracy in the world today. The United States and the European Union can reinforce the internal resilience of democracies, fortifying them against both domestic and foreign challenges by strengthening democratic structures and assisting emerging democracies in consolidating their governance systems.

Transatlantic allies can counter authoritarianism by actively defending pluralism, civically active organisations, and neutral civil information systems. The United States, alongside the European Union, can counter democratic decay by utilising authoritarian narratives to subvert democracy through the use of unifying narratives focused on upholding democratic values. Authoritarian-sponsored subversion and propaganda can be countered through fostering exchanges between people and helping build civil society networks. Such actions would enable grassroots movements championing democratic and human rights reforms to be strengthened.

The United States and the European Union, in light of the shifting global order, need to address human rights and democratic deficiency issues even outside their areas of direct concern. Transatlantic allies can coordinate and mobilise diplomatic action to address systematic human rights abuses and democratic erosion through engagement with international organisations and regional blocs. Such involvement contributes to promoting a rules-based international order that upholds the rights and freedoms of all persons without regard to nationality or any other consideration.

In the end, a robust commitment to human rights and democratic ideals is what brings the United States and the European Union together toward pursuing a just, more equitable, and inclusive world. The transatlantic partnership is an example of unity in advancing the collective hope of humanity by utilising the region's energies to protect fundamental rights and democratic governance. Their united resolve conveys an unequivocal message that while the defence of human rights and democratic values is borderless, it fortifies the foundation of a future anchored on mutual respect, dignity, and equality.

Balancing China's Influence: Coordinated Approaches to a Strategic Rival

The advance of China as a strategic competitor brings a multitude of challenges for transatlantic relations, particularly within the context of changing the world's geopolitical order. From the perspective of geopolitical competition, there is an increasing need to consolidate approaches to China's impact in multi-domain competition including economy, technological advancement, security, and even ideology. At this junction, the United States and the European Union have to navigate through the complexities of defending shared values, maintaining open societies, and ensuring that their interests are well protected.

Economic relations with China remain one of the critical front lines in which transatlantic partners are compelled to balance their relations with China and at the same time protect their industries, supply chains and patents. Disputes regarding trade relations such as access to local markets, provision of subsidies by the government, and protectionist policies have all brought to the fore the question of the need for economic unification through regulatory alignment. Adherence to the norms of competition and transparency has become a bonding factor within both the United States and the EU. The attempts to advocate for the TTIP and improve control upon foreign direct investment are central in managing the economic growth of China.

One of the concerns in the progress of global technology is the cooperation that seeks to contain China's rising power in emerging technologies and digital infrastructure. Policies aimed at fortifying R&D, fostering technological innovation, and implementing advanced cybersecurity defences have become imperative to restrain Chinese technological dominance. The governance of 5G networks, artificial intelligence, and data privacy demonstrates the resolve of the US and EU to build a technological ecosystem that remains competitive and resilient to China's stated objectives.

Security issues are another element of the comprehensive challenge resulting from the expansion of China's influence. The need for transatlantic cooperation to defend critical infrastructure, reinforce defence capabilities, and maintain strategic autonomy has increased in light of China's growing aggressiveness in the Indo-Pacific region and beyond. The US-EU alliance's resolve to counterbalance Chinese geopolitical ambitions while ensuring global peace and stability is evident in their coordinated joint military drills, intelligence sharing, and deterrence strategies.

Lastly, the ideological aspects of the cooperative policies on China outlines are essential for sustaining the framework of cooperation. The groundwork for cooperation to counter China's authoritarian influence and foster an inclusive international order which is value-based rests on the respect for democracy and the rule of law. Cooperation across the Atlantic seeks to defend human rights, support civil society initiatives, counter disinformation, and the US and the European Union seek to unite to defend values, protect freedoms within the context of changing power dynamics across the globe.

To address the multifaceted problem emanating from China's growing influence, the US and the EU are ready to revive their transatlantic partnership by reinvigorating multilateral engagements and devising a coherent structure for a shifting value system in a changing world. Through constructive discussions, strategic synergies, and leveraging their combined assets, the transatlantic allies stand prepared to address the challenges and capitalise on the opportunities posed by the strategic competition with China to foster enduring partnerships and bolster global resilience.

Future prospects: ongoing relations in a developing world

Sustaining relationships between the US and the European Union (EU) has always been of concern, particularly in the world we live in today. This is because the world is going through tremendous change due to shifts in technologies, new geopolitics and ever-evolving global issues. It is crucial to promote sustainable partnerships in order to mitigate quite a number of challenges that may arise globally. There are many approaches that can be taken, but one of the most important is the reformation of diplomatic relations, economic interaction and security cooperation in line with contemporary realities. Enduring partnerships that can surpass the test of time rely on innovation, collaboration, and adaptable frameworks. Strong action will be needed to effectively address the challenges of globalisation, digitalisation, and societal transformation. Lasting partnerships also cover the commitment toward shared values including democracy, human rights, and the rule of law. Fostering and promoting these timeless principles would shape the groundwork for transatlantic cooperation in responsive global affairs. In the coming years, these relationships would enable focus on sustainable development, inclusive growth and resilient infrastructure and enduring global partnerships.

This involves raising measures to support the adoption of new energy sources, steps for adapting to climate change, as well as eco-friendly policies to fulfil environmental obligations. Developing mutual security concerns for active collaborative defence strategies and information exchange will remain core components of protecting shared interests. The application of new technologies and promotion of innovation development pathways can foster new opportunities for sustainable collaboration. From digitisation and AI to space and other frontiers, the utilisation of scientific and technological innovations will determine the future of transatlantic collaboration. It is important to note that partnerships that last are dynamic in nature; rather, they need continual discourse, flexibility to change, and the ability to face the unexpected head-on. The US and the EU have developed strong and effective partnerships by prioritising, identifying common goals, recalibrating weaker links, and retuning methods. In a rapidly changing world, sustainable collaboration relies fundamentally on trust, understanding changing conditions, and working together for the good of all.

While the US and the EU grapple with the complex problems offered by the 21st century, they need to adopt an optimistic stance and work together to form flexible, sustainable, and proactive transatlantic partnerships.

8

Trump's Return
The rise of populism and nationalism in the West

Global shift to populism and nationalism

In the last ten years, there has been an increase in the adoption of nation-alist and populist ideologies around the world. This trend is associated with fervent rejection of established political elites alongside assertions of national self-determination and identity, leading to public political agita-tion and behavioural activism in many democratic societies. The causes of discontent are numerous and arise from complex socio-economic, cultur-al, and geopolitical factors. There is widespread feeling of discontent and dissatisfaction among diverse population segments. The rapid advance of technology, especially digital communication, has aided the consolidation and mobilization of nationalist and populist sentiments and enabled the wide-reaching support for leaders adopting such policies. The increasing use of nationalism and populism cannot be understood in isolation; rather, it indicates a broader shift in global politics with reconfigured power cen-tres and increased focus on national interests. Due to global politics ram-ifications, further examination of the ideological resurgence's historical roots, modern forms, and geostrategic impact is essential.

Analysing the principles of populism and nationalism, considering how they evolved and their sociopolitical effects, allows us to understand better how these ideologies interact with contemporary global politics. This study helps us determine what is driving these movements and what is their impact on democratic governance and international collaboration. Understanding the resurgence of populism and nationalism requires us to situate it in the context of globalization, economic disparity, and cultural identity, allowing us to identify the factors behind their persistent attractiveness to so many different people. These movements indeed require a sharp examination through the lens of sociological thought, historical reflection, and geopolitical reasoning to make sense of their great significance. Thus, in this chapter, I provide a rigorous assessment of the ideology, history, and dynamics underpinning the rising tide of populism and nationalism, emphasizing the consequences for domestic policy and international relations.

Defining populism and nationalism: historical and contemporary perspectives

Both populism and nationalism are political ideologies that at some point in time have sought to unify a particular segment of global society into a singular movement. As the social and political climates evolve, so too do corresponding ideologies. Nationalism pertains to the focus of a singular culture, people, and nation above other nations and cultures. It is usually fused with more aggressive, xenophobic, and exclusionary thoughts to entirely focus on self-preservation and prosperity, controlling all borders of a nation. Populism never stands alone; rather it is a complement to other ideologies where it is used rhetorically and sentimentally to appeal to ordinary citizens as against the perceivable elite.

From the development of nationalist movements in the 19th century and the rise of populist leaders in the 20th and 21st centuries, these ideologies have shaped domestic and international politics in profound ways. It is important to consider contemporary views in order to appreciate the complexities that lie within populism and nationalism. The heterogeneity of these perspectives results in an absence of an all-encompassing definition, which has caused contention among scholars, decision-makers, and citizens. Instead, the fusion of nationalism with other sociopolitical phenomena leads to such increased intricacies in its understanding and analysis. As these movements face new and more advanced technologies and communicative resources, such as social media and digital platforms, their modes of political mobilization change, and so their messages have to adapt as well. Tracing the history and the contemporary changes of nationalism and populism helps to comprehend their significance to societal dynamics and formulate calibrated counteractions to their growing prevalence.

Political climate: Key factors influencing Trump's comeback

The general public alongside their trust in political institutions are critical to any country's development. Within the US, any shift in policy direction impacts the western world, with nationalistic sentiments redefining the perception towards populism within the region and giving rise to Trump. Coupled with Global Warming, technological advancement, and wealth disparity, claim both America and Britain are vulnerable to strategic competition from the east. Markedly, social media along with the dispersal of the digital world has drastically impacted worldviews, pushing the narrative into a negative feedback loop detrimental to growth.

As new technologies emerged, so did the spread of populism and inflammatory speeches, as well as the agitation of the frustrated. The phenomenon of "echo chambers" in these digital spaces fostered prevailing opinions and added to the division of balance to discourse. In addition to these self-evolving elements, external factors like geopolitical conflicts,

immigration debates, and perceived aggressions toward national independence fuelled radical populist and nationalist agendas. Trump's return
to power can be interpreted within this web of sociopolitical intricacies,
where he is portrayed as a person who managed to make use of these
pre-existing conditions and found resonance in significant portions of
the electorate. Exploring the American political landscape helps explain
the shift in sentiments of a large portion of the Republicans and offers
in-depth insights into the implications of such a fundamental change in
political behaviour. These considerations are crucial in understanding the
consequences of Trump's return, particularly in regard to transatlantic
relations, international networks of authority, and the state and future of
democratic systems.

Comparative analysis: The rise of right-wing populists in Europe

The emergence of right-wing populism in Europe has greatly impacted the
continent's politics, creating rich discourse about its history and consequences. From the rise of the Alternative Germany party to the elevation
of Marine Le Pen's National Rally in France, populism's tide has been
felt everywhere. Understanding this phenomenon requires a thorough
socio-economic history and cultural analyses of each country in comparison to others. This analysis is vital to determine the similarities and
differences, and thus understand the bigger picture. There are a plethora
of reasons that can explain the success of populist parties in Europe. Ever
since the onset of globalisation and automation, there has been widespread
economic anxiety. Economic discontent, along with hatred toward elites
among certain groups, creates an ideal environment for populist promises.
The lack of effective action to control the immigration crisis and growing
fears concerning national identity and safety have further strengthened
the support for such extremist nationalist anti-immigration policies. These
problems, when not dealt with by established political institutions, strong-

ly bolstered the attraction of populist rhetoric, which marketed itself as a solution for ignored constituents' demands.

Though there are various ways through which right-wing populism might manifest itself in different states, there are certain aspects which require further analysis. One of the characteristics of such a rise is the use of social media and other digital channels for political mobilisation and propaganda. These avenues allowed easy access to supporters as well as the wide circulation of populist ideologies, which bypassed traditional gatekeeping media. The deepening of polarisation within societies has accelerated the erosion of politics premised on consensus, fostering conflictual politics that are increasingly fragmented. Given these circumstances, examining the implications of right-wing populism on democracy and societal fragmentation is crucial. These movements threaten dangerously the core pillars of a liberal democracy by undermining, for example, the protection of minorities, the rule of law, and the overall health of democratic governance. Hence, understanding the implications of the rise of right-wing populism in Europe and the future of the continent requires thoughtful comparative study.

Media Influence: utilising sociogenic platforms during political mobilisation

Currently, media—a syndrome that includes various forms of technology—appears to play a critical role in public debates, overriding partisan agendas, and even in election campaigning. Social media has revolutionised the way information is shared and has provided a plethora of contacts for political leaders to engage with and mobilise their followers. It is necessary to ask, what is the impact of social networks in advancing populism and nativism as well as nationalism on democracy, social order, and cohesion?

Many political figures as well as political movements have social networks at their disposal. These platforms have made it possible to communicate directly with their targets without going through the traditional gatekeepers of information. Social media enables political actors to tailor their stories for particular groups within the populace. This micro-targeting of narratives along with algorithmic content placement strengthens the chances of convincing and winning collective engagement. Nonetheless, as everyone paying attention to social media has access and can engage with the public through it—also leads to polarisation coupled with echo chambers, rampant misinformation, and a decline in honest discourse. This poses further problems to the very essence of democracy that many claim to champion.

The extreme evolution of social media has enabled the easy access and diffusion of populist and nationalist ideologies which use emotional sentiment and oversimplified stories to appeal to dissatisfied portions of the populace. This new reality fuelled the proliferation of divisive rhetoric, the increase in social divides, and the erosion of trust in social institutions, fundamentally transforming the political and social structure of states.

Social media has numerous effects that extend beyond individual nations because political actors have increasingly used these outlets as means of transnational interaction and collaboration to build joint agendas and promote them beyond the borders of a country. The shared spread of extremist ideologies and cross-pollination of populist movements demonstrate the new politically mobilised world order where advanced technology enables boundless non-regional political interactions.

Ever-changing social media presents a challenge for lawmakers and society that need to control the harmful effects of unrestricted digital conversation while protecting the principles of civil discourse and democratic citizenship. Differentiating the scope of governing speech as informing politically and socially active citizens while simultaneously controlling the discourse poses one of the greatest challenges today when Internet access is ubiquitous.

Policy Paradigms: Immigration, Trade Protectionism, and Foreign Policy

With regards to the political paradigms, the impact of right-wing populism along with nationalism has deeply affected immigration, trade jealousy, and foreign relations. In view of populism, the western leaders have re-considered policies around border control, taking a tougher stance on accepting refugees. Immigration is now discussed in terms of increased enforcement, heightened securitisation, and militaristic nationalistic rhetoric focused on protecting national interests.

Right-wing populism has been characterised by outbursts of trade jealousy, increasing tariffs, and coming up with new international trade agreements. Such policies are described as economic nationalism which has been debated at length regarding their effects on global supply chains, consumer prices, and more broadly, the already fragile system of international trade and cooperation.

Simultaneously, the agenda for foreign relations has undergone a shift as a result of populist and nationalist sentiments. Some key leaders have adopted an 'America First' approach, chiefly seeking to promote national priorities at the expense of multilateral undertakings, which has heightened tensions with international allies and organisations. This focus on unilateral action leads to increased scepticism about cooperation with the rest of the world, resulting in diplomatic difficulties.

The political paradigms ascribed to right-wing populism and nationalism tend to differ from conventional ones and generate heavy critique and discussion at both national and international levels. With such ideologies gaining traction, one must consider exploring their consequences in governance, diplomacy, international relations, and the overall globalisation landscape.

National consequences: Cultural and societal fractures

Populism and nationalism, particularly in western states, have led to notable consequences at a national level. This is particularly evident in the form of cultural shifts and societal fractures. There is evidence of political polarisation leading to social tensions and even disintegration of historic synergies. Monolithic views held by the general public on various issues such as immigration, ethnic plurality, and national identity are increasingly shifting to competing factions. This has created a situation in which societal disunity becomes a real possibility, providing significant hurdles to social integration and constructive interaction.

The surge of populism and nationalism has brought about significant changes in the culture of these societies. It is clear that traditional norms and values are being reconsidered and redefined, which has led to the rhetoric of populist leaders demanding a return to nationalist ways. Such changes trigger conflicts regarding national identity, multiculturalism, and the construction of a society around its diversity. Consequently, there is a striking clash between those who defend progressive and inclusive values against the advocates of a more protectionist and exclusive ethic.

The aftermath of these cultural changes is felt in almost every sphere, including education, the media, public discourse, and even civic engagement. Schools and media channels have transformed into arenas where competing narratives, reflecting deeper sociopolitical cleavages, struggle for dominance. Pervasive emotionally charged and polarising rhetoric has entered public discourse towards consensus becoming the most difficult objective to achieve while pursuing ideological entrenchment.

The rise of populism and nationalistic attitudes has changed the patterns of civic engagement and activism. In response to these changes, civil society has mobilised with grassroots movements and advocacy groups forming to protect pluralistic and diverse values. At the same time, there has been an increase in reactionary nativist and ethnocentric movements, thus deepening the societal divisions already created by the politics of the region.

Considering all the above-mentioned, it is necessary to evaluate the impact that the rise of populism and nationalism has on national systems within a country. Within these ideologies rests the need to resolve conflict and tension, and create unity making separation increasingly concerning. Strategically dividing society to further pit a culturally diverse populace cannot be made without considering the means to bring together, inclusively fostering a unified narrative of national identity.

Global Responses: Allies and Enemies Join Together

Global attitudes respond as the West resorts to nationalist and populist views, with the rest of the world studying how to adapt to these strategic shifts. Adversaries and allies alike have to consider how to react to the evolving political reality that holds serious consequences for international relations.

The European Union, Canada, and Japan, as traditional allies of western democracies, have noted with concern the emergence of populist leaders along with nationalist rhetoric. These concerns focus on the established multilateral frameworks along with trade and collective security agreements. The debates regarding the erosion of liberal democratic values and the rise of protectionist policies in certain western states have turned attention towards transatlantic partnerships and the liberal international order.

On the other hand, western opponents like Russia and China have been keen to study the fractures within western societies. They are trying to drive these wedges deeper by marketing themselves to nations fed up with the liberal west as alternative "partners." This serves the purpose of undermining western solidarity and their power, bringing new contestation to the international political arena.

Both allies and adversaries register a variety of responses that can be understood in different ways. Some countries appear to be cautiously attempting to accommodate the shifting political terrain while still up-holding shared democratic values and economic cooperation. Others have voiced their worries about the impact of populism and nationalism on global order and stability.

In western societies, the reaction has been quite notable, and so has been the reaction from civil society, as well as think tanks and even diplo-matic missions which have become proactive in the public and politi-cal discourse. They are trying to defend the pillars of liberal democracy, human rights, and international relations but, at the same time, seek to reconcile with the rightfully angry sentiments that have fueled the populist onslaught, acknowledging the deep social, economic, and cultural changes behind these movements.

The intertwined conflict of international response, politics, and domes-tic factors highlights the need to address the issues of populism and na-tionalism more thoroughly. Especially, the actions of allies and adversaries shape the contours of global governance, agreements pertaining to secu-rity, and economic relations in a very significant manner. Understanding these relations requires careful and decisive diplomacy, far-sighted strate-gies, and deep knowledge of history, current power relations, and trends.

Evaluating the economic consequences: Immediate ben-efits and enduring threats

The Covid-19 pandemic as well as the economic consequences of Rus-sia's invasion of Ukraine have increased the level of uncertainty in global and domestic economics. The protectionism, as well as inward-looking strategies being adopted by politicians across the globe, signals a revival of populism and nationalism. This shift, coupled with the election of former President Trump, moves right-wing political parties into power in many parts of Europe.

Trade protectionism, tariff imposition on imports, and the encourage-ment of domestic manufacturing are often showcased as ensuring quick and short-term gains. Advocates of such policies argue that such measures will stimulate activity in the domestic industries, generate employment opportunities and boost the national economies. The truth, however, is far more nuanced. Although protectionist measures could provide some relief to specific industries from external competition for some time, they tend to generate retaliatory actions from trade partners which result in trade wars that are detrimental to all economies involved. Such measures tend to change global supply chains, inflate prices for consumers, and weaken trust and collaboration on an international level.

Within this framework, the long-term effects of an isolationist approach continue to emerge as alarming. Nations that appear to turn inward to avoid international cooperation stand to lose the fundamental benefit of global interconnectedness. Focused collaborative innovations, shared resources, and trade relations that are beneficial to both parties become crucial for economic growth in a world that is becoming increasingly interdependent. Such economic nationalism acts as a threat, putting all such vital networks in danger for growth and prosperity.

The consequences of these economic policies deepening populism and nationalist policies will certainly create global instability that would, in turn, threaten the already fragile financial markets and increase geopolitical tensions. The shifts in strategies from global to local may perhaps deter cross-generational funding, but new technological advancements and dual-dip investment spectacles arising from the global focus, alongside forcing the world to address the reality of issues like climate change and pandemics, would put pressure in times of uncertainty.

As any responsible authority would note, short-term foresight based on publicity-driven funding would assume a lack of genuine support. Building the narrative would demand stronger reasoning based on investments focused on fostering long-term ventures. From both a capitalist and a global citizen's point of view - bolstering frameworks that support global connections interspersed with a sprinkle of extreme circumvention to gain popularity would give rise to challenges that need addressing in a world confronted with the absence of cohesive policies.

Conclusion: the consequence of a highly polarised political society

The solution for dealing with the consequences of a highly polarised political landscape is understanding the balance between the economic and geopolitical realities and the intertwining of nationalist and populist sentiments. The rise of Western populism and nationalism has not only transformed domestic policies; it has multi-dimensional repercussions for international relations, creating dilemmas for policymakers and leaders. As we try to make sense of this phenomenon, it is evident that the efforts require significant and coordinated action from several sectors simultaneously.

Above all, one must understand the realities and concerns that underpin these phenomena. Dismissing them as irrational and devoid of any logic only deepens the gap in society. It is important for leaders to approach the underlying issues using conversations, political processes, and socio-economic frameworks that strive for greater social integration and inequality reduction.

Fostering democratic resilience toward divisive discourse and democratic backsliding requires strong protective systems. Protecting democratic processes, upholding the rule of law, and ensuring responsible journalism play pivotal roles in counteracting the negative repercussions of polarisation. Upholding democracy is equally important to the effectiveness of governance and requires transparency and accountability, serving to obstruct the rise of authoritarian tendencies.

Concurrently, the initiative of fostering and practising constructive engagement and cooperative diplomacy both domestically and abroad stands to reduce tension and polarisation. Concentrating on shared ideas and goals serves to lessen the adversarial character of modern-day politics. The need to consolidate efforts to deal with climate change, global health issues, and economic volatility serves to unify and galvanise collective action while going beyond self-serving nationalism.

Fostering a culture of critical thinking, media literacy, and civic education is vital in cultivating an informed citizenry. By encouraging participation in civil society, factual debate, and empathy, the divisive nature of disinformation and echo chambers can be mitigated. Both formal and informal education are essential in providing individuals with the ability to distinguish truth from fiction, especially in a globalised and interconnected world.

In the end, we need to try reconciling two extreme positions and find a balance between the values of liberalism, which include inclusiveness and diversity, as well as considerations for some of the more disgruntled parts of society. Attempting to solve the problem of a politically divided society greatly requires not only visionary leadership but active participation from the constituents to bridge divides and willingly champion the greater good. Following this approach enables societies to balance the re-embrace of democracy alongside unity in diversity under a single foundation for a more just, equitable, and harmonious society.

9

Economic Cooperation and Competition:
Trade and investment

Introduction to transatlantic economic ties

The economic relations between the United States and the European Union (EU) are a testament to the intertwining of their markets. Spanning several decades, this partnership has evolved from post-World War II reconstruction efforts to the establishment of a sophisticated trade and investment network. Rooted in shared values of democracy, freedom and free markets, transatlantic economic ties have fostered unparalleled levels of collaboration, while also experiencing periods of tension and disagreement. The scale of mutual investment and trade flows reflects the depth and complexity of this relationship, which underpins the stability and prosperity of the global economy. From the automotive and aerospace industries to technological and financial services, both sides have benefited from transatlantic investment, technological exchange and access to markets. While historic alliances such as NATO have strengthened security cooperation, economic interdependence has played an equally vital role in strengthening diplomatic relations and soft power influence.

Harmonising regulatory standards and facilitating trade through agreements such as the Transatlantic Trade and Investment Partnership (TTIP) have sought to streamline transactions and improve market access. In the face of geopolitical change and rapid technological advances, the United States and the European Union have shown resilience by adapting their economic strategies, encouraging innovation and addressing common challenges. Despite occasional differences in trade policies or regulatory frameworks, the overarching commitment to fostering an open, rules-based economic order remains the cornerstone of transatlantic economic ties. As the global economic landscape continues to evolve, the United States and the European Union stand ready to break new ground, reaffirming their commitment to a strong and cooperative economic relationship that transcends temporal challenges and underscores the enduring strength of their bond.

Historical context: A legacy of collaboration and conflict

The historical relationship between the United States and Europe has been characterised by a complex interplay of collaboration and conflict, which has shaped the transatlantic economic landscape. The roots of this complex dynamic can be traced back to the aftermath of the Second World War, when the United States played a vital role in the reconstruction of war-torn Europe through the Marshall Plan. This act of generosity laid the foundations for a strong economic partnership and set the stage for future cooperation. However, the early post-war years were also marked by tensions, particularly in the area of trade, as both sides sought to protect their industries and farmers while adapting to the complexities of a rapidly changing global economy.

The creation of institutions such as the General Agreement on Tariffs and Trade (GATT) and, later, the World Trade Organisation (WTO), provided a framework for managing trade disputes and promoting greater economic integration. Throughout the second half of the 20th century, transatlantic relations experienced periodic tensions, particularly disagreements over agricultural subsidies, intellectual property rights and market access. Nevertheless, the shared values of democracy, free enterprise and the rule of law remained the pillars of common ground that fostered the maintenance of economic ties.

The end of the Cold War ushered in a new era of globalisation, opening up new prospects for transatlantic trade and investment. The growth of multinationals on both sides of the Atlantic has strengthened economic interdependence, leading to an increase in cross-border mergers, acquisitions and joint ventures. At the same time, the expansion of digital technology and commerce has posed new challenges in areas such as data privacy, cybersecurity and e-commerce regulation, adding new layers of complexity to transatlantic economic relations. At the dawn of the 21st century, the historical context of collaboration and conflict continues to shape the contours of transatlantic economic cooperation, providing valuable insights into the complex dynamics at play and laying the foundation for future trade and investment efforts.

Trade agreements: Evolution and impact

Trade agreements between the United States and the European Union have played a vital role in shaping transatlantic economic relations, with a significant impact on the dynamics of world trade. The evolution of these agreements reflects changes in the geopolitical and economic landscape, as well as the shifting priorities of both parties.

The historical context of trade agreements dates back to the aftermath of the Second World War, when the Marshall Plan laid the foundations for economic cooperation and the recovery of war-torn Europe. Subsequent agreements, such as the General Agreement on Tariffs and Trade (GATT) and its successor, the World Trade Organisation (WTO), paved the way for multilateral trade rules and negotiations. Bilateral agreements, including the Transatlantic Trade and Investment Partnership (TTIP) and current efforts to negotiate a comprehensive trade agreement, have sought to deepen economic integration while addressing regulatory differences.

The impact of these trade agreements goes beyond tariff reductions and market access. They have facilitated the movement of goods, services and investment across the Atlantic, bringing businesses and consumers closer together. Harmonisation of standards and regulations aims to improve the compatibility and efficiency of transatlantic trade, making it easier for companies to operate in both markets.

Challenges have also emerged in the wake of these agreements. Disputes over agricultural subsidies, intellectual property rights and non-tariff barriers reflect the complexity of reconciling diverse economic interests and regulatory frameworks. The rise of protectionist sentiments and nationalist policies has posed new obstacles to the advancement of free trade.

Going forward, the evolution of trade agreements will continue to be shaped by emerging issues such as digital trade, climate considerations and the intersection of trade and geopolitics. The impact of future agreements on job creation, innovation and sustainable development will be closely scrutinised, particularly in the context of evolving global supply chains and economic uncertainties.

In short, the evolution and impact of trade agreements between the United States and the European Union are emblematic of the complex interaction between economic cooperation and competition. As both partners face the challenges and opportunities of a rapidly changing global economy, the importance of trade agreements as instruments of prosperity and strategic alignment remains undeniable.

Investment flows: Mutual benefits and challenges

As trade between the United States and the European Union has become increasingly interconnected, investment flows have played a crucial role in strengthening economic ties. Foreign direct investment (FDI) between these two major economies has generated mutual benefits and opportunities, but it has also posed significant challenges that require careful consideration. The exchange of capital, technology and expertise has stimulated innovation, job creation and economic growth on both sides of the Atlantic. This mutually beneficial relationship has strengthened the competitiveness of industries, facilitated knowledge transfer and encouraged cross-border collaboration. Diversification of investment portfolios contributed to greater financial stability and resilience to global market fluctuations. However, the growing interdependence of transatlantic investment flows has raised concerns about national sovereignty, security and strategic interests.

The influx of foreign capital into key sectors such as telecommunications, energy and infrastructure has prompted debates on ownership, control and potential vulnerabilities. Differences in regulatory frameworks and policy approaches have created obstacles for investors seeking to navigate complex legal environments and business cultures. Issues related to intellectual property rights, labour standards and environmental regulations have emphasised the need for increased cooperation and coordination.

Despite the shared benefits arising from investment flows, the emergence of protectionist measures and geopolitical tensions has cast a shadow of uncertainty over the future trajectory of transatlantic economic relations. The search for reciprocity and equity in investment policies remains an ongoing challenge, requiring thoughtful dialogue, transparency and a commitment to promoting a level playing field. As the United States and the European Union seek to recalibrate their economic strategies in a rapidly changing global landscape, the balance between promoting open markets and safeguarding national interests will be critical to ensuring the continued prosperity and stability of their intertwined economies.

The role of multinationals in policy-making

Multinational companies play a key role in policy-making and influence the dynamics of trade and investment at the global level. As key players in transatlantic economic relations, these entities have a considerable influence on government policies, trade agreements and regulatory frameworks. Their extensive reach, diverse activities and considerable financial resources enable them to engage actively with policymakers, defend their interests and contribute to the formulation of economic policies. Through their lobbying activities, multinationals often seek to align regulatory environments with their commercial objectives, advocating for initiatives that promote better market access, streamlined business procedures and favourable tax regimes. These efforts are motivated by the pursuit of competitive advantages, operational efficiency and profitability. Multinationals frequently engage in public-private partnerships, leveraging their expertise and resources to collaborate with governments on initiatives related to infrastructure development, innovation and sustainable practices. By participating proactively in policy dialogues and fostering cooperation between the public and private sectors, they strive to create an environment conducive to unimpeded cross-border trade and investment.

Despite their potential for positive change, multinational enterprises are also under scrutiny regarding their impact on labour standards, environmental sustainability and social equity. Critics argue that their pursuit of profitability can lead to labour exploitation, environmental degradation and exacerbated socio-economic disparities. This dynamic emphasises the importance of responsible corporate conduct and ethical business practices.

In the context of transatlantic relations, multinational companies operate in a complex landscape characterised by varied regulatory approaches, divergent tax systems and constantly evolving trade dynamics. As such, they face multiple challenges arising from geopolitical tensions, protectionist measures and technological disruptions. The interaction between multinational companies and government bodies emphasises the complex nature of their influence on policy formulation and implementation. In the ever-changing landscape of international trade, it is imperative that stakeholders engage in constructive dialogues that address the various interests and concerns at stake. Achieving a harmonised approach that reconciles economic imperatives and the well-being of society remains an ongoing endeavour at the intersection of multinational corporations and policy-making.

Tariffs and Trade Wars: Lessons from Recent History

The transatlantic economic landscape has been influenced by the imposition of tariffs alongside the commencement of trade wars within the past few decades. As world economic powers, the United States and the EU have experienced periods of fracture and conflict, battling over fair competition, intellectual property, and access to markets. The application of tariffs has almost always invited counter-trade measures that initiate conflict and impact several industries on both sides of the ocean. Businesses and consumers are, knowingly or unknowingly, influenced by such actions, as well as trade more broadly in the world's markets today.

Investment may worsen due to the instability created by heightened tariffs, and disrupt supply chains. The uncertainty extends beyond a single industry to the entire economy, including trust from the private sector. Relations between countries can become strained, participation in international agencies and coalitions may be disrupted, and collaborative initiatives on important challenges in the world may also become impaired.

In order to construct mechanisms more sophisticated for resolving issues and fostering economic growth, it is crucial to evaluate the implications of recent trade conflicts and their conflicts in greater detail. Such trade encounters and their repercussions will guide future trade relations and minimise protectionist tendencies. Furthermore, they highlight the need for solution frameworks to trade conflicts and for strategies that promote shared growth. Stakeholders, policymakers, and businesses will be able to navigate through the intricate systems of tariffs and trade wars constructively, encouraging sustainable economic collaboration through having the right information and insight.

Innovations in Technology and Ownership of Intellectual Properties

The intersection of ownership of intellectual properties and innovation in technology has etched a particular mark in the transatlantic economy. Patent protection, which is critical for spearheading entrepreneurial breakthroughs in Europe and the United States, assumes a new dimension with the advent of new technologies. The issue lies in the myriad constituents of the relationship between innovation and property rights. The Technology Innovation and Proprietary Rights are essential to understanding the fine line that exists between encouraging invention and protecting individual ownership rights.

The acceleration of technological advancement provides numerous chances for companies and entrepreneurs to invent exceptional goods, services, and processes. Moreover, the intellectual property protection landscape has also evolved due to the heightened competition. Unapproved application or duplication policies can weaken incentives for pursuing research and development this makes protecting IP all the more imperative. The EU and USA deeply appreciate the creation of innovations while respecting the law. Subsequently, the legal systems of such countries provide for adequate protection of inventions, trademarks, copyrights, trade secrets, and patents in order to reward innovation.

Besides offering protective policies, bilateral collaboration on intellectual property rights is essential for the deepening transatlantic economic relationship. Coordinated actions to enhance the patent system, boost enforcement, and address emerging digital challenges demonstrate the commitment to innovation-led growth. Participation in international forums and discussions enables the US and the EU to champion robust IP protection and shape the international trade and investment landscape.

In the wake of new technologies, new challenges are being recognised in the realm of intellectual property rights. The digitisation of information and the increase in the use of online services has created difficulties in regard to enforcing restrictions on copyright, piracy of digital content, and privacy breaches. In response, the U.S. and the European Union implemented specific policies geared towards modifying the rules of intellectual property to incorporate the digital innovations while balancing the needs for fundamental innovation alongside global safeguards.

The Joint Consideration of Advanced Practices of Artificial Intelligence, blockchain technology, and biotechnologies necessitate the application of futurist outlooks on governance of intellectual property. In order to respond to the need for growth fostered by the potential these developments hold, there has to be mobilised effort to design appropriate and flexible legal structures that support innovation for economic growth. This way, the U.S. and EU will aid in addressing the change in the technological world and the intellectual property framework thereby sharpening the synergy of their innovation ecosystems to enhance their global competitive standing.

The present debate on technological innovation and intellectual property rights marks a meeting of the interests and concerns of the United States and the European Union. The creation of strong systems of intellectual property protection and cooperation in research and development activities, together with an aggressive attitude to new technologies, enables transatlantic partners to propel their innovation economies and determine the future of international technological dominance.

The digital economy: Opportunities and regulatory concerns

For both sides of the Atlantic, the digital economy presents numerous opportunities for collaboration and growth. With advancements in digital technologies, businesses on both sides of the Atlantic have increased their scope and transformed the traditional industrial landscape. To name a few, e-commerce, cloud computing, data analytics, and the IoT have changed business and consumer operations and interactions. The expansion of digital platforms has allowed Small and Medium Enterprises (SMEs) to access international markets, thereby encouraging entrepreneurship and innovation. Despite the availability of these opportunities, there are challenges that pose a risk in the digital space. The privacy and cybersecurity of data, alongside the protection of consumers, have forced policymakers to assess existing regulatory measures and create new ones to safeguard against the dynamic shifts in the digital era.

Attempts to protect the privacy rights of individuals and the responsibilities of organisations in the European Union and the United States are portrayed in the Union's General Data Protection Regulation (GDPR) and California Consumer Privacy Act (CCPA) respectively. Significant power and allegations of monopolistic behaviour have placed scrutiny on the tech giants regarding antitrust and competition policies. The debate between the European Union and the United States on the regulatory frameworks for the digital economy showcases the tension between innovation and regulation.

While addressing the complex problems stated above, transatlantic partners could strengthen the foundations of a digital economic partnership by defining global standards through cooperation and aligning regulations. Both the European Union and the United States stand to gain from the development of a digital market, provided that basic rights, as well as just and transparent business practices, are safeguarded. These partnerships require effort from all participants in order to resolve existing disputes, establish trust, and create a consistent system that supports innovation while upholding fairness, responsibility, and inclusivity. If effectively coordinated, the transatlantic alliance will enhance its role as a key player in shaping the digital economy and demonstrate its engagement in fostering responsible and ethical transformations in digital technology.

Transatlantic divergence: Tax and antitrust policies

Previous relations across the Atlantic have marked the cooperation of harmonised economic systems; however, there have been gaps in the alignment of taxation and antitrust policies in recent years. There has been growing contention over corporate tax slabs, digital taxes, and global tax reform efforts. Recently, the US and EU seem to disagree about the taxation policies of multinational technological corporations. The EU has started implementing taxes on digital services, while the US has countered with the ATSDMA, raising concerns about discriminatory policies and their impact on US businesses.

This gap in taxation has intensified existing conflicts and underlined the urgency of having a coordinated international approach to the challenges brought about by the digital economy. Antitrust policy is a further area of conflict between the US and the EU. Although both aim to ensure and maintain healthy competition by preventing monopolistic behaviours, the methods adopted to achieve these goals are quite different. The EU has been much more interventionist with technology companies, imposing heavy fines and calling for more regulation. On the other hand, the US is accused of being too lenient in enforcing rules and too accepting of a dominant stance from some operators in the system. All of these issues create conflict over how regulations should be set and arguments over which countries control which parts, raising concerns about the division of international standards and the distortion of competition in the market.

When navigating the differing policies of taxation and antitrust, it is important to seek a middle ground that is based on cooperation alongside fairness, transparency, and competition. Solving these issues collaboratively will be crucial for the health and solidity of the transatlantic economic relationship alongside the global economy. Such policies should be designed in a way that balances the needs of all parties, thus ensuring a harmonious partnership for all stakeholders.

Towards a sustainable economic partnership: Future directions

Future actions Northwest Europe has to take regarding fostering a collaborative ideal between the US and the EU need to be strategically addressed concerning the evolving economic structures of Northwest Europe and transatlantic relations, in hope of developing actions that will provide sustainable and reciprocal economic benefits. Certain areas require immediate attention. Regulatory cooperation has to be broadened alongside reducing restrictive measures governing the functionality of different market sectors to increase trade activity and have a unified market structure. This requires the unification of industry standards alongside regulations pertaining to product safety, environmental protection, and finance services, giving equal opportunity for enterprises to thrive on both sides of the Atlantic.

The advancement of an innovative as well as a cooperative approach towards technology is fundamental in defining the future scopes of the economic partnership. Technological emerging investments, in particular, focus on strategising sustained economic growth, job opportunities, and overall global competitiveness. Advances in clean energy, artificial intelligence, and digital infrastructural technologies provide promising prospects for synergistic collaborations that ensure collective benefits.

Collaboration and active participation are essential in pursuing resilient climate initiatives as well as holistic sustainable development goals. Through joint innovative research, tackling diverse environmental challenges, as well as investing in renewable energy and sustainable alternatives, societal wellbeing is enhanced while economic prospects are utilised for efficient environmental management. Thereupon, Delta can excel in green technologies and environmental sustainability escalation, showcasing the transatlantic economic partnership as powerful eco-friendly proactive industry leaders.

Transatlantic economic partnerships have the opportunity at hand to display remarkable proactive eco-friendly initiatives by improving responsible business approaches, further driving innovation towards ameliorating climate change, and enhancing renewable energy usage. Transformations in logistics and global supply chains are characterised by the need to fulfil flexible coherence policies, increasing adaptability and efficiency emphasis. Improvement of any supply chain strengthens the resilience benchmark and magnifies virtualisation interdisciplinary sourcing, therefore enhancing operational efficiency. Conducting such risk management measures ensures stable economic opportunities.

Ultimately, the attainment of an equitable and comprehensive economic collaboration entails resolving societal issues such as employees' rights and inclusivity. Addressing social issues like the equitable treatment of women, proper representation of different races and ethnicities, and inclusive workforce demographics enhances the unity and moral character of the Transatlantic Economic Partnership. Applying social responsibility regarding economic policymaking indicates that the policymakers are committed to the values of equity and growth, hence progress.

To these future steps, both the United States and the European Union could develop a strong, innovative, and sustainable economic alliance that acts as a driver for global wealth and advancement.

10

The EU's Pursuit of Strategic Autonomy

Trade policies in a multipolar world

Understanding Strategic Autonomy

The European Union aims to embed a strategic autonomy feature into its policy framework in an attempt to strengthen its active presence in the international sphere and assert its influence globally. Perceiving the EU's security and strategic interests as hinges towards other international actors, the EU attempts to enhance its self-sufficiency through international security relations, integration processes, and foreign policy initiatives involving defence and security. This aim not only requires military capacity development, but also economically, technologically, and institutionally self-governing policy sufficiency. Weak power seeks, through a strategic autonomy approach, to strengthen its foothold devoid of heavily relying on foreign supremacy, allowing the EU to project its policies and secure its interests. This is a portrayal of adjusting to changing international circumstances in order to adopt a more profound approach to international policy-making.

Embracing multi-levels of autonomy seeks usability to holistically tackle pressing international affairs that define the EU's strategic objectives.

Strategic autonomy is an ever-evolving endeavour that necessitates the EU to heighten its coherence and integration among Member States, as well as to build closer relationships with partners of a similar ideology. Achieving strategic autonomy is a meticulous act of balancing self-sufficiency with cooperation, sustained by the will and unity of European Union countries. While the European Union is still working to adjust to new global realities, strategic autonomy remains a vital focus area of its policy framework, defining the nature of its international relations, and showcasing its efforts to be more assertive and resilient.

Predecessor contingencies relative to the autonomy of the EU

The idea of European strategic autonomy has a rich history that has transformed over time due to geopolitical shifts, security concerns, and global changes. The European continent was devastated after WWII, leading to the formation of institutions that would foster cooperation and prevent conflicts and wars in the future. The economic downturn was revitalised through the signing of the Treaty of Rome in 1957, which branched the construction of the European Economic Community (EEC). With the EEC came deepening economic relations with member states aimed at stability and prosperity for all. But it was not until after the Cold War that the idea of strategic autonomy started to gain traction as Europe tried to gain control over its foreign and security policy.

Fundamental changes to the international system following the dissolution of the Soviet Union encouraged the EU to internationalise its role as a global actor. During this time, the evolution of the Common Foreign and Security Policy (CFSP) and Common Security and Defence Policy (CSDP) showcased Europe's aspirations to independently manage security and defence matters. The increasing geopolitical complexity resulting from the enlargement of the EU to accommodate new Member States also poses new opportunities and challenges for strategic autonomy.

EU Balkan conflict crisis management and the neighbouring region crises brought to focus the dire need for efficient sophisticated conflict prevention mechanisms. This severe imbalance reinforced the need for greater autonomy in terms of security. The European Security Strategy of 2003, along with its revisions, outlined the pre-existing gaps in governance that the severe geopolitical imbalances created and envisioned a holistically comprehensive approach the Union engages in to global—internationally claiming cooperative engagement solutions to the dire challenges the world faces. The evolution of increasing autonomous power for the EU showcased attempts to tackle the intricate, highly fluid international system, continuously shaping Europe's strategic identity as an actor in global politics.

Strategies on Defence and Security

The struggle for strategic aloofness of the European Union is intricately connected with its defence and security strategies. With the strategic rivalry of the United States and China receiving considerable attention to defend interests, the focus of the EU has been systematically to redress its position in the world to improve its defence capacities and secure more coherent EU methods of security policy. The volatile geopolitical context, bearing uncertainty as well as the emergence of new phenomena, is compelling the Union to reconsider its policies in regard to defence and security. The need for an integrated and comprehensive posture for defence is increasingly apparent, given the persisting traditional security challenges and new hybrid threats, the evolutionary possibilities of cyber attacks, and multiple other vulnerabilities.

Increasing the military potential of the European Union and greater collaboration among the Member States are among the key perspectives in its defence policies. Steps have been taken towards increasing interoperability and cooperation in the modernisation of defence materiel and the procurement of defence systems. The signing of the Treaty of Lisbon marked the beginning of Permanent Structured Cooperation (PESCO), which is an important milestone in the evolving defence structure of the participating EU countries. This Collaborative Project intends to enhance cooperation in the structure of defence related to the induced research, the standardisation of defence capabilities, and aid industrial cooperation to strengthen autonomy and supremacy in defence.

While fortifying conventional defence abilities, the EU is also focused on addressing non-military concerns such as terrorism, cyber threats, and hybrid warfare. The evolution of distinctly military and civilian components of security systems suggests the EU's determination to meet the security needs of its Member States and citizens. Cybersecurity enhancements, disinformation countermeasures, and improved crisis management capabilities all exemplify the EU's preparedness and intention to defend its security concerns.

The European Union's security and defence policies have a strong interrelation with its relationships with outside partners, including NATO and other international organisations. While transatlantic cooperation develops, the EU tries to maintain strong alignment with NATO and further the European Union's Defence Policy at the same time. The complementarity of defence efforts from the EU and NATO serves to strengthen the need for shared defence planning and burden-sharing in Europe.

The continuing discussion on defence and security emphasises the need for cooperation between the Atlantic partners in dealing with shared security issues. The EU seeks to promote order and global peace and security by fostering synergies and complementarity within the EU, between the United States and other allies on the other side of the Atlantic, which aids the functioning of a rules-based international order. In the end, the strategies of the EU in the domain of defence and security are equally important for the strategic autonomy of the EU and defining the Union as a responsible global security actor.

Economic Resilience and Industrial Policy

Fostering economic resilience while designing industrial policy in the context of the rapidly changing global environment is strategically important for the European Union in realising its autonomous goals. To face economic and geopolitical headwinds, the EU has attempted to strengthen the undermining pillars of its autonomy, sharpening its vulnerabilities. A vital part of this effort is the creation of a robust industrial policy that fuels innovation and competition while safeguarding the critical industries of European sovereignty.

Economic resilience is understood as the capability to endure and recover from economic shocks, whether they stem from internal or external sources. The focus the EU places on economic resilience highlights the importance of risk mitigation, supply chain diversification, and building national self-sufficiency. The EU seeks to enhance its economic structure through strategic investments, regulatory policies, and supportive frameworks for emerging industries while attempting to avoid disruption, sustain growth, and increase prosperity.

The EU's strategic autonomy agenda relies on an industrial policy framework. The EU aims to establish advanced manufacturing and digital technology renewable energy sectors by fostering the adoption of public-private partnerships, which will enable R&D and encourage the use of new technologies to develop Europe's industrial foothold globally, thus allowing Europe to build a resilient industrial base that will ensure innovative and high-quality job creation.

When pursuing economic resilience and formulating an industrial policy, the EU has to contend with numerous problems, particularly those involving the international sphere, environmental sustainability, the digital transformation, and ethical and regulatory frameworks. In this regard, collaboration and cooperation between EU Member States, industry actors, and policymakers is necessary to develop an autonomous, cohesive, and systematic industrial strategy based on strategic autonomy.

As it moves ahead, behaviourally proactive economic resilience and industrial policy within the EU demonstrates the intent of the Union to defend its economically vital interests, while also indicating a desire to shift towards greater self-reliance when it comes to trade, technology, and innovation. Integration of the industrial policy with economic multifunctions at the centre of globalisation and technological advancement transforms the economic landscape of the Union and strengthens its position in the international economy.

Technological sovereignty: Developments in digital technologies and AI

As the European Union strives for strategic autonomy, the pursuit of technological sovereignty has become especially important concerning digital advances and AI. To keep pace with rapid innovations around the world, the EU understands the need to preserve its digital capabilities and minimise reliance on external providers of technology. Considerations on the various aspects of technological sovereignty will include governance of data, cybersecurity, digital infrastructure, and AI development.

The goal of the EU's technological sovereignty policy is to guarantee that European companies and citizens have access to cutting-edge technologies while also protecting privacy, security, and ethical values. In this regard, the EU sets and implements policies and regulations intended to create a favourable digital ecosystem within the Union's borders. In particular, the EU is facing the challenge of protecting critical digital infrastructure, which has prompted the development of strong cybersecurity policies and the response of countermeasures against potential threats and vulnerabilities.

The EU appreciates the impact of AI on many fields and is therefore heavily investing its resources into artificial intelligence R&D. In order to manage the risks posed by new technologies, the EU promotes the development of AI in a manner that does not infringe upon fundamental rights and values. The European AI Act is an example of the attempts made by the EU to legally bind AI development to humanity, nurture innovation, and simultaneously ensure responsible use of power.

The EU's concerns surrounding data governance issues are crucial to achieving autonomy over technology. The EU has enacted data protection laws like the GDPR, which enables the protection of individual privacy while regulating the international circulation of personal information. With data becoming increasingly essential for promoting innovation and growth, the EU is also striving to create and implement a data governance strategy that safeguards, controls, and allows transparent access to data while reducing the risks associated with uncontrolled use.

As a final point, the EU strives to take control of its digital future through AI innovation and value-based construction, as highlighted in "technological sovereignty". In the document "EU Digital Strategy", it aims for achieving self-sufficiency by integrating industrial policy, innovation, investment, and regulations to provide a sense of leadership in global competition.

Trade Policies within a Multipolar World

In attempting to read the paragraph's headline *Trade policies in a multipolar world*, one could assume it's an overly simplistic description of a highly complex global phenomenon. As it appears, the relations between countries and trading blocs become more and more derived from politics and the internal relations of their participants instead of merely being economic interactions. The understanding of a multipolar world clearly indicates the existence of this enhanced complexity given by multiple competing economic pillars.

New factors are emerging in global markets, many of them needing advanced strategic approaches towards dealing with them.

The European Union, for instance, faces challenges with regard to trade in the dynamic relationship with its new partners like China, India, Brazil appearing on the list of accepted world economies. To cope with the on-going transformation and protect its geopolitical interests and withstand socio-political threats coming from the geopolitical landscape surrounding Europe, the EU is increasingly aiming at implementing a value-based trade strategy.

These opponents act in compliance with clearly outlined laws of international trade which the EU intends to strengthen and defend actively in common with other nations. Along that, the EU dedicates efforts in counteracting using state-sustained economy systems, which help unfounded authority and rivalry on international trade matrix trade's resources, principles and assets set up to provide balance.

Constructive coalition bloc approaches outlining the benefits including the reciprocal advantages principle regarding free trade zone agreements. These are turned into preconditions for supporting the European identity diagnostics facing fierce identity lesion hostilities to billing developments on the continent alongside the founding member states principles of law while respecting environmentally friendly practices.

Simultaneously, the European Union (EU) understands the importance of shifting its trade options to reduce reliance on one single market. This strategic form of diversification helps the EU adjust to shifting geopolitical changes along with the possible threats that come with them. The EU seeks to improve its economic strength by fostering trade relations in multiple areas, and at the same time, retain a certain level of power when negotiating for better trade deals.

The EU's global trade strategies and policies regarding a multipolar environment are guided by the need to capitalise on the latest digital and technological advancements while ensuring the privacy and safety of personal and corporate data. The EU aims for a balance between the integration of the digital economy and traditional commerce by encouraging free trade and protectionism concerning sensitive data, intellectual property, and proprietary information. The EU focuses on uniting regulations and establishing alignment with cooperative countries to accomplish their goals of sustainable, technology-centred, and driven trade, which is essential for boosting the economy.

The changing geopolitical context of strategic partnerships and rivalries also impacts the EU's trade policies. The Union's relations with other global powers have to balance the economic priorities and the politics of the world power system. In a context of geopolitical tensions, conflicting interests pose difficulties which require advanced diplomacy and comprehension of trade and security interrelationships.

To sum up, negotiating trade policies within a multipolar world aimed at achieving strategic autonomy reflects for the EU a blend of economic considerations married to normative engagement and strategic visionary thinking. Upholding EU interests and values while engaging in global trade requires a high level of diplomatic skill, agility in policymaking, and proactive interaction with multiple actors.

Governance and the Institutional System

With regard to the strategic autonomy of the European Union, institutional frameworks and governance are pivotal in the formation of policies and strategies. The EU functions within a sophisticated institutional system, which contains numerous decision-making and bureaucratic bodies as well as mechanisms representing the Member States. This intricate system embodies the interests and priorities of the 27 EU Member States that participate in formulating and implementing policies pertaining to strategic autonomy. An important component of the EU's institutional system is the European Commission that exercises executive power to draft the laws, implement EU policies, and represent the EU in international treaty negotiations. In partnership with the European Parliament, the Council of the European Union, and the European Council, the Commission attempts to move forward the strategic autonomy agenda within the complicated interplay of EU governance. The European External Action Service (EEAS) has outstanding importance in the fusion of foreign and security policies of the EU and in the provision of diplomatic assistance and, thus, in the global projection of the EU. The European Defence Agency (EDA) has been working together with the Member States on the research and development of defence capabilities and underscores the institutional efforts to bolster EU defence capabilities.

The principle of subsidiarity permits these institutions to function at their level without undermining central governance or national freedom. The EU's system of governance also includes collaboration with international organisations like NATO and strategic dialogues with other important international actors, which reflects the EU's commitment to multilateralism while developing strategic autonomy. The EU's established initiatives like Permanent Structured Cooperation (PESCO) and the European Defence Fund (EDF) express the EU's intentions toward greater cooperation and investment in defence. The attempts to simplify the decision-making processes, increase synergy amongst Member States, and promote coherent actions in the domain of security and defence illustrate the pace of changes in the institutional frameworks and governance systems of the EU. Nonetheless, there are still gaps such as the lack of a strong consensus among Member States, the diverse and at times conflicting national interests, and aligning strategic goals with emerging shifts in global power relations. Addressing these issues calls for a carefully crafted approach in which collective decision-making takes place alongside respecting the sovereignty of nations, supported by clear, accountable, and robust governance structures.

The development of the European Union toward strategic autonomy moves forward in parallel with the effectiveness of its governance system and institutional frameworks, which will shape Europe's security architecture, prosperity evolution, and global role.

Transatlantic strategic relations and autonomy

For centuries, transatlantic relations have been one of the fundamental pillars of world geopolitics, profoundly influencing both the international environment and global order. The interplay between the European Union's grappling with strategic autonomisation and the United States merits consideration in relation to the contemporary international framework. The EU's reinforcing strategic autonomy is inevitably entangling the Partnership with an oceanic ally, where the collective security shield clashes with the design for independence and sovereignty.

The transatlantic alliance has often served as a bulwark for Western values and principles on fundamental democratic freedoms, human rights and market economy, and has anchored common initiatives of the EU and USA. A certain divergence of priorities and approaches to transatlantic cooperation has emerged in the last years. The EU's assertion of strategic autonomy tends to be viewed as a skeptical development for transatlantic relations, particularly concerning defence, security, and trade.

From a security standpoint, the EU's attempts to bolster strategic autonomy have provoked concern about how Europe can regionally and globally autonomously respond to security issues without US reliance. The EU's own security concerns along with its dependency on the US as the main security provider for Europe elucidate the need for transatlantic European security relations reconceptualisation. While the US continues to be important for Europe, disagreements about defence expenditures, commitment to NATO, and military engagements highlight the need to reconstruct the transatlantic security architecture. Initiatives by the EU to construct autonomous defence capabilities and structures have engendered discussions about burden sharing and NATO's role in Euro-Atlantic security.

In the lower levels of the strategic autonomy hierarchy, a new space for consideration is a normative balance with transatlantic interdependence and the pursuit of enhanced economic independence. Struggles regarding digital taxation, data privacy, and associated regulatory trade policy frameworks reveal the difficulties accompanying the creation and implementation of different policies at different levels. The protection of economic interests alongside the promotion of fair competition marks a new interaction area of strategic autonomy and transatlantic trade policy that deserves more attention.

It is critical to point out that the EU's strategic autonomy is not at odds with the United States. Instead, it demonstrates the evolution of international order and the need to respond to an unprecedented global reality. Within the context of transatlantic relations and strategic autonomy, the EU and the US face the complex problem of balancing divergent interests alongside reciprocal values, which has traditionally acted as the glue of the alliance. In the end, how the transatlantic partners balance self-defined strategic autonomy and collective defence will define the global order in the 21st century.

Challenges and Critiques on Strategic Autonomy

While the European Union (EU) attempts to achieve strategic autonomy, there are a number of hurdles and criticisms that deeply affect this growth. One notable problem is in the area of security and defence. The development of the strategic autonomy of the EU tends to create complications for NATO and its efforts, raising concerns about the coherence and transatlantic security cooperation. The absence of a common European approach to defence and the varying degree of military capabilities of the EU Member States poses great challenges towards a unified security policy. The reliance on outside providers of crucial defence technologies and equipment systematically obstructs the ability of the EU to claim full autonomy in its defence capabilities.

A different challenge has to do with economic resilience and industrial policy. As previously mentioned, attaining strategic autonomy requires a strong economy that is equally robust and resilient to withstand external shocks and pressures. Still, economic interdependencies with global powers, especially in trade and investment, raise concerns about the possibility of the EU fully disconnecting and acting independently in its own interest. Competing national interests and regulatory differences, alongside the activities of multinational enterprises and their interests, create complex obstacles to the cohesive policies designed to fortify the economic autonomy of the EU.

Sovereignty in the digital realm is perhaps the most prominent in the contemporary context. The European Union has to confront the escalating power of non-European technology monopolies, along with the dangers relating to dependence on foreign technologies in critical infrastructure areas like national security, cybersecurity, artificial intelligence, and telecommunications. For the European Union, the imbalances created by efforts to attain innovation, alongside the need to safeguard sensitive data and infrastructure, make the pursuit of strategic autonomy highly paradoxical.

The discussion of strategic autonomy goes hand in hand with trade relations in a multipolar system. On the one hand, the EU is trying to create new trade relationships, as well as encourage an international order that is based on rules, but at the same time is dealing with geopolitical and other world power tensions, protectionism, and competition, which make autonomous trade policies difficult for the EU. The EU is caught trying to balance rules and norms with economic interests, along with the asymmetric nature of global trade, which underscores the complexity of the challenges for the EU.

The absence of an institutional framework and governance structures is an additional challenge to strategic autonomy. The lack of central coordination and coherence among EU institutions and Member States creates an enormous challenge considering the plethora of interests and policy approaches existing in the Union. The never-ending disputes regarding the decision-making authority, the allocation of funding, and the division of powers add to the criticism of the EU claiming strategic autonomy.

The list of challenges and criticisms of strategic autonomy is boundless – security, economic overreliance, tech fragility, trade intricacies, and governance issues. Confronting these challenges demands a precise balancing act that reconciles internal and external intricacies with competing interests in order to fulfil the goal of EU autonomy.

Optimistic and Pessimistic Forecasts of European Sovereignty

As the European Union works towards achieving strategic autonomy within the globalised world, European sovereignty is simultaneously expanding and contracting. Throughout the next few decades, the EU is likely to encounter several opportunities and constraints which will significantly impact its capacity as a sovereign unit.

The European Union's enforcement of a more integrated defence and security focus aims to shift the sovereignty balance towards the EU. The consolidation of defence research, development, and acquisition collaboratives such as PESCO (Permanent Structured Cooperation) reinforces the belief towards achieving strategic autonomy. The enhancement of external and internal security threats motivates the EU to increase its role as a security provider. Furthermore, the alignment of member states towards common defence expenditures will be crucial in determining the decisiveness of EU autonomous action in security matters.

The economic self-sufficiency of the European Union, as well as its industrial policy, will heavily rely on the sovereignty of Europe. In an attempt to strengthen its independence, the EU is actively working towards economic self-sufficiency by mitigating policies and alliances that externally dictate its decisions and controlling spearhead industries. The EU will have to make advancements in critical technologies, innovation, and infrastructure in order to achieve economic independence; this includes dominating emerging global markets. The goal is to nurture innovation-driven internal competition in the EU to sustain growth and accelerate digital transformation.

The other major issue is related to the sovereignty of the EU in technology, especially regarding AI and digitalisation. As digital technologies permeate other areas of the economy, for global competitiveness, Europe's ability to self-administer is crucial in setting frameworks for regulating new technologies and data exploitation laws in alignment with its cultural norms. For achieving technological sovereignty, the EU needs to focus on the human-centric angle of AI, ensuring strong protective measures for identity data and enhancing cyber defence systems.

Alliances and trade policies will affect the expansion of European sovereignty in a multipolar world order. With globalisation, the EU's attempt to build strategic alliances and effectively use its economic power will be important in the international arena and will determine the autonomy it has in global trade. The dispute over international trade, the promotion of strong supply chains, and the EU's capacity to regulate its business with the regional economic powers will define how the EU impacts the sovereignty it retains regarding trade.

In conclusion, the forecast of European sovereignty will rely on how spatial the geopolitical shifts are along with the EU's internal counterbalancing interests. If the EU strategically plans and invests in borders through security, economic fortitude, technological advancements, and commerce, it could change the narrative of being a mere actor to an autonomous influencer on the global stage. Still, the ambition towards strategic independence should go hand in hand with recognising interdependence and effective cooperation to promote shared interests and protect collective sovereignty within the context of globalisation.

11

Policy Divergences
Data Privacy, Taxation, and Regulation

Foundation of the Political Differences

The foundation of the Transatlantic relationship between the USA and the EU has always been mutual values, shared objectives, and economic relations. However, there is a widening gap in political attitudes towards data sovereignty, taxation, and regulation. This is emerging as one of the most considerable challenges to the longstanding partnership. This chapter looks at the complexity of the differences in relations between the USA and the EU, in particular the differences in the treatment and regulatory frameworks of privacy laws.

Differences in regulations are rooted in fundamental rights such as an individual's privacy and the degree to which a state can intervene and safeguard it. The EU has taken the lead in formulating comprehensive legal instruments geared towards the protection of data like the General Data Protection Regulation (GDPR). GDPR is famous for its strict requirements in data withholding, processing, consent, and allowing people to control their personal information. On the other hand, the USA takes a multi-layered approach to data protection with a sectoral character at the national level and variable state laws at the subnational level. A significant example of this is the California Consumer Privacy Act (CCPA).

This gap regarding regulatory approaches illustrates not only the underlying ideological differences, but also the varying cultures regarding privacy and data protection. These gaps have led to problems in transatlantic data flows which affect businesses, consumers and policymakers on both sides of the ocean. The international transfer of personal data and the operation of global companies have become politically sensitive topics highlighting the necessity to resolve these issues.

These differences include also tax policies, especially concerning international businesses and digital services. The EU has been trying to reform the tax system in a way that aims to make sure digital corporations contribute adequately, which has led to discussions on the taxation of digital services and the need for coordinated action against tax avoidance. In contrast, the United States has raised concerns over these unilateral actions, advocating for a comprehensive approach through the OECD's work on 'taxing digital economy' initiatives.

These disputes continue to strain international relations as they underscore the intricate web of global capitalism blended with competition for resources and national autonomy. The problems caused by such discrepancies are not merely of a legal technical nature, but rather much more fundamental issues of state, control and power relations in the contemporary world order. To understand this multi-faceted challenge, it is necessary to analyse the underlying political divergences in the context of shifting geopolitics and differing visions for a rules-based world order. In any case, resolving such conflicts of policies is achievable through coordinated effort, discussion, and agreement on protecting the interests of the opposing citizens and businesses along the transatlantic region.

The principles of privacy regulations in the EU and the USA

Borders and technological advancements gave birth to a new issue; data privacy. The respective laws in the EU and the USA are deeply rooted in their unique cultures, legal, and historical contexts. To address the growing concern regarding data privacy, the EU instituted the General Data Protection Regulation (GDPR) in 2018, which set forth strict requirements regarding consent, individual rights, and data access. Under GDPR, there is a fundamental right to digital data privacy which underpins commercial and organisational data processing activities. Adopting policies enforcing privacy by design and by default has expanded the scope of business operations which need to comply with data privacy laws, raising global standards for data privacy regulations. Unlike the EU, the USA has not passed a comprehensive federal law for personal data protection akin to the GDPR. The USA deals with data privacy issues through a fragmented approach with state-specific laws, as seen with the California Consumer Privacy Act (CCPA). The CCPA does provide a framework for individual data rights along the lines of the GDPR, enabling consumers to know, delete, and refuse the sale of their personal information, but it does come with restrictions.

The American approach towards privacy has historically been based on ancillary laws as a result of specific industries like healthcare, finance, and even children's online privacy. This model is more diverse and industry-based in nature as compared to the EU's consolidated and rights-based approach. The differences in attitudes, legal traditions, and cultural interests have shaped the gaps in privacy laws between the EU and the U.S. To put it simply, the EU tends to view privacy as a fundamental human right while the U.S. focuses more on commercial innovation alongside freedom of speech. Business, government, and individual frameworks regarding standards of privacy create different perceptions and cause opposing regulatory philosophies concerned with ownership over privacy and data.

These considerations outline the challenges with coming to an agreement on issues of transatlantic data privacy. In essence, these differences demonstrate the need for more collaboration in regards to tackling the issues formed due to the digital ecosystem.

Comparative analysis: GDPR versus CCPA

Studying the General Data Protection Regulation (GDPR) and the California Consumer Privacy Act (CCPA) together shows how differently the EU and US regulate data privacy. GDPR, adopted in 2018, is the world's most comprehensive and authoritative piece of legislation concerning data protection owing to its aim at empowering individuals and coordinating data privacy laws across Europe. Its main principles are centred on consent, minimisation, purpose limitation, and accountability stressing the rights of data subjects and imposing strict obligations on data controllers and processors. On the contrary, CCPA, which came into effect in 2020, constitutes a significant milestone in the American system of regulation by giving Californian consumers more control over the personal data that companies hold about them. While CCPA is similar to GDPR in some respects, it also contains new provisions such as the right to opt out of sales, non-discrimination rights, and a private cause of action for data breach.

The GDPR and CCPA laws differ with respect to scope, applicability, enforcement mechanisms, and the specific rights assigned to individuals. Territorial scope is an area where notable differences can be discerned. The GDPR has extraterritorial provisions that concern personal data processing by entities that offer goods and services to individuals living in the EU. In contrast, the CCPA is much narrower in focus because it is concerned only with certain businesses operating in California that meet particular revenue or data handling thresholds. Compared to the CCPA, GDPR has a narrower definition of personal data and sensitive data. This is due to the differences in legal cultures and attitudes towards privacy between the EU and the US. Another area of difference is enforcement mechanisms. The

CCPA relies on the California Attorney General and to a limited extent private lawsuits, while the GDPR grants significant powers to supervisory authorities to impose harsh penalties for non-compliance. The rights assigned to individuals under each framework differ in emphasis, with the GDPR focusing on informed consent and the right to be forgotten, while the CCPA focuses on the right to disclosure and the right to opt out.

The consequences of these different legislative systems are ever evolving and transcend jurisdictional boundaries. Businesses with footprints in the European Union (EU) and California encounter intricate complications concerning meeting compliance prerequisites, shifting operational definitions, and managing cross-border data movements. These gaps in the law add to the already complicated nature of transatlantic data transfer, thus the need for rigorous or substantial equivalence tests to allow the flow of data while guarding it with strong legal protections. The comparison of GDPR and CCPA acts as a reference point for policymakers, companies, and citizens in European countries and America in understanding and trying to merge the split in policies at a time when data privacy is a crown issue policy due to rapid technological advancement alongside societal demand.

Tax policy: Bridging the transatlantic differences

Tax policy remains one of the most significant divides between the European Union (EU) and the United States, highlighting both challenges and opportunities for transatlantic relations. The disparities in tax policies, focused especially on taxes on corporations, have been a constant bone of contention not just for multinational firms but also in relation to economic competition and international commerce. On one hand, understanding the delicate relationship between these two regions from this angle is critical in developing and fostering cooperation that will serve to bridge the gap between the two regions' opposing divisions.

The European Union (EU) was the first area in the world to develop a digital economic tax having regard to the imbalance in tax revenue and taxes paid by digital companies operating in the region. This 'digital services tax' proposal has been aimed at the revenue derived from the digital economy. Simultaneously, the discussions surrounding the Common Consolidated Corporate Tax Base (CCCTB) came as an attempt to unify the corporate tax system within EU Member States for the purpose of curtailing tax competition and profit shifting. It is equally important to assess the impact of such measures on US-based technology companies and the global economy transatlantically.

On the other hand, the United States has actively pursued its own tax reform initiatives, as illustrated by the 2017 Tax Cuts and Jobs Act (TCJA), which made substantial changes to the corporate tax structure by lowering the federal corporate tax rate and transitioning to a territorial taxation system for multinationals. These reforms have ignited fierce contention over the effectiveness of the US's investment competitiveness, investment global flow, and overall international market position in relation to other countries.

In trying to solve these disparities, all parties involved from policymakers, economists to business leaders try to balance competing interests while taking into account the distinct jurisdictional priorities and boundaries. For example, the effort to harmonise transatlantic divergences in tax policy utilises dialogue forums like the Transatlantic Economic Council, which promotes the sharing of ideas and seeks areas of agreement. These cooperative research projects, along with joint economic impact assessments, contribute to analysing the effects of specific changes in tax policies on trade and investment between regions across the Atlantic.

OECD and G20 are also important in supporting international cooperation in tax matters and drafting universal policies for responding to the issues of taxation resulting from digitalisation. Continual work on the OECD Base Erosion and Profit Shifting (BEPS) policy and setting a universal bottom limit for taxation are supportive strategies in the re-establishment of norm-setting and equalising competitive taxation between countries.

In summary, the differences in transatlantic policies require a delicate mix of stimulating a competitive business landscape and ensuring that a reasonable contribution is made toward public revenue. The discourse of tax policy in question continues to adapt – the ever-changing interplay between geography and politics, economics on one hand, and technology on the other requires unified attention to alleviate gaps and bolster the strength of transatlantic economic relations.

Debates on digital taxation: Contested terrain

The digital economy has created new and innovative ways to conduct business around the world, which presents difficulties with regard to the policies and their implementation. As economies on either side of the Atlantic try to figure out how to tax the various digital services and products, the debates concerning digital tax have heightened for policymakers, multinational firms, and stakeholders across the Atlantic.

Each of the groups described above has at least one dispute that stems from the user-based versus a physical address-based approach to taxation. The digital economy's cross-border nature increasingly erodes traditional tax jurisdiction boundaries where value is purportedly created and how it ought to be measured for tax estimation

Taxes in the EU and the United States have differing impacts on the debate regarding digital taxation. The EU has been the frontrunner in trying to implement taxes on digital services, trying to ensure that the digital corporations adequately pay taxes based on the interactions that offer value, data collection, and many other activities within the ecosystem. Because of concern over the consequences such policies would have on American technology firms, the U.S. has preferred a collective approach through the OECD.

Certain nations unilaterally imposing taxes on the digital services of multilateral corporations have invariably caused tensions in international relations and trade. The retaliation threats that have emerged provoke concerns about trade wars, making it clear that geopolitical affairs, economics, and politics are irrevocably linked.

These technological shifts during the last few decades have necessitated collaboration and a unified stance between nations to face the problems created by the adapting digital economy. Nonetheless, while valid concerns like economic competitiveness, innovation, and tax equity emerge, these disputes have to be directed towards balancing taxation policies and fostering growth.

In creating a digital economy, stakeholders should work to integrate all concerns into a single structure or model that encompasses all interests. It will be important to create a cohesive and sensible approach that balances fairness with economic growth, and ensures reliability in taxation principles.

Regulatory Approaches: Convergence or Divergence?

Developing a holistic approach to regulating data privacy, taxation, and other aspects of the digital world has been a focal point of attention on both sides of the Atlantic for some years now. One hallmark of the European Union (EU) and European Economic Area (EEA) datacentre's exposure to personal data is the General Data Protection Regulation (GDPR), which serves as a comprehensive legislative framework to safeguard the personal data and privacy rights of individuals. The GDPR obliges organisations to follow stringent guidelines regarding the collection, processing, and storage of their data, thereby empowering individuals over their personal information and data.

In comparison, the United States has approached this issue differently, with disparate federal and state-level regulations. While the country's sector-specific laws provide some degree of coverage via HIPAA and COPPA, there is no overarching federal personal data protection legislation analogous to the EU GDPR. Instead, operational control of data privacy and security in the United States is mainly administered through laws specific to a given industry or self-regulation by the respective sectors.

The differing ways in which the two regions regulate important issues raise concerns about the compatibility and interoperability of data protection regulations within the EU and the US. Such differences affect the privacy rights of individuals and create difficulties for businesses operating on a global scale. For multinational corporations, the need to comply with both sets of legal requirements can prove to be painfully intricate and expensive, raising the glaring issues of access to markets and transatlantic trade.

In the same breath, overseas digital taxation remains one of the strategically unresolved problems, as the EU and the US part ways over the methods of imposing taxes on digital companies achieving keen revenue figures in international markets. While the OECD tries to negotiate a composite approach to deal with the tax issues resulting from the economy's digital transformation, clashes of opinion on the allocation of taxing rights and thresholds for taxable presence continuously fuel debates on just and equitable taxation.

With the evolution of new technologies comes content moderation, platform responsibility, competition policy, and these topics have drawn the most prominent differences in regulation. The EU's frontier approach manifested in the Digital Services Act and the Digital Markets Act aims to regulate the behaviour of online platforms, while the US still struggles with debates on the two-hundred and thirtieth section of the Communications Decency Act, as well as antitrust actions against the most powerful tech companies.

The policies on both sides of the Atlantic, as well as their accompanying businesses and stakeholders, must come to a consensus about managing differences in social norms, legal frameworks, and economic factors - something which deceptively appears simple but is in fact very challenging. To balance the fundamental rights of the people and the concepts of innovation, active transatlantic relations, and guarding free market competition, finding balance is essential.

The consequences of policy differences on transatlantic trade

Transatlantic trade has faced challenges due to the conflicting regulatory frameworks that the United States and the European Union impose. The clash of data protection laws, taxation policies, and other regulations poses risks for multinational corporations operating within both jurisdictions. These differences have added burdens to business operations while simultaneously adjusting the balance of transatlantic trade to be more fragmented and costly, which drives up compliance expenses. Within the separate EU and U.S. markets, competing data privacy laws such as the GDPR and CCPA have emerged, forcing corporations to maintain disparate data compliance structures and management frameworks, achieving compliance at the expense of strategic agility as a result of intricate organisational data management ecosystems. Differences in fiscal policy, especially the disputes concerning digital taxes, complicate international commerce and strain the financial systems of global firms. These developments make it extremely difficult for enterprises to manage diverse tax policies across national borders due to the risk of encountering multiple taxation jurisdictions. Standards and policies, including those governing the development of technical efficacy and market access, have also been affected by the dissimilarity in regulations.

Competing regulations have created problems pertaining to market access and the movement of goods, reducing the overall competitiveness of businesses in both regions. The lack of convergence on certain policies has inhibited growth and dissuaded investment alongside the fragmentation of cross-border economic collaboration. The consequences of policy fragmentation on transatlantic trade have added challenges at the enterprise level and extend to more basic economic impacts, which brings economic tension and hinders the potential of transatlantic trade from being fully realised. There is a need to more actively address the negative impacts of regulatory divergence, which calls for the attention of the EU and the US to better work towards alignment and cooperation. These concerns require collaboration to streamline regulations and enhance transparency as well as sponsorship of regulatory consistency to create an optimal climate for transatlantic trade and investment. Achieving desired outcomes is possible through reducing outdated restrictions and sponsoring economic and environmental Pavlovian conditions to shield shared EU-US interests.

Multinational companies: Navigating the regulatory landscape

Like nearly all areas of business, data privacy and data protection in a multinational context poses unique challenges for multinational companies. From a cross-border perspective, the United States and European Union present a decidedly stark juxtaposition in terms of regulatory *taxation secrecy, as well as the boundaries of confidentiality*. Multinational businesses operate across borders and face an almost endless and often conflicting set of laws. This maze of regulations, which govern not only data and digital privacy, but also tax compliance, business legislation, and sectoral regulations, creates a gradually tightening noose around a business's head. With the shift towards greater policy harmonisation, it is increasingly becoming a prominent consideration straddling the transatlantic area for ease of doing business. As businesses shift their attention on the school of policy, they also end up with a slew of data privacy laws to navigate through. The EU's General Data Protection Regulation develops distinct rules regarding the collection, retention, and processing of personal data, and every firm that deals with data pertaining to the residents of the EU is subject to it, irrespective of its geographical location. In contrast, a patchwork approach characterises the regulatory landscape of the United States, and the California Consumer Privacy Act (CCPA) stands out as a key legislative element. The disparity creates difficulties in formulating standard policies for data processing across multiple jurisdictions. Strategic tax policies create barriers for companies due to the fact that corporate tax rates, transfer pricing, and the American and European digital tax legislations change frequently. The taxation of digital services in Europe as well as the discussions on a universal minimum corporate tax add to this complexity. Other primary and secondary regulations such as those related to the environment or the pharmaceutical industry have steep differences between the EU and US leading to custom strategies for each region. To navigate these obstacles, multinationals employ legal, compliance, or regulatory affairs teams who manage the red tape coming from various legislations. These teams are indispensable for developing and executing the firm's corporate compliance strategy and managing compliance risk. Such businesses expend significant resources on lobbying and stakeholder engagement to shape policies in order to bring about convergence of regulations. The development of international relations and forums for transatlantic regulatory cooperation enhances multilateral advocacy for unified regulations. Some businesses adopt voluntary initiatives and membership requirements to reduce legal ambiguity and ensure that their operations are conducted in accordance with industry best practices.

Navigating the regulatory mazes of multinational enterprises culminates in understanding the specific legal contours of each jurisdiction, thereby demonstrating the need for policy alignment to achieve smooth intercontinental trade at the same time.

Diplomatic channels and policy alignment

While multinationals shift from one operational region to another within the EU and the US, it becomes obvious that there is a dire need for policy alignment and harmonisation. The imposition of an all-encompassing system regarding data privacy, taxation, and regulation is imperative for increased transatlantic commerce devoid of discrimination for competitors on either side of the Atlantic.

These policies regard the alignment of legislative actions or regulations to remove gaps and bring efficiencies to the compliance burden within these frameworks. This requires significant mobilization of government, industry, and international bodies to facilitate effective law and policy dialogue. There is a perpetual need to build coalitions towards the achievement of common regulatory goals and cooperative approaches to the resolution of policy conflicts.

Diplomatic avenues are paramount in dealing with discussions around policy harmonisation. Instruments of bilateral and multilateral diplomacy such as the EU and USA summit enable policymakers to consider possible contours of concordance in data protection, taxation, and interfacing standards. Such diplomacy enables exchanges of or at least agrees on guidelines of best practices, identifiable challenges, and mutual benchmarks of regulatory divergence.

Diplomacy, in this sense, goes beyond government to include the active involvement of private citizens. Trade associations, business associations, or lobby groups are important in bridging the gap between the developed world transnational corporations and the policymakers. These groups participate in diplomacy that helps in the development of more realistic responses to the complexities of transatlantic policies.

Apart from diplomatic discussion, attempts at policy harmonisation at the international level through institutions seek to intentionally bring about uniformity to the policies. Joint action in the OECD, WTO, or G20 aids agreement on international norms and best practices in data protection, taxation, and regulation. These institutions offer the possibility of setting forth shared standards and frameworks that aid in achieving a higher level of consistency policymaking across different jurisdictions.

In the end, as shared governance advances, the policies must be woven together with strategic insight, dedication, and sustained effort. Efforts by the EU and the United States to solve these policy conflicts through diplomacy and a partnership on international issues could foster a more coherent transatlantic marketplace. Stimulated collaboration and engagement can effectively strengthen the partnership between the two economic powers regarding a coordinated approach to data privacy, taxation, and regulation.

Conclusion: Towards a unified framework?

To recapitulate, developing a unified approach to data privacy, taxation, and regulation within the European Union and the United States is undeniably intricate. Despite both sides being adamant in upholding their positions, the realities of our interconnected world emphasise the necessity of finding a balance. In this regard, the shared governance endeavours and the diplomatic efforts detailed in this book provide the slightest hope of mitigating the transcontinental divides.

Taking into account the historical, legal and economic aspects of each policy enables stakeholders on both sides of the Atlantic to understand the rationale and issues that have contributed to today's policies. Comparative examination of fundamental documents such as the General Data Protection Regulation (GDPR) and the California Consumer Privacy Act (CCPA) exposes the existence of divergences, but also of alignments and convergence opportunities.

The Protection of Personal Information Act (POPIA) and the GDPR present a direct relationship between ensuring data privacy, data security, fostering technological advancement, and stimulating economic growth. The discourse regarding digital taxation underscores cross-border concerns within a distinctly borderless digital marketplace that undergoes rapid transformations as multidisciplinary divisions.

There is no doubt that business executives and public policymakers need to discuss more cooperatively concerning the issues of discrepancy among divergent national regulations. For companies doing international business, the problem of engineering disparate measures becomes an organisational inefficiency and a cumbersome compliance task. A shared legal framework would alleviate these issues and facilitate smoother transatlantic business relations.

Noted however, the balance between prioritising stakeholders and national concerns requires care when focusing towards convergence. This balance actively seeks to ensure beneficial outcomes while safeguarding control to authorities. There needs to be proactive consideration towards the implications policy and governance structures as they relate to technological advancement.

This raises a significant question: Can innovation and economic competitiveness be maintained while individual rights within the US and EU are not infringed upon in a singular framework? While attempting to answer this question, it becomes apparent that pursuit stems from a legal and regulatory angle is seeking to deepen the connections across the Atlantic alliance and reaffirm shared ideals within an ever-evolving context.

Some challenges remain to be resolved. However, the possibility of developing a unified approach gives us an opportunity to take the lead in the creation of global policies and regulations. This suggests an effort to manage the opportunities that come with digital technology while upholding essential values. By doing this, the EU and the US could lead international activities aimed at fostering a safe, pro-innovation, and ethically grounded digital infrastructure. As we pursue such strategies, we approach the vision of a unified transatlantic approach which symbolises the sustained alliance and shared goals of two powerful partners.

12
Geopolitical Pressures
China's Rising Influence

Introduction to China's Global Strategy

The rise of China as a global economic power is accompanied by a vision that goes beyond its geographical limits. Initiatives like the Belt and Road Initiative (BRI) and the Asian Infrastructure Investment Bank (AIIB) showcase China's willingness to mould the geopolitical order and expand its reach around the world. These undertakings have been guided by a clear plan to facilitate economic growth, foster relationships and strengthen interconnections with countries in Asia, Africa, Europe, and other parts of the world. The win-win cooperation policy, which seeks to promote shared gains, is at the core of China's international strategy. It seeks to move towards a new order of international relations grounded on respect, equity, and inclusion.

As part of this strategy, China intends to employ its economic strength to cultivate various relationships with different countries through trade and investment while deepening the diplomatic and cultural ties with them. In this regard, the BRI, in particular, epitomises China's dedication towards infrastructure advancement and its commitment to foster economic synergy regionally on a wide scale and intra-regionally on narrow scales. Through the investment in important transport corridors, energy infrastructures, and Information Technology, China hopes to improve the economic development of its partners and at the same time facilitate their access to trade routes and markets.

Outside of the economy, China aims to wield its soft power through culture and other areas as a part of its global soft strategy. This incorporates aspects such as aiding the global expansion of the Chinese language and promoting Chinese traditional medicine and martial arts. The growing influence of the media and entertainment industries is also being deployed to project its culture overseas along with the diplomatic policies of China.

China's overarching strategies include the implementation of technological advancement for global competitiveness. The country's primary focus is placed on new artificial intelligence, telecommunications, and infrastructure technology with the aim of increasing its digital foothold, which leads to China being viewed as a potential frontrunner in innovation and technology as well as its advocate globally. China's active participation in international organisations and multilateral meetings depicts the country's resolve to transform global governance frameworks according to its interests and to establish rules and norms that define its worldview.

China's unfolding global strategies spark various reactions from world powers, which in turn undergo ongoing discussions regarding their impacts on existing sociopolitical standards as well as shifts in power balances. Thus, providing insights into the intricacies of China's global strategies provides an understanding of global politics as well as the interaction between countries.

Economic Growth and the 'Belt and Road' Initiative

China's rapid growth and development, along with its ambitious 'Belt and Road Initiative' (BRI), has gained global interest and remarkably stimulated contemporary geopolitical, economic, and growth discussions. The Belt and Road Initiative (BRI), a proposition made by Xi Jinping, the current president of China, aims to revive the ancient trade routes of the Silk Road and establish infrastructure systems across Asia, Africa, and Europe. This initiative is intended to strengthen China's influence and increase trade and investment among participating countries. This initiative is considered one of the most important foreign and economic policy projects initiated by China, showcasing its attempts at claiming global hegemony.

The scope of the BRI encompasses transport networks, energy pipelines, telecommunications infrastructure, as well as ports, offering immense opportunities for participating countries in the creation of employment, economic advancement, and regional integration. However, those in the Western world who are sceptics and critics remain anxious about issues of sustainability of debt, transparency, environmental concerns, geopolitical consequences, and the possibility of fostering dependency among the beneficiary countries. Adherence (or the lack of it) to international governance principles set by the West have fuelled debates about the real intentions behind the Chinese drive.

The expansion of the economy in China, along with the BIS's planful strategies, has led to drastic counter-strategies and responses from other world powers such as the USA and the European Union. These countries view the growing economic power of China as an asset, but one that needs to be dealt with cautiously. This has resulted in competition, engagement or even assertive alternative strategies in the BIS territories. The fusion of economic interests and global power struggle leads to a complicated system where the expansion of China's economy is deeply connected with international relations and the governance of the global economy.

With these varying and interrelated topics, it is essential that policymakers, analysts and every other relevant stakeholder put their efforts into formulating the right approach to dealing with the expansion of China's economy alongside the BIS. Detailed studies are greatly needed to analyse how changes will impact international and regional trade, as well as development, technological cooperation, energy security and even financial services. Finally, as China works towards achieving the outlined goals, constructive discussions are necessary to help in forming strategies based on sustainable development and transparent collaboration.

With regards to the "digital diplomacy" angle, one can see the increasing scope of China's "soft power reach" through its investment in 5G networks, satellites, and other digital infrastructure projects.

Advancements in technology and China's digital diplomacy initiatives

Considerable leaps under artificial intelligence, quantum computing, and 5G, as well as China's space programmes and other spheres, put China miles ahead of many nations. For China, advancing digitally is just one of the many benefits of robust domestic policies such as "Investing in cutting-edge technologies" that enable the country to harness "digital diplomacy" for augmenting its global influence.

Strategic deployment of digital tools serves as an effective lens to view and interact with other countries. Using technology, China has been at the forefront of changing perceptions of China in the world. It uses technology to transcend geographic boundaries as well as connect overseas citizens, enabling collaboration with citizens around the world as well as further serving its interests in foreign territories.

By using its technology, China has tried to establish digital links and connectivity across continents using projects such as the Digital Silk Highway, which aids in the country's Belt and Road Initiative. However, the deepening integration of digital technologies into China's diplomacy has given Western countries reason to worry about 'data security, intellectual property rights, and possible geopolitical exploitation'. The interaction between advancements in technology and digital diplomacy has become increasingly important in Sino-Western relations, taking the form of discussions on data privacy, cybersecurity, and the regulation of cutting-edge technologies. China's aggressive action to expand its digital strategy internationally has fuelled the call for stronger coordination and collaboration within the West to collectively manage those influences and promote shared interests and values. To grasp China's shifting position on the global stage and the complexities of contemporary geopolitics, it is crucial to comprehend the technological dimensions of China's digital diplomacy and foreign policy framework.

Military modernisation and strategic challenges

In conjunction with China's rapid economic development, the country has also sought to strengthen its strategic capabilities through military modernisation. The People's Liberation Army (PLA) has been acquiring cutting-edge weaponry like hypersonic missiles, anti-ship ballistic missiles, and stealth aircraft, in addition to expanding and modernising its naval and land forces. This increase in military spending is gradually changing China into a fierce regional power that is capable of sustaining military might beyond its frontiers.

China's spending in the domains of cyber and space warfare technologies is further complicating traditional security paradigms. The sophistication of military strategies is reflected in the PLA's focus on a strategy defined by integrated joint operations and network-centric warfare. This modernisation is not restricted to conventional capabilities; China is also growing its nuclear stockpile, making advances in missile defence systems, and developing offensive cyber warfare capabilities.

The developments in China have raised concerns among US and European defence planners who are trying to grasp the scope of China's strategic goals. The problem presented by China's modernisation of military capabilities goes far beyond the traditional military bounds. China's military expansion into strategically important regions, such as the South China Sea, has further strained relations with the United States. Additionally, China's aggressive posture toward territorial claims, along with attempts to safeguard sea routes and maritime interests, has heightened anxieties from rival global naval powers. China's maritime development and expansionist strategies have sparked a critical reevaluation of security frameworks and military defence strategies throughout the Indo-Pacific region. While China broadens its military presence, the post-WWII (1945) geopolitical structure within this crucial region is undergoing profound transformation, complicating security calculations for the United States, Europe, and regional allies. In this context, the delicate balance of security systems, advanced technologies, and diplomatic initiatives is forming the frontline of international rivalry for the years to come. Crafting effective policies to tackle these shifts requires analysis of China's developing military strategy and its consequences on international security frameworks.

Impact in the scope of international organisations

With China undergoing expansion of its influence across the globe, its role in international organisations has been of great importance to nations across the globe. China's activity in multilateral organisations like the United Nations (UN), World Trade Organisation (WTO), International Monetary Fund (IMF), and World Bank has received a lot of consideration regarding its participation concerning global governance and set standards. Given China's economic clout and growing diplomatic power, it is only rational that China attempts to utilise its position in these forums to pursue its strategic goals, often countering West-dominated initiatives and advocating for changes aligned with its objectives like its rivals do.

Perhaps one of the most crucial activities where we can vividly see China's impact is through funding of development and infrastructure projects. China has set up initiatives to serve as other alternatives to aid fund infrastructure development in emerging economies such as the Asian Infrastructure Investment Bank (AIIB) and New Development Bank (NDB), which serves to question impact on international financial institutions.

China's assistance in international aid and peacekeeping operations highlights its self-portrayal as a responsible stakeholder in assisting stability and development at a global level.

In the case of international organisations, China actively looks for opportunities to assume control of specialised agencies or to shape the policies of entire branches like telecommunications, intellectual property, environment, public health, and many others. The Belt and Road Initiative (BRI), which is China's flagship foreign policy endeavour, touches on various multilateral frameworks and regional concerns for collaboration while simultaneously raising Western fears over geopolitical and economic consequences.

The involvement of China in global organisations illustrates its willingness to reshape international policies and institutions in an attempt to accommodate its newly emerging status as a superpower. With the ongoing changes in the dynamics of multilateralism set against geopolitical contestation and shifting coalitions, it is critical to understand China's role and influence within these frameworks for the competing policymakers, scholars, and practitioners of modern international relations of the 21st century.

Soft Power: Culture, Education and Media

The growth of China's international influence has certainly made clear the application of soft power tools such as culture, education and the media. China has attempted to promote its language and cultural understanding through Confucius Institutes which could help shape public sentiment across the world.

The increasing number of international students studying at Chinese universities poses potential avenues for Chinese influence due to the relationships and networks formed. This is facilitated by China's investment in educational scholarships and exchanges. The expansion of state-owned Chinese media, such as CGTN (China Global Television Network), has furthered the spread of Chinese perspectives on world events. This shifts international narratives and discourses while raising concerns in the West regarding the control of information and propaganda, leading them to rethink the impact Chinese media has on the credibility of Western political and media discourse.

China's soft power became, for the first time, palpable to Western countries like the United States and European Union countries. Attempts to find a balance between fostering cultural and academic exchange and unwarranted foreign influence have sparked discussions on the regulation of Confucius Institutes on transparency in educational partnerships. As a response to China's attempts to spread soft power, Western countries have strengthened their cultural diplomacy by promoting educational programmes, independent media, and alternative perspectives to counter China's influence.

The use of soft power to win over people has now become an integral part of the dynamic political struggle between the West and China.

US and European responses to China's assertions

China's attempts to cement its place as a world superpower have made the US, alongside Europe, respond in unison as they seem to unanimously worry about Beijing's attempts to dominate global politics. This perception has triggered an evolutionary reshaping of foreign policy strategies and alliance systems to counter China's rise from multiple angles.

At a more fundamental level, US-European responses have sought to emphasise a single front for defending a rules-based international order that is transparent, equitable, and reciprocal in its dealings with China. This includes supporting multilateral agreements alongside strengthening domestic regulatory frameworks aimed at protecting against trade-dumping practices.

In security and defence, there has been some aligning of purpose in regard to constraining China's military modernisation programme and its impact on other arms of regional equilibrium. This has led to greater cooperation in the areas of intelligence sharing, joint military training and exercises, fortification of defence capabilities, and military buildups in the Indo-Pacific region. The deepening cooperation between the United States and its European allies in this regard demonstrates a common understanding of and commitment to the remnants of security structures set up after World War II, whether obsolete and no longer meeting the people's demands, expectations, or hopes.

After understanding China's power in international forums, the US and Europe have tried to use their diplomatic strength to push reforms that align with their traditional beliefs and attributes. Their strategy is to highlight socio-political narratives that focus on the importance of liberalism and individual freedom, which stands in stark contrast to China's argument of the effectiveness of socialism for developing nations.

Particular reference can be made for the strategy that emphasises the fostering of economic interdependence while seeking to lessen the impacts of over-dependence on Chinese supply chains and foreign investment. For instance, some negotiations aim at broader alteration of the trade relations toward tighter control of exports, increased screening of investments, and protection of critical infrastructure and technology from external control.

The Importance of Indo-Pacific Security Agreements

With China trying to expand its influence in the Indo-Pacific, there is growing focus on how security arrangements stabilise the region and mitigate strategic competition. The security dynamics in the Indo-Pacific remain contested due to the confluence of economic, military, and geopolitical activities, with great powers competing for dominance. The United States, having been an ally in this region post the World War II, has once again affirmed its attention to 'order' by re-committing to control the system it instituted, and to ensure the unimpeded movement of vessels in important maritime routes.

To counter China's aggressive actions, the U.S. heightened its security relations and increased its presence in the Indo-Pacific region by conducting joint military exercises, selling arms to allies in the region, and enhancing defence agreements with allies. The Quad, consisting of the

U.S., Japan, India, and Australia, has emerged as a strategic platform to enhance security cooperation and articulate a collective vision of 'a free, open and inclusive Indo-Pacific'.

At the same time, the European Union has gradually acknowledged and set out its vision for the Indo-Pacific strategic region, focusing on the enforcement of international law, international relations, sustainable development, and connectivity. Dialogue and fostering trust-building initiatives among regional participants are facilitated by multilateral institutions like ASEAN and the East Asia Summit. However, these changes in the security environment within the Indo-Pacific region also present some problems, particularly with China's increasing territorial and military expansionism, which deepens the concern of Western powers over potential destabilisation.

China's relationship with developing countries

Within the world's second largest economy, China has established extensive diplomatic and economic relations with developing countries across Asia, Africa, and Latin America, which deeply influences the world geopolitical framework. This has been the focus of global conversations lately. It is strategic in nature as it aims to strengthen China's global footprint, influence, market reach, and access to essential natural resources.

A critical part of interacting with developing countries is the economic collaboration fostered by China's Belt and Road Initiative (BRI). This multifaceted programme aims to bolster infrastructure investment, trade, and promote partnerships with several countries across different continents. China seeks to finance and construct primary infrastructural facilities, including ports, motorways, and railways, to facilitate economic development in the participating nations while economically and geopolitically strengthening its self-interests.

Alongside economic collaboration, China's relationship with developing countries covers a wide range of areas, including, but not limited to, technological, educational, health, and agricultural sectors. With a Chinese scope of goodwill, technology transfers, educational exchanges, and medical assistance programmes extend the frontier of international compassion. Chinese investment coupled with the transfer of agricultural knowledge helps alleviate food insecurity issues in developing areas, enhancing economic development and strengthening bilateral relations.

Nevertheless, China's expanding presence in developing nations is receiving criticism from other countries. The financial support being offered through infrastructural loans has provoked concerns about sustainability, dependence, and even greater debt for borrowing nations. Public and political focus has also been drawn towards investment transparency, environmental effects, labour rights, and governance issues regarding Chinese investments.

In conjunction with developed nations, the modification of China's relations with developing countries has drawn attention for its geopolitical consequences regarding pre-existing coalitions and power balances. The strengthening of China's strategic partnerships and cooperation with Southeast Asia and Sub-Saharan Africa intersects with established Western control, thus creating debates regarding shifts of influence and potential geopolitical reconfigurations.

Therefore, the developing country focus of China's foreign relations studies becomes an important focal point to scrutinise under diplomacy, international relations, global governance, and international political economy. Bridging the gaps and understanding the complexities behind these relations requires consideration of the intricacies of geopolitics, developmental goals, and collaboration on the world stage.

Conclusion: Maneuvering Sino-Western Relations Tensions

With the change in the world order, it is more pertinent than ever for both officials and stakeholders to carefully navigate the intricacies of tensions between China and the West. The relations between China and Western nations have been and will continue to be a source of both challenges and opportunities that require deep diplomacy and strategic thinking. It is important to understand that as much as engagement is crucial for resolving differences and areas of persistent tensions, constructive dialogue is equally important if cooperation is to be built across divides. An even more moderated stance on Sino-Western relations works best in an environment that synergises the geopolitical, economic, technological, and security domains.

In summation, a balanced approach, or a single framework strategy for both Western and China relations, integrating economic interdependence, strategic dialogue, and principled engagement yields the best results. Attempts to restore balance need to focus on the attainment of clearly defined goals alongside balancing interests. A cohesive strategy needs to improve transparency and compliance with developing international rules addressing points of disagreement with firm, yet constructive dialogue. A united stance for the United States, European Union, and other Western allies of China is the fundamental approach needed, for unified input from shared strategic alliance values. This is best achieved by deft management of trade, technology, security, human rights, and regional stability.

This conclusion highlights the need to utilise multilateral forums and alliances to proactively manage the Sino-Western relations. Strengthening partnerships in the Indo-Pacific region, leveraging the transatlantic relationships, and engaging supportive democracies around the world could foster collective resilience to counter China's growing assertiveness. Both bilateral and multilateral actions aimed at strengthening sustainable development and advancing human rights are efforts to impose some dominant norms and principles in light of the Western–China tensions.

As mentioned earlier, it is important to recognise the competitive dimensions alongside the cooperative aspects while addressing the Sino-Western tensions. The relations between China and the West will benefit from a balanced, pragmatic, yet principled strategy. Wisely managing these tensions, as strategically manoeuvred by China and Western nations, becomes crucial in nurturing the stability, understanding, and sustainable global prosperity.

13

Climate Policy
Striving for Global Leadership

Climate policy in transatlantic relations

The geographic scope of cooperation on climate policy is an important factor for the development of the transatlantic partnership and for the exercise of global leadership. Collaboration on an international scale is critically important in solving the current challenges of the world, including the need for global climate policy. The keywords climate policy and transatlantic relations together suggest a deep meaning resulting from the will of the EU and the US to do something urgently about the environmental problems. The concern as it is translated into concrete actions to manage climate change is aimed at adapting the relationships to make them deepen and broaden instilling more flexible synergies in the collaboration between the partners. The historical timeline dedicated to climate action illustrates the increasing coexistence of these powerful actors to give directions to the global agenda on sustainable development and environmental governance. The transatlantic partnership symbolises political and military alliance strategic confluence which does not stick to the single issues approach of bilateral deals but instead shows the united attitude concerning responsible global identity. On the background of severe environmental issues, the transatlantic relationship becomes a major determinant not only for climate issues but for international policy as a whole. Such context positions the two leaders to lead the global fight against climate change. In the rest of the chapter, I will analyse and try to provide answers to the questions of the geography of climate policy as one of the factors of transatlantic partnership development and the geopolitical angles of analysis of the unity of the US and EU in policy designs.

This analysis attempts to clarify the synergy of interests and values that fuel the competition for global primacy in policy on climate change through the history of international agreements on the environment and the current state of international cooperation towards common goals. It aims to underline the significant impact of transatlantic relations and cooperation on the construction of relations for international sustainability and climate justice. As a final point, such an explanation goes far beyond a detailed account of the climate policy 'tangle' – the enduring storyline is about the 'America' and 'Europe' solving together one of the defining problems of our era while grammatically linking the narrative to partnership.

Historical context: Evolution of environmental agreements

An overview of the history of agreements within the context of transatlantic relations shows the changing perception of climate change and sustainability on a global level. The history of international collaboration on environmental issues began in the 1970s with milestones such as the Stockholm Conference and the establishment of the United Nations Environment Programme (UNEP), which provided a framework for a multilateral approach towards tackling environmental challenges. This was followed in later decades by global recognition of the interrelated nature of environmental problems, which resulted in landmark treaties like the

Montreal Protocol and the Kyoto Protocol.

Within the transatlantic context, the evolution of international environmental agreements was responding to shifts in the structural features of geopolitical alliances and the economic focus of the world. There was a growing appreciation of the need to coordinate on environmental issues from the transatlantic perspective during the 1980s, but it was in the 1990s that notable developments such as the Transatlantic Agenda and the New Transatlantic Agenda came into being, aimed at strengthening US-European relations with an emphasis on environmental issues.

The attainment of the Paris Agreement in compliance with the United Nations Framework Convention on Climate Change (UNFCCC) in December 2015 symbolised an escalation in global initiatives towards combating climate change. The agreement emerged from a convergence of interests between the US and the EU that balanced emissions controls with economic growth. There was clarity offered in terms of responsibility and needed actions which formed the basis for international treaties on economic growth stimulus systems.

Changes in public scientific understanding of climate change, combined with increases in public awareness, move backward and forward, while simultaneously advancing technology, have significantly increased pressure for more effective international agreements aimed at addressing climate change. As noted in the first section of this paper, climate change is defined as a problem in need of an urgent solution, and this paradigm has inspired the creation of powerful policies such as the European Green Deal alongside the rejoining of the Paris Agreement by the Biden Administration.

The historical context regarding climate agreements in transatlantic relations serves as a guide for contemporary climate policy. The development of international cooperative efforts indicates that the formation of agreements has paralleled and has simultaneously been influenced by the emerging knowledge of the environmental crisis within the context of the underlying politics, economy, society, and global relationships.

European Green Deal: an overarching synthesis

The European Green Deal stands as a path towards a transformative and ambitious vision that seeks to achieve a climate-neutral economy within the European Union (EU) region. The European Green Deal is fundamentally concerned with addressing the imperative challenge of climate change juxtaposed to sustainable economic growth and therefore is focused on environmental protection. This framework is comprised of several policy initiatives and regulatory actions aimed at reducing greenhouse gas emissions and improving resource efficiency. The unique approach that the European Green Deal takes goes beyond environmental issues to include economic, social, geopolitical, and development policies that indicate sustainable development. The European Green Deal is self-explanatory in its wording; its basis is European and features a goal to be achieved by the year 2050 that incorporates the commitments set by the Paris Agreement. The effort made by the European Union is to clearly and strongly reduce emissions in various sectors, including energy, transportation activities, and industrial processes, thus providing substantial reductions to the carbon footprint.

The European Green Deal pays special attention to fostering clean technologies as one of the components that requires the expansion of the economy. This includes promoting eco-friendly investments along with developing new research initiatives for renewable energy and other green technologies, as well as environment-friendly initiatives. From a regulatory standpoint, the European Green Deal entails the overhaul of laws within the framework of accompanying policies and creates new policies within the scope of its overriding sustainability objectives. This includes actions like the Circular Economy Action Plan, Biodiversity Strategy, and the Sustainable Finance Programme, which aims to foster systemic ecological resilience and the strength of green business. The European Green Deal also highlights the causes of social inequality and the measures for a just transition for the workers and communities impacted by the shift to a green economy. In achieving this, the balance between environmental needs and social aspects attempts to preserve the ecosystem while protecting social equity and justice. Geographically, the European Green Deal demonstrates global leadership in sustainable development goals. The EU is setting the pace for international climate action while supporting initiatives for climate-neutral strategies in the EU to encourage collaboration among countries in addressing climate challenges.

Ultimately, the European Green Deal serves as proof of the EU's intent to lead the transition towards a more sustainable economy while simultaneously providing a paradigm of cohesive policymaking and globally transformative action.

America's Pledge to the Paris Agreement

America's "renewed" participation in the Paris Agreement, as from 2021, is suggestive of an adjustment in mental paradigm concerning the environment, climate policy, and global leadership. The re-engagement with the Agreement came into effect on 3rd August 2021 following the United States withdrawal, which was effective from 4th November 2020. This is indicative of global leadership on climate policy, which had been perceived as a lack during the period in which the US had withdrawn. The constraining factors associated with it had a decelerative effect on international attempts to combat climate crises. The participation serves to not only position the United States strategically in international negotiations but also afford opportunities to inspire transatlantic collaboration on strengthening the frameworks of global climate policy. The United States coming back to the Agreement is also expected to vertically shift the prospects of the climate action ecosystem through enhanced wielding of power and venting potential it holds in vital areas such as reduction of carbon emissions and financing clean energy ecosystems. In supporting international frameworks, the US emerges to credibly empower collaborative interventions. This shows its commitment towards fostering an environment conducive to technological developments through multi-directional international relations. Returning to the Agreement acts as motivation for other states to pump additional efforts into their own climate targets to encourage widespread international collaboration.

The United States and the European Union can work together to advance efforts to adapt to climate change, promote climate resilience, increase ambition for climate change, and mobilise funding for climate change adaptation.

The US's renewed involvement in the Paris Agreement represents a landmark shift in the context of climate change governance, indicating that there is an increased willingness towards a collective approach in tackling the fundamental challenge of climate change. From a global economic perspective, the US is the world's largest economy, and the US is always a big player in setting policies across the globe. American leadership is also crucial when it comes to the economy. This change marks a shift in US leadership and their policy focus towards climate change. These steps help deal with decisively low efforts put into climate changes. This renewal of commitment can also help restore diplomatic relations and partnerships between both sides of the Atlantic and unlock innovation and resources necessary for a sustainable low carbon future. The renewed US commitment puts American leadership back in the global climate view, increasing the opportunity for efforts towards a sustainable world focused on climate reduction, and calling for joint efforts aimed at planetary protection for future generations.

Transatlantic Conversations: Mobilising Joint Political Activity

The need to facilitate transatlantic discussions on the issue of climate policy is of utmost importance. Due to the multifaceted nature of climate change, the United States and the European Union require in-depth deliberations aimed at uniting their efforts on approaches to this problem.

These discussions enable best practices to be implemented, regulatory frameworks to be tailored, and innovation to be fostered in pursuit of sustainable devise solutions. Such dialogues afford policymakers, scientists, industry leaders, and other stakeholders an opportunity to share their perceptions and formulate innovative initiatives towards devising sustainable policies for climate change. Climate action both regionally and globally can be achieved through the dialogues by adopting a leadership paradigm that sets the pace for the rest of the nations to emulate. The development and implementation of an effective policy is made possible by access to information and expertise made available in these dialogues, thus aiding the setting of aggressive deadlines and targets for emissions reductions. The European Union and the United States can strategically use international decision-making bodies to tailor a joint platform that strategically influences prevailing international climate change policies and has a concrete impact on the globe.

In the context of Transatlantic Dialogues, cooperation for the acceleration of low-carbon economies is identified, including shared research activities, investment partnerships, and technology transfers. Through the optimisation of their impact, the coordinated effort of both parties stimulates change towards cleaner vehicles, sustainable energy systems, resilient infrastructure, and transforms the economy towards renewable energy. Apart from the positive environmental impacts, the proactive collaboration on climate policies offers additional value by further enhancing as well as offering employment opportunities and, overpowering centre-stage businesses in green technologies. All in all, Transatlantic Dialogues are crucial in closing the gap and creating synergy of the American and European Union climate policies. Working around the common goals of mutual reinforcement, these Dialogues shape the pathway to the global lead in emission reduction and construct a foundation for enduring sustainability.

Technological Innovation and Green Energy Transition

The pursuit of sustainability and the reduction of carbon emissions have become paramount in the realm of transatlantic relations. As the world faces the challenges posed by climate change, both the United States and the European Union are increasingly turning to technological innovation and green energy transition as pivotal solutions. This section delves into the intricate developments and initiatives within this domain.

Technological innovation holds the key to unlocking a greener future. Advancements in renewable energy technologies, such as solar, wind, and hydroelectric power, are reshaping the energy landscape on both sides of the Atlantic. Moreover, the emergence of breakthrough technologies like carbon capture and storage (CCS) and advanced battery storage systems are revolutionizing the way we harness and utilize energy resources. These developments underscore the commitment of the US and the EU to invest in research and development while fostering an environment conducive to technological breakthroughs.

Furthermore, the green energy transition is not confined to the energy sector alone. It permeates various industries, including transportation, manufacturing, and construction. Electric vehicles (EVs), for instance, are gaining prominence as viable alternatives to traditional combustion engine vehicles, thus driving the need for robust charging infrastructure and sustainable battery production. Additionally, smart grids and energy-efficient buildings are central to optimizing energy consumption and reducing environmental impact.

Partnerships and collaborative ventures play a crucial role in propelling this transition forward. Transatlantic cooperation in research and development, knowledge exchange, and joint investment initiatives has accelerated the pace of technological innovation and deployment. The sharing of best practices and lessons learned has facilitated the scaling-up of green technologies and increased their accessibility.

It is imperative to recognize that embracing a green energy transition is not merely an environmental prerogative but also a strategic economic pivot. The transition presents unparalleled opportunities for job creation, enhanced global competitiveness, and sustainable economic growth. Equally important is the potential to mitigate geopolitical tensions stemming from traditional energy dependencies and enhance energy security through diversified and decentralized energy sources.

In summary, the convergence of technological innovation and the green energy transition epitomizes the shared commitment of the US and the EU towards combating climate change and forging a sustainable future. This collaborative endeavor underscores the significance of leveraging cutting-edge technologies to address the complexities of climate mitigation while concurrently fostering economic prosperity.

The Economic Implications of Climate Policies

Climate policies have become a focal point in shaping the economic landscape of nations, with significant implications for industries, job markets, and overall economic growth. As countries strive to meet their climate targets, the transition to a low-carbon economy presents both challenges and opportunities for economic transformation. The shift towards renewable energy sources, such as wind, solar, and hydroelectric power, has sparked innovation and investment in clean energy technologies. This transition creates new employment opportunities in the renewable energy sector while also necessitating the reskilling and retraining of workers in traditional energy industries. Moreover, the increased adoption of energy-efficient technologies and sustainable practices across sectors can lead to long-term cost savings and improved productivity. On the other hand, some industries heavily reliant on fossil fuels may face disruptions and require targeted support during the transition. Furthermore, the adoption of carbon pricing mechanisms and emissions trading schemes introduces new financial considerations for businesses, influencing investment decisions and operational strategies. Beyond the domestic sphere, the economic implications of climate policies extend to international trade and com-petitiveness. As countries implement climate regulations and standards, cross-border trade dynamics are influenced by environmental considera-tions, leading to potential adjustments in global supply chains and market demands. Additionally, the pursuit of climate goals can foster internation-al cooperation and partnerships, creating opportunities for joint research and development, as well as the exchange of green technologies and exper-tise. However, disparities in the implementation and stringency of climate regulations across countries can give rise to concerns regarding market distortions and competitiveness, prompting the need for harmonization efforts and dialogue. Overall, the economic implications of climate policies underscore the interconnectedness of environmental sustainability and economic prosperity, necessitating a delicate balance between achieving climate objectives and safeguarding economic stability.

Balancing National Interests with Global Responsibilities

Achieving a delicate equilibrium between national interests and global responsibilities is a pivotal challenge in the context of climate policy within transatlantic relations. Nations are inherently driven by their individual priorities and economic imperatives, leading to divergence in policy ap-proaches and commitments. At the same time, the interconnectedness of environmental issues necessitates a coordinated, global response to miti-gate the impact of climate change. This section delves into the complexities of reconciling national autonomy with the imperative to act collectively for the greater good.

The tension between sovereignty and shared responsibility is a recur-rent theme in international negotiations on climate action. Countries often face internal pressures to prioritize short-term economic gains over long-term sustainability, especially when confronted with the need to transition away from carbon-intensive industries. This dilemma is particularly pronounced in sectors that have traditionally fueled national prosperity, such as fossil fuel extraction and heavy manufacturing. Striking a balance requires astute leadership and foresight to navigate this intricate landscape of competing interests.

Moreover, geopolitical considerations further complicate the pursuit of global climate goals. Strategic alliances, security concerns, and power dynamics influence the willingness of nations to commit to ambitious climate targets. The differential impact of climate change on diverse regions also leads to disparities in perceived urgency, complicating efforts to achieve consensus on binding agreements. The evolving transatlantic relationship adds another layer of complexity, as the dynamics between the US and the EU shape the broader global climate discourse.

Addressing the inherent tension between national interests and global responsibilities demands a multi-faceted approach. First and foremost, fostering a sense of shared purpose through dialogue and diplomacy is essential. Building trust and understanding among nations can help transcend narrow self-interests and promote cooperative solutions. Aligning climate objectives with economic incentives and offering support for transitioning industries can assuage fears of economic repercussions, fostering greater buy-in from stakeholders.

In addition, the role of multilateral institutions and frameworks cannot be overstated. Platforms such as the United Nations Framework Convention on Climate Change (UNFCCC) provide avenues for negotiation, collaboration, and monitoring of climate commitments. Strengthening these mechanisms and reinforcing the principles of equity and common but differentiated responsibilities can help bridge the gap between national sovereignty and global climate imperatives. Furthermore, leveraging technological advancements and knowledge sharing can incentivize participation and facilitate the diffusion of sustainable practices across borders.

Ultimately, striking a harmonious balance between national interests and global responsibilities necessitates visionary leadership, genuine cooperation, and a recognition of the interconnectedness of our planet. It is an intricate dance that requires astute navigation, continual reassessment, and unwavering commitment to steering towards a sustainable, collective future.

Diplomatic Challenges in Multilateral Climate Negotiations

Multilateral climate negotiations present a myriad of diplomatic challenges that require astute navigation and strategic decision-making. At the heart of these challenges lie the divergent priorities and interests of participating nations, each seeking to safeguard its own economic vitality while contributing to global climate action. The intricate web of cross-border dependencies, historical emissions, and future development trajectories further complicates the negotiation landscape, necessitating adept diplomacy to foster consensus and collective action.

One of the foremost diplomatic challenges is the tension between developed and developing nations regarding burden-sharing and responsibility for emissions reduction. Developing countries often argue for the preservation of their right to industrialization and economic growth, pointing to the historical emissions of industrialized nations as the primary cause of the current climate crisis. Conversely, advanced economies emphasise the need for equitable contributions from all parties, acknowledging the imperative of shared responsibility in mitigating climate change. Bridging this gap demands adroit negotiation skills and an acute understanding of the nuanced dynamics at play.

Moreover, the issue of financial assistance and technology transfer amplifies the complexity of multilateral climate negotiations. Developing countries frequently underscore the necessity of financial support and technological cooperation from developed nations to facilitate their transition to low-carbon economies. Addressing this concern entails delicate diplomacy centered on trust-building, transparency, and the alignment of diverse interests and capabilities.

Additionally, the diversification of national priorities complicates the crafting of unified approaches in multilateral settings. Each nation enters negotiations with distinct domestic agendas, be it energy security, agricultural sustainability, or industrial competitiveness. Balancing these disparate considerations within a cohesive framework necessitates exhaustive dialogue, compromise, and principled leadership. Furthermore, geopolitical tensions and strategic rivalries can impede collaboration, underscoring the diplomatic acumen required to navigate contentious political landscapes and foster inclusive engagement.

In conclusion, navigating the diplomatic challenges inherent in multilateral climate negotiations demands a deft understanding of complex interdependencies, the ability to reconcile conflicting national interests, and the vision to catalyze collaborative action. It necessitates fostering an environment that encourages open communication, mutual respect, and shared commitment to the common goal of addressing climate change. The intricacies of international diplomacy underscore the pivotal role of skilled negotiators and leaders in steering the course towards sustainable, collective climate action.

Prospects for Collaborative Leadership in the Climate Arena

As the pressing challenges posed by climate change continue to escalate, the prospects for collaborative leadership in the global climate arena have become increasingly critical. The transatlantic community, comprising the United States and the European Union, stands at a pivotal juncture in shaping the future trajectory of climate policies. With the reengagement of the United States in the Paris Agreement and the ambitious targets outlined in the European Green Deal, there exists a unique opportunity for these two influential entities to take the lead in driving meaningful change.

Collaborative leadership in the context of climate action entails not only a shared commitment to mitigation and adaptation measures but also an integrated approach to addressing complex environmental, economic, and social interdependencies. Through sustained dialogue and cooperation, the transatlantic partners can harness their combined expertise in technological innovation, sustainable development, and policy implementation to foster a culture of proactive environmental stewardship.

Crucially, the prospects for collaborative leadership hinge on the ability of the United States and the European Union to leverage their influence in mobilizing broader international cooperation. By setting high standards for emissions reduction, promoting clean energy technologies, and advancing climate finance initiatives, the transatlantic alliance can serve as a catalyst for inspiring global momentum in combating climate change.

Moreover, the collaborative leadership model necessitates a holistic approach that extends beyond traditional diplomatic channels. It involves engaging diverse stakeholders, including civil society, private sector actors, and local communities, in driving inclusive and sustainable climate action. By championing a bottom-up approach to climate governance, the transatlantic partners can cultivate a sense of ownership and shared responsibility among a diverse array of societal actors.

Nevertheless, the realization of collaborative leadership in the climate arena also faces inherent challenges. These include navigating divergent national interests, balancing regulatory frameworks, and ensuring equitable distribution of the burdens associated with transitioning to a low-carbon economy. Overcoming these hurdles demands concerted efforts to bridge policy disparities and cultivate a common vision grounded in mutual respect and understanding.

Looking ahead, the prospects for collaborative leadership in the climate arena hinge on sustained political will, strategic alignment of priorities, and a steadfast commitment to driving transformative change. As the United States and the European Union seek to navigate the complexities of this evolving landscape, the potential for them to emerge as unified frontrunners in addressing the global climate crisis remains formidable.

14
Challenges and Opportunities in Space Exploration

Chronology of space exploration: Laying the foundations

The beginnings of space exploration are the epitome of the endeavour and courage of human civilisation. It began with ancient civilisations observing the sky and mapping the movements of the heavens. But the real leap came in the 20th century, when mankind began to push the boundaries of the Earth. The space age began after the Soviet Union launched Sputnik 1 in 1957. This triggered a space race between the superpowers. This event led to the creation of NASA in the United States, which set ambitious goals for manned missions to the Moon. The Apollo programme culminated in Neil Armstrong's first steps on the moon in 1969, captivating the world and marking space exploration as the Everest of human achievement. In the decades that followed, robotic explorers such as the Voyager spacecraft gave us unprecedented and invaluable information about our solar system. The end of the Cold War ushered in an age of cooperation in the field of international conflict, which extended into space with the International Space Station (ISS), built by a collaboration of several nations. This cooperation has not only advanced scientific research, but also fostered international diplomacy.

The private sector has fully integrated space technology into its operations with the commercialisation of satellite launches and the proliferation of telecommunications satellites, greatly expanding human activities beyond Earth. In the early decades of the 21st century, China, India and private space companies such as SpaceX and Blue Origin began to participate in space exploration, indicating increased international involvement in space activities. New space technologies, such as advanced propulsion systems, advanced materials and miniaturised spacecraft, are now enabling increasingly ambitious future missions, including manned missions to Mars and beyond. The milestones achieved in space exploration are a testament to human ingenuity, determination and boundless curiosity. It symbolises a shared, coordinated effort that transcends political boundaries and brings humanity together in the quest to understand the universe.

Incremental innovation and reusable rockets

The renewed drive for space exploration technology has transformed the new age of space exploration, bringing us closer to new frontiers. It has culminated in engineering marvels such as innovations in scientific discovery; the global foray of space exploration is largely driven by technological advances. Recent breakthroughs in the construction of reusable rockets by SpaceX, Blue Origin and several private companies are a case in point. An unprecedented reduction in the cost of rockets that can be recovered and reused has made conducting scientific research in space more accessible. Space travel has become much more affordable, increasing the frequency of missions and the breadth and depth of scientific research conducted in space. Other technological advances that have changed the scope of space exploration include innovations in jet propulsion in transverse and lateral jet propulsion mechanisms, more popularly known as ion propulsion, which have expanded the range of space missions.

The integration of jet propulsion has significantly improved the distance that spaceflight can reach, into the deepest pockets of space. With ever-increasing demand and fuel efficiency, these innovations have changed the face of deep space exploration, allowing spacecraft to reach new frontiers with much less propellant. At the same time, the development of robotics and autonomous systems has enhanced the ability of spacecraft to perform complex manoeuvres, make repairs and collect scientific data in environments that are inhospitable or hazardous to human life. Robotic explorers, such as rovers and landers, have provided unprecedented information about the composition and geology of celestial bodies, laying the groundwork for future human missions and expeditions.

Innovations in materials science and additive manufacturing have made it possible to develop spacecraft components with greater durability and multifunctionality, enabling the construction of structures and instruments tailored to withstand the harsh environment of space. The advent of 3D printing technology has improved the efficiency of space missions by enabling on-site manufacturing and repair, reducing reliance on terrestrial supply chains and increasing the sustainability of long-duration missions.

Artificial intelligence and machine learning, coupled with big data analytics, have significantly advanced the ability to process the vast amounts of scientific data collected during missions, and to detect patterns, anomalies and correlations that traditional analytical methods cannot. The potential of these approaches for accelerating scientific discovery, optimising mission planning and improving astronomical understanding is immense.

In the near future, further developments in areas such as quantum computing, laser communications and interplanetary navigation will enable new levels of space exploration and provide unprecedented opportunities - dramatically improving the ultimate levels of computing, communications and laser precision for future missions. The advancement of these innovative technologies will surely usher in an epoch of powerful scientific

achievements and groundbreaking endeavours in the field of space exploration.

Transnational interactions: Encouraging cooperation for a global partnership

The effort to travel and explore space has become a joint endeavour across
nations in recent years, as international cooperation has strengthened
global partnerships. Different countries aim to develop joint initiatives
focused on exploring the universe and exploiting its resources. International teamwork in space activities multiplies the progress of science and
technology, as well as diplomatic relations and understanding between
the countries involved. The international community has demonstrated
rudimentary space cooperation through the International Space Station
(ISS), built and operated by the United States, Russia, Europe, Japan
and Canada. The ISS has been used primarily as an outpost in space and
has become an example and symbol of international human cooperation,
enabling many nations to further join efforts to develop international
cooperation in space exploration. Joint space activities have shown how
many partners around the world are joining forces to strengthen their
international partnerships in space exploration. Other space projects, such
as ESA's Rosetta mission, which successfully placed a probe on a comet,
and the Mars rovers from NASA and foreign partners, are other examples
of how collaborative efforts work.

Moreover, these partnerships go beyond scientific relationships and include attempts to achieve a shared vision of using space for non-hostile
activities.

In seeking and solving internationally shared scientific problems, pooling the resources, skills and infrastructure of nations leads to better allocation of funding and technology. New discoveries, environments and
advances are gained from the collaborations that are formed. As international collaboration increases, different nations are working together to

solve complicated problems, using their unique strengths to explore the possibilities for the development and use of space.

In one way or another, working together on space exploration missions builds trust and goodwill between nations and fosters the teamwork needed to tackle other global issues. As other spacefaring nations recognise these gaps and seek to work together, partnerships are made available through missions, technology and research. Such efforts not only facilitate progress in space exploration, but also build a more united future for humanity beyond Earth by bringing all nations together.

The involvement of the private sector has been a major feature of space exploration, ushering in a new era of competition, innovation and collaboration. In addition to space exploration, a huge transformation is taking place in various fields with the help of advanced technologies now provided by the private sector. Private sector investment in the space sector, together with the skilled workforce, is helping to drive new developments throughout the space industry.

Emerging commercial space companies are at the forefront of this change. Companies such as SpaceX, Blue Origin and Virgin Galactic are some of the pioneers using reusable rockets and setting their sights on the moon for space tourism beyond the imagination. These goals are becoming a reality thanks to a new, fierce competition that is accelerating progress and innovation in the commercial space sector.

The involvement of the private sector has opened up new ways of working with government space agencies. Public-private partnerships have been effective in mobilising resources, sharing knowledge and leveraging complementary assets to achieve common goals. For example, NASA's collaboration with private companies on human spaceflight, cargo resupply missions, and potential lunar landings demonstrates the benefits of collaborative efforts to expand the scope of human exploration in space.

In addition to their technological capabilities, the private sector brings a commercial perspective focused on cost efficiency, flexibility and responsiveness to change. This has led to the emergence of cutting-edge technologies such as advanced propulsion systems, satellite miniaturisation and in-orbit servicing capabilities. The commercialisation of space activities has stimulated the expansion of services provided in space, including telecommunications, Earth observation and scientific research, and has increased the economic footprint of the space industry.

Both ethics and regulation have become a priority as private organisations work to redefine the frontiers. There is a significant gap in the governance needed to address the collision of security concerns, environmental impacts, intellectual property and global commitments that require communication from around the world. The concerns of private sector innovation and regulatory control is an urgent issue that requires policy change to allow healthy competition while protecting the important aspects of society.

The emerging involvement of private organisations in space activities around the world will certainly influence the future of space exploration. It is these organisations that will ensure sustainable competition and growth in the space sector, leading to remarkable achievements for the future and great opportunities for the world and humanity.

The Future of Space Exploration: Visionary Projects and Long-term Goals

As we gaze towards the future of space exploration, it becomes increasingly evident that humanity stands on the cusp of extraordinary achievements in our quest to explore and colonize outer space. Visionary projects and long-term goals hold the promise of transforming our understanding of the cosmos and expanding the frontiers of human civilization.

One of the most ambitious long-term goals of space exploration is the establishment of permanent human settlements on other celestial bodies, such as the Moon and Mars. This endeavor not only presents profound scientific and technological challenges but also raises fundamental questions about the sustainability and adaptability of human life beyond Earth. Envisioned as interdisciplinary missions involving international cooperation, these ventures aim to lay the groundwork for a multi-planetary society while contributing to our knowledge of planetary science and astrobiology.

Furthermore, visionary projects like space telescopes, such as the James Webb Space Telescope, promise to revolutionize our understanding of the universe by peering into the depths of space and time, unveiling the origins of galaxies, stars, and potentially habitable exoplanets. These instruments exemplify our relentless pursuit of knowledge and our commitment to unraveling the mysteries of the cosmos.

In addition to these endeavors, the future of space exploration also encompasses the development of advanced propulsion technologies that could enable faster and more efficient travel within our solar system and beyond. Concepts like solar sails, ion propulsion, and even theoretical warp drives captivate the imagination and inspire scientists and engineers to push the boundaries of what is deemed possible.

Moreover, the exploration and utilization of space resources, such as asteroid mining and in-situ resource utilization, hold tremendous potential for supporting sustained human presence in space. From extracting valuable minerals to harnessing water and other essential resources, these initiatives lay the groundwork for establishing space-based industries and enabling self-sufficient off-world colonies.

Ultimately, the future of space exploration hinges on the collective efforts of government agencies, private enterprises, academic institutions, and international collaborators. A harmonious synergy of visionary projects and long-term goals, underpinned by sustained investment and unwavering dedication, will drive humanity's expansion into the cosmos and pave the way for a future where space is not just a realm of wonder but an extension of human civilisation itself.

Use of Space Resources: Opportunities for Mining and Development

Space resources claim to mark a new era in advancing space exploration. A step beyond the fantasies associated with travelling to other planets, the possibility of utilising resources that exist beyond Earth is attracting novel interest from both governmental and corporate sectors. The prospect of discovering and utilising spaceborn resources offers numerous considerations as well as challenges especially with regard to sustainability and economic development. Dramatic advances in technology coupled with an increase in the frequency of space missions is heightening the likelihood of exploiting water, minerals, and metals from asteroids, the Moon, and even Mars, no longer a distant dream. In terms of space mining opportunities, it is critical to appreciate the technological, legal, and ecological aspects that are crucial to properly harness these options. Above all, the development of numerous innovative extraction techniques and resource processing technologies is imperative for infusing new life into current paradigms of resource utilisation on extraterrestrial bodies.

The intertwining issues of international space law still remain an obstacle and a point of concern when one considers space property rights, allocation of resources, and balance within the legal framework of space exploration. The environmental and long-term consequences of mining activities on celestial bodies are crucial to the effort of achieving sustainable use of space resources. At this stage, innovation and responsible standards for resource use must be driven by collaboration between the private and public sectors. The development of new approaches to problems related to Earth resources will enable expansion and improvement of space infrastructure and support scientific endeavours, thus resulting in sustainable solutions to the sustainable development of space resources. Adequate ethical frameworks and responsible international cooperation over the use of space resources will enable the next stage of humanity's transition to living beyond Earth. With the development of space resource strategies, humanity has the opportunity for transformative change, which enables multi-faceted sustainable development of space presence.

Geopolitical implications: The new space race

In the 21st century, different countries have shown an intensifying interest in space exploration with an intention to innovate for domestic needs. This interest comes both from the perspective of scientific research and modern geopolitics. The once explorative venture in the scientific field has turned into an international competition called 'the new space race.' This modern space race is marked with competition coming from above the Earth's surface, seeking opportunities that would radically improve inter-country relations. Numerous nations are heavily funding space projects based on their expectations for future economic and military dominance.

At the forefront of this competition, states like the US, China and Russia along with other space superpowers like Japan, India and the European Union have emerged. These states understand what is at stake for them economically, concerning resource acquisition and it greatly helps them immensely extend their political power and influence across the globe.

As nations develop and deploy dual-use space capabilities, the militarisation of space further complicates geopolitical concerns. The constellation of military satellites that provide communication, reconnaissance, and navigation services have now become essential components of warfare, raising concerns over the militarisation of space and the possibility of conflicts extending beyond the boundaries of Earth.

Competition over satellites and other space assets fuels existing rivalries and invents new ones, blurring the lines between geopolitical conflicts and space activities. Some countries have begun to treat celestial bodies like the Moon and Mars as strategically important, leading to a new kind of political rivalry that mimics the harsh competition of the Cold War space race.

Conflicts and rivalries are accompanied by space law problems, such as boundaries, sovereign rights, intellectual property, and environmental conservation. There are increasing legal gaps as regions and orbits of airspace become more crowded with satellites and devices. International treaties and documents are needed to formally define space and its components so as to govern any relationship with it.

In order to examine the geopolitical dimensions of the emerging space race, it is necessary to integrate diplomacy, cooperation, and the creation of distinct regulations and standards of behaviour. Cooperation among space-faring nations can reduce the chances of conflict and promote a shared appreciation of outer space as an asset that has a peaceful and benevolent nature from which all humanity can benefit. Developing responsible policies on the governance of space will be crucial to ensure that space continues to be used for the advancement of human civilisation while minimising the conflict and threats that may arise.

Policies and strategies: Developing measures for the enhancement of security and collaboration

The prospects of space exploration and utilisation pose certain complexities that call for the formulation of policy or regulatory approaches to deal with security, sustainability, and global cooperation. With the advancement of capabilities by space-faring states and private entities, the value of clearly defined rules governing the concerned activities in space is increasing. There is also a need to promote collaboration among the parties with the aim of promoting and conducting scientific and exploratory activities beyond the orbit of Earth.

The development of an all-encompassing framework for space policy and regulation requires consideration of orbital space debris, satellite communication spectrum allocation, planetary protection, space-related conflicts, and intellectual property rights. In light of the variation in these elements, international agreement and cooperation are necessary.

A fundamental aspect of space policy is controlling space debris, as it presents enormously destructive risks to active satellites, spacecraft, and manned missions. Policies should outline space operational boundaries concerning decommissioned spacecraft removal and additional debris generation reduction through collision avoidance, sustainable mission planning, and enhanced skillful manoeuvring.

There are international boundaries to satellite communication that require certain satellite frequency space international agreements to prevent collision interference and achieve uniformity across nations. Moreover, the need for spectrum harmonisation extends beyond satellite communication to include various space services like remote sensing, navigation, and telecommunications.

Another major concern is planetary protection, which is intended to prevent biotic contamination of celestial bodies and Earth, safeguard viable extraterrestrial life, and maintain the integrity of scientific endeavours in future missions. Respecting principles entails developing comprehensive sterilisation protocols for space vehicles intended for other planets and conducting ethical scientific research.

As companies begin to offer services in space, as well as investment and research opportunities, the intellectual property frameworks, licensing structures, and liability legislation must be tailored to meet the requirements necessary for fostering private investments. Defined boundaries have the potential to encourage appropriate competition, supporting commercial endeavours and the greater scientific public interest.

Arriving at new solutions for the problems identified calls for the growing blend of the commercial space industry and space-faring nations. The presence of various state and commercial space actors emphasises the need to develop mechanisms to resolve emerging conflicts. Legal frameworks focusing on the governance of space should prioritise conflict prevention and resolution, possibly utilising existing international components, with consideration for the particular nature of space activities.

In any case, the creation of guidance policies for space endeavours within the context of international cooperation requires balancing the risks of safety, security, and innovation. Initiatives intended to address these intricate multifaceted issues will enable the exploration and utilisation of the universe's resources in a sustainable manner, preserving them for future generations.

Public perception and support: The role of citizen engagement

Public perception and support are critical for the future of space exploration. As the society of the world becomes interstellar inclusive, it is increasingly necessary to capture the confidence and enthusiasm of the citizens globally. The conception and approval of the citizens on consideration of space activities not only assist in sustainable provisions and political backing, but also garner interest among youth, scientists, engineers, and explorers of the country.

Perception and engagement are vital components in the implementation of space activities. As a result, Science Centres, Museums and other Educational Institutions can form a repository for knowledge about space activities and can help promote interest among the various audiences. In addition, working with the public to increase the popularity of space missions, their discoveries, and the advances made in technology assists in arousing the imagination as well as building pride and wonder for the existing endeavours of humanity.

The use of digital technologies and social media allows both private companies and space agencies to communicate with the public directly at a whole new level, providing real-time updates, interactive content, and behind-the-scenes access to space missions. The use of virtual reality and other immersive storytelling techniques can place people in the breathtaking realm of space, helping to develop a sense of collective support for space exploration.

Enabling the public to take part in particular projects under defined parameters allows citizens to participate directly in space research and exploration. Through collaborative projects and platforms, amateur astronomers, citizen scientists, and other space enthusiasts can contribute towards the collection, analysis, and even some discoveries of information pertaining to celestial bodies. With the incorporation of diverse communities in scientific projects, space agencies are able to foster inclusion and belonging which will help strengthen the bond between citizens and the universe.

Trust, particularly public trust, can be easily gained and maintained by fulfilling the ethical and societal aspects of space exploration. The responsible initiatives revolving around the sustainability of space, the environment, and pacifism appeal to global citizens who do care for the sustainability of resources and peace. Space activities, responsibly shared and communicated about their risks, benefits, and societal impacts do provide for an informed public that connects with the greater story of humankind's journey into space.

Ultimately, citizen engagement can be termed as not only useful in supporting the advocacy for space exploration but for enriching the journey into the unexplored known to real life.

Five In-Depth Perspectives Discussing Current Trends And Innovations Ideas For Space Technology

We stand at the brink of extraordinary achievements set to be accomplished in the coming years when looking at the future of space exploration. Innovative ideas exploring and colonising outer space blend optimistically with the long-term goals transforming the existence of humanity while pushing the boundaries of human civilisation.

Constructing human bases on Mars or the moon is one of the goals set far in the future when humankind expands into the cosmos. There are still many scientific problems to solve and technologies to develop before such a goal becomes possible, and it raises the question of whether life can be sustained beyond our planet. International cooperation within astronavigation bodies and planetary sciences may enable humans to further develop boundaries and give rise to astrobiology.

Aimed at machine learning and AI, the James Webb Space Telescope marks the beginning of new space exploration. It is an example of visionary projects that humanity manages to achieve. It, along with other space telescopes, allows us to reveal secrets that lie within galaxies, stars, the universe, and exoplanets deemed habitable.

Beyond currently available tools, the future of space exploration includes solid advancement goals. Concepts such as solar sails or ion motors would spread the boundaries of the solar system, and even hypothetical warp devices may one day allow humans to further explore galaxies.

The dynamic use of resources in space such as asteroid mining and in-situ resource utilisation has outstanding promise for sustaining human presence in outer space. These initiatives, from extracting precious minerals to exploiting water and other essential resources, serve as the stepping stones for the establishment of space industries and self-sufficient colonies beyond Earth.

Humankind's future in space will rely on the collaborative strides of government bodies, private organisations, academic partners, and cross-border cooperatives. Optimal integration of visionary ideas with sustainable plans backed by consistent funding committed to realising long-term goals will enable humans to venture into outer space, nurturing a future where it transforms from an endless enigma into human civilisation.

15
NATO and Security Concerns
Balancing Commitments

Understanding NATO's strategic purpose

As the cornerstone of the collective defence and security of member countries, NATO, the North Atlantic Treaty Organisation, is important in defining the geopolitical balance of the Euro-Atlantic area. Established in the Cold War era, NATO has turned into a powerful strategic partnership to curb aggression, instability, and foster democratic principles across the territory under its jurisdiction. The core principle upon which these obligations and commitments are based is that of collective security, in which allied states agree to defend and support one another, which drastically raises the costs of potential attacks. Threatened by aggressors such as Russia and the conflict in Ukraine, NATO is strategically integrating military force, diplomacy, and intelligence to respond to the challenges faced by the region. Through fostering greater integration and collaboration between allied nations, NATO ensures a high state of military preparedness. These capabilities enable NATO to support strong deterrent and rapid reaction forces. The equipment and training of NATO forces is not limited to traditional areas of military focus, as it also addresses emerging risks like cyber warfare, terrorism, and hybrid warfare. In a nutshell, NATO remains a very important element in fostering the security and stability of the globe and its regions, managing the risks involved, and functioning within the framework of the system of international relations.

Through NATO's persistent undertaking, it leads in ensuring the safety and stability of its territories and members while developing relations with other global actors. In light of this, NATO has not overlooked forging trust, cooperation, and resilience among its members, and NATO strengthens its position as the foundation for security in the Transatlantic area and as a defender of democratic and peaceful values.

Historical Context: The Development of NATO's Mission

The chronological development of NATO's mission within global international relations is directly linked with its strategic functional role and defines its importance in the international security system. NATO, which was created in the midst of the Cold War after the Second World War, aimed at forming a North American-European bloc military alliance in order to contain the Soviet Union and its imperial policies. The initial document, the North Atlantic Treaty, signed in 1949, provided the framework of a military-political alliance aimed at ensuring the security of its members, which has survived through diverse geopolitical and global transformations.

During the Cold War, NATO prioritised preventing Soviet hostility and maintaining stability within Europe. The organisation actively participated in constructing a security system for the continent, providing reassurance to its members and containing the advance of communism. NATO's military transformation during this time strengthened its position as the base of Western security policy and reinforced the alliance's readiness for collective defence.

The winding down of the Cold War marked another period in NATO's development, as it had to review the alliance's strategic objectives. The dissolution of the Soviet Union brought new, volatile security concerns in the form of ethnic strife and regional instability. These shifts created a fundamental change in the objectives of NATO, empowering it to undertake a more proactive role in international affairs, shifting from territorial defence to crisis management, cooperative security, and expansion.

From terrorism, cyberattacks, hybrid warfare, and the renewed conflict between states, there is no end to security threats in the 21st century. These and more have prompted NATO to make further adaptations to strengthen its capabilities and globally expand partnerships. The Alliance's involvement in Afghanistan, tackling terrorist conflict, and support for stabilisation operations manifest its commitment to contemporary multi-dimensional security challenges.

NATO's history is laden with shifts in the organisation needed for adaptive changes in security. This demonstrates NATO's ability to maintain its resonance with evolving threats. The evolution of NATO's mission showcases the organisation's effort towards maintaining peace, safeguarding democracy, and enabling transition across the Euro-Atlantic region. Grasping and analysing the history is crucial when trying to understand the intricate engagements of NATO in modern-day politics, especially when it comes to managing security and balancing obligations in a world brimming with ambiguity.

The current security landscape: Overview of threats

The current security landscape combines highly intricate and adaptive sets of threats that endanger the stability and welfare of the transatlantic countries. Emerging non-traditional security risks as well as traditional ones continue to develop in a world that is becoming increasingly interlinked. In general, all these factors require comprehensive assessment as well as strategic responses. Along with state-based threats like geopolitical competition, regional conflicts and military aggression are some of the key challenges NATO and its member states face. Such threats continue to challenge the alliance's collective defence obligations and underscore the relevance of the alliance's founding principles. The existence of asymmetric threats, such as terrorism, cyber attacks, and disinformation campaigns has further complicated the security equation and common interest, which in turn has made adaptable and innovative approaches imperative. It is important to understand how all these factors and regions are interconnected. There is no dividing line when it comes to geography and coordinated action from both sides of the Atlantic is crucial.

Global phenomena such as climate change, resource depletion, and pandemic events require attention as they may worsen pre-existing vulnerabilities and create new security concerns. There is no single approach to manage these risks, therefore understanding their interplay is crucial for fostering cooperation amongst the Allies and addressing the root causes of instability. NATO needs to take a proactive approach to deal with potential challenges that require changing the responsiveness and innovative measures of the Alliance. This involves collaborating with civilian sectors and employing a combination of military force, diplomacy, intelligence, and civil-military actions to more effectively manage threats. Utilizing non-NATO partners, international organisations, and civilian contractors strengthens the Alliance's response capabilities and counters advanced contemporary threats by expanding resources outside traditional defence frameworks. These diverse sets of approaches are made possible by the underlying principles of shared values and trust towards NATO's commitment to defend the existing international order. Cohesive action from NATO and partner states enables the maintenance of peace and security necessary to sustain the transatlantic alliances.

Transatlantic defence capabilities: Evaluation of commitments

It is critical to analyse the defence capabilities and commitments of partners across the Atlantic in NATO's framework context as the world security situation is changing. The alliance members experience a whole spectrum of security challenges, including inter-state and intra-state as well as non-state actors, and asymmetric warfare. Therefore, mobilisation of the military capabilities and contributions from each member state needs to be evaluated in order to sustain the alliance's collective power and resilience.

Evaluating commitments requires attention to the differences in the demographic structure of defence which are possessed by NATO member states. Such defence capabilities have land, air and naval forces and sophisticated technological and strategic assets. If all these contributions are put together, NATO will be able to comprehensively evaluate the level of its readiness to address thrusts and conflicts.

The evaluation of commitments goes beyond analysing operational military capabilities to include financial commitments towards defence and security. The even distribution of the burden among member states has been a goal for quite some time, where some allies do more than others. The calculation of financial commitments and defence expenditures against the GDP gives a snapshot on the total spending of the alliance on its integrated defence and security systems.

Alongside assessing defence capabilities, alignment of strategic priorities and the readiness of other Member States to participate in collective military action is equally significant. Cooperation regarding intelligence, logistics, and rapid response increases the level of interoperability and efficiency in transatlantic defence efforts.

Assessment of commitments requires an acknowledgment of the shifting landscape of security threats including new dimensions in cyberspace and hybrid warfare. The realm of cybersecurity is a new domain of operational defence and requires spending on resilience, cyber defences, and information warfare. The rise of hybrid threats based on combination of conventional and unconventional approaches calls for more dynamic defence policies.

While assessing defence obligations, NATO should also make good use of diplomacy and strategic conversations to build common security agreements. Understanding the transatlantic bond, or link, is vital when tackling issues pertaining to global security. In light of the current dynamic security landscape, careful consideration of the defence capabilities is vital to sustain relevance in the NATO mission.

Emerging Cybersecurity Threats for NATO

Hybrid warfare tactics combine conventional military operations with disinformation, cyber-assaults, and economic coercion. This form of conflict exploits weaknesses in a nation's defences to create ambiguities and challenges traditional responses. The NATO alliance is actively dealing with these types of emerging dangers by enhancing cyber defence systems and bolstering responsive capabilities. This is needed as the digital world is greatly interconnected, making it easy to infiltrate a nation's digital infrastructure. Democracy, critical sovereignty, and other sensitive elements that make a country safe face severe repercussions due to cyber threats. The continuous boost in technology usage offers non-state and state actors the upper hand in penetrating essential facilities and services. Moreover, NATO and its allies are also faced with the consequences of a non-NATO ally employing hybrid warfare exploiting existing fractures within the alliance in a show of dominance. It is crucial for member nations to build a single and coordinated approach for the proper management of cyber threats and build detailed strategies to deter and respond to them. Without well-defined universal rules that mitigate the escalation of conflicts that are created from hostile cyber acts, control over cyberspace will remain a dangerous dilemma internationally.

It is important to incorporate cyber elements into wider defence strategies and military exercises in order to enhance readiness and create coherence in addressing more sophisticated threats. NATO's adaptive policy shifts concerning modern conflict are not limited to traditional domains, but also include all the complex components of cyber and hybrid warfare. Collective cyber defences and resilience efforts show the Alliance's intent on defending its members from tampering security risks while keeping guard of adversaries' approaches to undermine critical infrastructure. The changing geopolitical landscape requires that these emerging threats are addressed with enduring collaboration, new approaches, and flexibility of the Transatlantic Partnership for the protection of common interests and values.

How The Ukrainian Conflict Impacted NATO's Strategy

The Ukrainian conflict has certainly been a crucial turning point in many of NATO's strategies. Russia's annexation of Crimea and the conflict in southeastern Ukraine poses a threat to the stability and security of Europe which has brought into question the operation and NATO's functions. The crisis demonstrated the necessity of the alliance for immediate military and united response which resulted in aggression. As a building response, NATO aimed to bolster deterrence and strengthen the defence posture of its member states. NATO also reassured its Eastern Flank Allies that Baltic states would receive ground battle groups and increased air policing. Together these steps restored NATO's assurances. The Ukraine crisis was an alarm signal for NATO countries to restore the alliance's commitment to collective defence and increase military readiness. This growing focus on defence has resulted in an increase in the initiatives conducted by NATO such as the Readiness Action Plan which intends to increase the rapid deployment of allied forces and improve their integration.

The war in Ukraine has highlighted the need to deepen NATO's engagement with non-member countries like Georgia and Ukraine to foster building their resilience and capacity. The crisis brought attention to NATO's multi-faceted warfare hybrid intelligence and early warning systems because of the growing use of disinformation warfare. In particular, NATO had to improve situational awareness and response capabilities to more effectively counter strategic communication and hybrid threat responses. The conflict in Ukraine also sparked discussion within NATO about the Alliance's adaptation to an increasingly volatile and intricate security landscape, leading to an increased focus on resilience as well as the integration of emerging technologies into defence planning. In general, the conflict in Ukraine has been a central axis for NATO strategic planning and has further consolidated alliance cohesion and adaptability towards shifting security dynamics.

Balancing US leadership and European autonomy

The United States of America, as the premier nation of NATO, has always taken the lead in modelling the strategies and military functions of the alliance. With the change of times, however, there seems to be an increasing focus on balancing US preeminence with European self-sufficiency in the control of the alliance. This is brought about by a number of reasons such as varying geo-political interests, the transformation in the patterns of security threats and Europe's quest for self-sufficiency in decision-making. To attain this balance, however, requires complex navigation as well as dialogue between the US and European leaders and reconsidering the balance of power within the alliance.

Widening gaps in the transatlantic relationship has crucially been debated under the term burden sharing particularly with regards to the level of defence expenditure and military contributions. Despite the fact that the United States has consistently "carried the bigger stick" in fulfilling NATO's collective defence obligations, there is renewed recognition among European allies that they need to, at the very least, start enhancing their military spending to more appropriately secure their defence capabilities. Albeit slow, this recognition is initiating debates on appropriate burden sharing, redistribution of defence responsibilities, and accommodating new resolution changes to the evolving security threats.

The movement in question does not mean that Europe seeks NATO autonomy at the expense of the United States completely disengaging from transatlantic relations. It aims more profoundly at exercising greater strategic and decision-making power over certain activities that affect European security infrastructure, including the provision of supplementary defence industrial bases, regional defence promotion, and the use of EU resources for collective NATO defence.

The pursuit of European autonomy should be framed as part of the stronger transatlantic alliance working in unison. It allows NATO to evolve while enhancing its cohesion and resilience, by enabling the European members to take a more active role in self-defence. Integration of control, coordination, planning, and intelligence distribution are vital under this revised framework, aimed at protecting the United States and Europe's opposing security interests.

When considering American hegemony and European independence, as noted before, cohesion and NATO's unity are paramount for security in the Euro-Atlantic region. With this in mind, any pursuit of autonomy ought to be done in a manner that reinforces alliance cohesion. Effective diplomacy and active transatlantic conversations are pivotal in shaping a consensus, fostering shared understanding, and evolving perceived responsibilities within NATO. The quest for balance in the transatlantic alliance rests on the assumption that the U.S. and European allies framework embraces divergent strategic views and capabilities and collaborates actively accepted in partnership.

Fixing alignment and internal conflict issues

In the web of relations under the term 'transatlantic', members tend to differ from the external bond of the bloc, or rather internal issues of NATO – the alignment of its members – strive to solve in a way in which NATO or its member states work as a coherent unified body. It is clear that allied nations do not share a common sense of adaptation as their view on the security landscape differs with regard to perceived national priority, threat level, and strategic goals. This gap often shows itself in the form of discrepancies regarding defence budgets, military capabilities, and any new approach to emerging security challenges or threats.

Reconciling the different levels of commitment and preparedness of the Member States remains one of the primary difficulties, particularly with regard to asymmetric and non-conventional security threats. Some Allies prioritise Territorial Defence and Deterrence while others focus on

International Peacekeeping Operations and Crisis Management. These differing priorities can create intra-alliance tensions and limit the ability of the Alliance to respond effectively to emerging security challenges.

In addition, differing regional geopolitical approaches within the Euro-Atlantic region aggravate the problem of NATO cohesion. The dynamics present in the eastern and southern flanks have unique security concerns, and attempting to unify approaches to the Baltic, Black Sea, and Mediterranean regions requires careful and skilled diplomacy.

To better these challenges, NATO needs to take a multifaceted and comprehensive approach that considers all views from within the allied member states. This helps resolve the disparity between national security strategies and collective defence and crisis management through constructive dialogue. Innovative mechanisms of burden-sharing along with capability development could help overcome imbalances in spending, military readiness, and provide strength to the unity and resilience of the Alliance.

Enhanced information sharing, interoperability, and joint training exercises are important to mitigate cohesive alignment challenges within NATO and foster a mission-oriented organisational culture. Viewing diversity not as fragmentation but as a strength, the Alliance will be able to utilise the wealth of skills and arms offered by its members to improve adaptability to respond to complex security threats.

Forward looking on dealing with the intra-organisational differences and alignment challenges will be crucial in maintaining NATO unity and relevance.

Beyond the Atlantic: Strategic Partnerships

Strategic Partnerships will aid in addressing the multilayered international security issues. In the changing nature of threats, strategic partnerships beyond the transatlantic boundaries have cultivated international security and stability. This chapter looks into the relevance of these relationships and how they can change NATO's strategic positioning.

The interest NATO has with the non-member states and particularly with the security-challenged region is one of the most relevant cases. NATO engages non-transatlantic states to increase its sphere of influence and tackle international security issues. These partnerships aim at refining intelligence sharing and the use of available resources, which eventually improves the strategic defence structure of the alliance.

In particular, these strategic partnerships incorporate non-military alliances, identifying economic and political spheres, and associating technological ones. Enhanced counter-terrorism activities, hacking and increasing terrorism barriers are parts of these partnerships. With the available resources and interests converging, NATO and its partners are aiding in building a new world order that is more secure and resilient.

NATO's partnerships with emerging international powers and regions outside the Euro-Atlantic area allow the alliance to manage its geopolitical complexities. Cooperation with Asia, Africa, and the Middle East exemplifies the alliance's flexibility and proactive nature in the ever-evolving context of global security. Such cooperation enhances democracy, human rights, and the rule of law while also strengthening the organisation's respect for international norms and principles.

The emerging alliances pose new relevant challenges and opportunities within the context of the transforming international security framework. Such transformations increase the need for strategic partnerships within NATO's context. They enable alliance members and partner nations to formulate shared objectives while also facilitating burden sharing, thereby reducing security risks. NATO fosters partnership by aiding mutual understanding and interoperability through a collaboratively defined structured dialogue and joint exercises for more effective responses to emerging threats.

In the future, NATO's existing partnerships as well as new ones formed outside the transatlantic region will be critical in shaping policies on global security governance. Such partnerships are likely to strengthen NATO's pillar role in world security. The organisation's evolution, along with changes in its commitments and strategic posture, will be discussed in the context of an interdependent world in the subsequent section.

Future trajectories: Expansion prospects for NATO

NATO's enlargement has been widely discussed and considered in light of the shifts in global security concerns. There remains significant debate over whether new countries should be added to the alliance's existing members, considering the constantly changing geopolitical environment. A blend of political, military, and strategic concerns gives rise to the debate over the alliance's proposed enlargement, each element being vital in defining the commanders of the alliance for its future path.

The Alliance's attempts to broaden its operations fuel discussions that indeed point towards a desire to improve security and stability in areas beyond the existing scopes. NATO membership is often sought by potential candidate countries because it greatly improves western defence alignment and means of self-defence. Potential candidates are incentivised with prospects of NATO enlargement as they tend to push for the implementation of democratic reforms, improvement of the rule of law, governance standards, and bolstering geopolitical objectives.

While discussing NATO enlargement further, geopolitical and security constraints must be taken into account, and need to be explained carefully. Prior to adding new members, regional dynamics and relations with bordering countries need to be given serious consideration. Infrastructure, spatial defence, and deployed forces all require extensive budgeting and manpower on logistics, which is an issue when NATO plans to expand the geographical scope of the Alliance.

Scenarios whereby internal cohesion erodes alongside NATO's decision-making system, which works on consensus, have been associated with amplifying restraint on expansion efforts. New members would have to strengthen the Alliance but could worsen operational synergy, thereby balancing efficiency against unit cohesion. Different member states attempting to manage diverging interests through varying strategic alignments would ultimately readjust the balance of collective security and cohesion.

The developments in hybrid threats and cyber warfare, along with other non-traditional challenges, escalate the need to reevaluate how new prospective members could enhance NATO's capabilities. This entails an examination of the member's democratic values, rule-based international order, and their military, technological, and strategic assets.

Additionally, NATO's future expansion will be driven by geopolitical shifts, regional security changes, and evolving transatlantic relations. NATO's open-door policy remains but requires expansion to be carefully considered along with the impact on NATO's collective defence and strategic goals.

16
Domestic Political Shifts
Populism and Globalisation Scepticism

Domestic Political Dynamics

Global political affairs transform the world and dominantly influence the international arena and crucial diplomatic relationships. Within the scope of a single nation exists a myriad of forces: politics, governance, administration, domestic security, social order, economy, and foreign affairs, all of which are components of international relations. These internal shifts shape a country's foreign policy and dictate how relations are formed and upheld with other nations.

Additionally, this chapter will paint the international picture in which the interplay and balance of global authorities are intricately intertwined with national systems, all governed by a singular force. This helps in understanding the phenomenon of transatlantic relations which is dependent on a multi-dimensional framework considering the interwoven dynamics of national policies and exceeding factors.

The diversity of issues that resonate with the citizens is a problem on its own in regard to national politics. Factors such as social, economic, and cultural constructs simultaneously shape a nation and the nation's psyche, which in turn affects the political landscape of the country. The rise of populism, the widespread growth of social media, and the changing nature of globalisation have added further dimensions to political discussions. All of these factors inject unforeseen complexities into the internal politics of states, and in return, affect international relations.

For the purpose of this chapter, we will look at the historical evolution of national political dynamics and consider the focus on the rise of populist movements and the shift of politics from traditional frameworks to more modern frameworks. It will trace the factors that explain the rise of populism, emphasising the scope of impact these movements have alongside the governance and diplomatic relations of countries. This chapter will also underline the case against globalisation and the underlying scepticism of global connections that infiltrates local politics, hence drawing attention to the intertwining currents of domestic politics and international relations.

The fundamental objective of this chapter is to explore the political dynamics of a nation that defines the relations of regions as complex as transatlantic ones while assessing the actual geopolitical state of the relations.

Context: The escalation of populism

The advancement of populism, in relation to its history, is connected to the development of society alongside its multiple factors. Populist movements typically emerge at times of significant economic, cultural, or social change, when various sections of society feel excluded and wish to express their discontent with the system. In the United States and Europe, for example, the 20th century witnessed a shift towards populist rhetoric driven by nationalistic leaders, culminating in the formation of the People's Party in the US, which aimed to radically alter the status quo. The interwar periods were marked by politically unstable economies that spawned enthusiastic leaders whose hopes were based on societal disillusionment.

In modern times, the resurgence of populism draws upon the unequal ramifications of globalisation, particularly following financial crises and rapid technological innovations. This context reveals that populism is more complex than merely a temporary phenomenon. Instead, it seeks to highlight the shifts and challenges within society, indicating that it has roots in historical disruptions.

Understanding the historical foundations of populism uncovers its origins and significance, including its impact on contemporary politics and international relations.

Study of the allure of populist movements

Both Europe and the United States have experienced a rise in populist movements in recent years. These political changes are driven by various societal, economic, and political factors. One contributing factor to the popularity of populism is the alienation experienced by particular sections of society. This sentiment often arises from the perception of being economically and politically marginalised by the elite and established economic systems, political systems, institutions, and processes, compounded by feelings of economic uncertainty due to globalisation and technological advancement.

Populist leaders tend to master the craft of forging strong emotional connections with their followers, often branding themselves as the champion of the so-called 'forgotten' or 'ignored' voters. They sell unrealistic straightforward remedies to angered and alienated masses. Populist rhetoric tends to be strongly nationalistic, protectionist, and anti-internationalist, appealing to people who oppose global integration and the erosion of national identity and sovereignty.

Populist rhetoric often paints a vivid picture of an attack on an immigrant, a global corporation, or some other external force that has been singularly identified to be the root cause of all societal problems. This narrative is particularly attractive to those looking for simple solutions to complicated problems, further solidifying the appeal of populists. It is precisely the promise of dismantling the entire system and changing everything about politics that attracts frustrated voters who are ready to try anything different.

The rise of social media has been instrumental in broadening the audience of populist movements. Social media is arguably the most popular outlet for broadcasting raw and sentimental content, enabling leaders of populism to reach their followers without going through mainstream media. This form of communication allows for a closeness in dishing out information, where attention looks like it is very close, fueling populism.

In order to understand the different reasons why populism is on the rise, it is critical to study them all at once. Understanding the sociopolitical realities that come with the development of populism allows for a better approach from policymakers and analysts to address issues that citizens struggle with in a way that sustains and fosters democracy and society.

Criticism of Globalisation: Economic and Cultural Viewpoint

There is little doubt that globalisation has transformed the economy by providing a new level of access to markets for the trade of goods, services, capital, and even labour. This phenomenon, however, has dealt with some critics on various cultural and economic fronts. Economically, it can be said that globalisation has deepened the gap between rich and poor countries. Western multinationals have made significant profits from outsourcing and offshoring, but working-class citizens have suffered job losses and stagnant wages due to heightened competition from low-wage countries. The resentment and disillusionment with globalisation is from the imbalance in its perceived benefits.

Globalisation has been accused of heavily prioritising profits against dimming social welfare and environmental concerns, which results in resource extraction and environmental pollution. Critics argue that free trade and deregulation of the economy facilitated the unchecked power of corporations to the detriment of the working class, small businesses, and the environment. These economic criticisms have generated scepticism toward transatlantic and regional partnerships and trading blocs that are believed to perpetuate unequal relations in the global economy.

Globalisation has raised issues relating to the erosion of a nation's identity and the vanishing of traditional values at a cultural level. The increase in the world's media and technology consumer markets and industry, known as 'Technological homogenisation', has also raised worries about the decline of cultural distinctiveness and commodification of its rich past. The immigration surge and multiculturalism that come with globalisation have raised fears of cultural dilution and social fragmentation among certain segments of society. These cultural critiques have turned into stronger nationalist and protectionist attitudes aimed at defending local cultures and customs from supposed foreign incursions.

The merger of such cultural and economic critiques has triggered populist movements and strengthened protective, nationalist, and anti-globalist currents. Most importantly, these views are important for the debates concerning relations of the Atlantic Basin for policy direction. To address such challenges requires an analysis of the relationship between restructuring of the economy, the preservation of culture, and global geopolitics in a networked economy.

Effects on the alignment of transatlantic policies

The escalation of globalisation, populism, and animosity towards international integration has resulted in the greatest divergence in the political alignment of the United States and Europe. The rise of populist sentiments on both sides of the ocean has dramatically changed the long-standing agreement on many defining constituents of international relations, which included trade, migration, and security policies, to name a few. This divergence in the approach towards international relations has complicated transatlantic collaboration and requires a rethinking of the interplay between the two geographical powers.

The United States and European integration have differing views on these topics as there is a growing gap in the attitude towards trade and economic unification. Resistance to globalisation has given rise to populism and an increase in antipathy towards previously accepted trade pacts. This has created friction between the US and EU, particularly evident through the conflict over tariffs and trade restrictions. Strained relationships are further complicated by differing opinions on immigration, as debates on border control and refugee resettlement bubble over conflicting national interests.

Multidisciplinary changes in data politics have instituted new strategic considerations for conflict and defence cooperation. Unilateralism and compulsive nationalism have transformed transatlantic military alliances alongside wider global security frameworks. These developments have strained collective defence constructs, particularly in NATO, which has differing views on emerging threats.

Populism promoted on social media bypasses sophisticated filtering, serving to intensify already divided public sentiments across the Atlantic. The dissemination of false narratives and inflammatory propaganda deeply damages efforts at mutual understanding and collaboration within the US and Europe. As bipartisanship is weaponised and political silos deepen, addressing common emerging problems becomes exceedingly difficult.

Therefore, the effect that has been caused regarding the alignment of policies on both sides of the Atlantic has been significant, stranding a host of policymakers in a web of complex competing priorities and diverging interests. Efforts to bridge these gaps require a new focus on dialogue and engagement in finding pathways towards rapprochement, although divergence of opinion has to be respected. Transatlantic partners need to understand shifting paradigms of domestic politics and work towards constructing a more robust collaborative approach to policy action designed for responsive adaptability, where enduring values and goals sustain the alliance.

The influence of social media on public opinion

Having social media at our fingertips provides ease of access to news in real-time, especially with regards to politics and global affairs. In today's world, countries are closely interconnected, enabling individuals to consume information globally through social media, which has now become a primary source of news. This rapid sharing of content can support multiple people in sharing their ideas and perspectives at unprecedented rates. As a result, social media greatly helps broaden the scope of public opinion; however, it also has the ability to polarise societies. In addition, the potent targeting tools that social media algorithms offer aid in spreading tailored messages regarding specific political ideologies and xenophobic expulsions to influence public sentiment for particular political agendas.

The rise of user-generated content and influencer culture has changed the media landscape, merging reporting with commentary. This intermingling makes it harder to evaluate the credibility and reliability of the information, significantly heightening the exposure to misrepresentation and unchecked misinformation. Social media helps to quickly coordinate and amplify grassroots dissenting movements, changing the discourse on globalisation, immigration, and national identity.

The phenomena of echo chambers and filter bubbles that grant a user content only previously displayed deepen divides in society, strengthening polarising perspectives that socially exist. Such phenomena profoundly impact transatlantic relations, as differing public opinions and ideologically driven perceptions from within the US and their European counterparts affect the perception and formulation of policies dealing with international cooperation and diplomacy.

Given these changes, policymakers and other relevant actors need to evaluate the impact social media has on public opinion, as well as its effects on national policy changes, populism, and globalisation scepticism. To achieve those goals, it is necessary to understand how social media affects public discourse and mitigate risks associated with disinformation and narratives driven by polarisation, while taking advantage of the opportunity presented by social media to steer dialogue towards an informed, inclusive, and constructive discussion on transatlantic and global issues.

Case Studies: The Primary Populist Figureheads and Their Movements

In order to understand the growth of populism, as well as scepticism towards globalisation, it is important to look into specific case studies of notable figures and movements that have impacted global politics. One case study that stands out is the rise of populist movements and leaders across Europe, which include Viktor Orban in Hungary, Matteo Salvini in Italy, and Marine Le Pen in France. These populist figures have sustained support by appealing to economic worries, cultural fears, and a yearning for self-governance. All of these leaders are said to have capitalised on simmering discontent by embracing anti-establishment populism. They managed to gain support by addressing issues tied to immigration, national identity, and economic disparity. Equally, the Brexit campaign in the United Kingdom, spearheaded by Nigel Farage from the UK Independence Party, showcased a striking outburst of populism that culminated in a defining decision with significant consequences. Not forgetting, the rise of Donald Trump and his political campaign across the continent marked a sharp shift from conventional politics, encapsulated in his 'America First' programme, signalling a fierce endorsement of protectionism and nationalism.

His out-of-the-box approach and unique messaging struck a chord with a segment of the American electorate, revealing the power of populism in shaping electoral choices. The case studies offered help to understand the phenomenon of populism, the tactics its leaders adopt, and the social context in which they are considered appealing. These examples demonstrate the intricate relationship between the narrative of dissatisfaction within the country, external forces, and the shifting lens through which politics is viewed, illustrating the impact of populism on modern governance systems.

The decline of mainstream political parties

Populism fused with growing scepticism towards globalisation has challenged the traditional political parties that for years have underpinned democracy in Western countries. The decline of these populist institutions is transforming the political landscape, creating new challenges for transatlantic relations and altering global equilibrium.

Disillusionment and political apathy, resulting from the inability of parties to adequately represent and respond to citizens, is one of the main factors contributing to the erosion of traditional political parties. In their eyes, economic elites have introduced policies that have further deepened gaps such as immigration, the economy, and job availability. This has resulted in the rise of grassroots and insurgent movements that seek to unbalance the established order of old political parties.

Changing methods of communication alongside the creation of social media have opened up new avenues for non-traditional political figures and groups to reach voters, which poses a challenge to the traditional centres of power. Information saturation adds to the issue by fragmenting the focus of the public with ease, resulting in citizens who are not aligned with the established political order. All of these factors make it harder for traditional political parties to serve the different segments of the population.

Shifts in socio-economic structures have revealed new divisions that cut across existing party lines. There is an increase in voter fragmentation across industries and along technological lines, as voters now have different attitudes towards economic protectionism, the resilience of a socially sustainable environment, and social values. This disintegration of cohesiveness among groups of voters who supported traditional political parties has led to conflicts of identity and ideology.

The decline of traditional political parties has major impacts on the cooperation and diplomacy of states. Transatlantic relations are managed by an intricate web of leaders and policymakers, and understanding the shifting dynamics of a country's political ecosystem is crucial in developing viable plans. The diminishing influence of established parties is likely to increase the unpredictability of how decisions are made and in what context. Non-orthodox political figures and groups could adopt conflicting means of addressing international issues, making it exceedingly difficult to develop a unified consensus and plan of action.

To conclude, the decline of the classical political party system marks an essential shift in the model of democracy in the West. This will profoundly change the ways in which these institutions will be able to shape transatlantic relations and global governance in a manner that is adaptive to the needs of their electorate. Understanding the emerging realities of these changes is essential for policymakers and political analysts concerned with the multi-dimensional dilemmas of 21st-century politics.

The Impact on International Relations

The changes in the global scene related to the waning of conventional political parties and the emergence of populist movements have profound repercussions for international relations. Diplomatic and multilateral commitments are changing significantly, with a broad focus on international relations. These changes might alter the balance of power associated with transatlantic relations as well as dramatically transform the traditional alliances essential for enduring global prosperity and stability. The trade, climate, and global crisis resilience that comes under collaborative efforts is equally challenged alongside the populism-infused scepticism towards globalisation. The integrative governance of diplomacy and international treaties, amidst rising unpredictability, brings colossal challenges to assembling cohesive foreign policies, driving strategic shifts in neighbouring nations. With these shifts, traditional diplomacy is forced to adapt to integration and reliance where these complex changes in governance and policy take place. Significant initiatives by civil society, the promotion of cultural exchange, and local level action to bridge political voids are vital to soften the impact of this political disturbance while fostering understanding and collaboration at the societal level.

As a matter of utmost importance, international organisations should be restructured in a manner that safeguards global collaboration while addressing the concerns and priorities of emerging populist movements. This might also require some dismantling of the existing decision-making frameworks, as well as restructuring the allocation of power within them. To effectively deal with such changes, diplomats can consult populist leaders and their followers through strategic engagement to offer them clearer narratives that soothe their fears related to global governance. Fostering international cooperation would be made easier by formulating complete and accurate policies that take into account the diversity of national self-determination and global challenges. Even with the difficulties introduced by populist ideologies and scepticism towards globalisation, the deeper interests and common principles that underpin transatlantic and international partnerships continue to reinforce each other. It is still feasible to pursue sustainable strategies for international cooperation and shared prosperity by recognising shifts in the political environment and tailoring diplomacy accordingly.

Fifth Stop: Reflections on Future Dynamics in Politics

In synthesising the shifts in the national political framework, it is also critical to consider the emerging transatlantic political tendencies that will mark the future. The emergence of populist movements alongside increasing sceptical attitudes toward globalisation have greatly transformed the political landscape of the US and the EU. Looking into the future, a number of certain trends are identified which are expected to continue shaping these regions' dynamics and interactions, with significant consequences on international collaboration and policy integration.

The contribution of digital media and technology into the sphere of politics has profoundly transformed the political discourse and it is here to stay. Social media channels offered great accessibility to a range of populist and anti-globalisation sentiments which are easy to propagate. Technology's role in shaping public discourse, influencing opinion, and providing means for socio-political activism is rapidly evolving, which makes this issue important for policymakers and analysts.

The existing forms of political parties and their respective systems of elections are so volatile that one is likely to observe more of these shifts occurring in the years ahead. In the face of persistent populist and nationalist sentiments, established political parties are under constant pressure to respond to changing voter demand or fade into irrelevance. These newly emerging coalitions and ideologies are likely to change the contours of transatlantic partnership.

The evolving economic context, especially after global challenges and social media influenced technology, is bound to affect political views and focus areas. The discussion around economic imbalance, protectionist tendencies, and labour market upheavals will continue to dominate policymaking and public opinion across the Atlantic.

The aspirations aimed towards self-sufficiency and self-governance within the context of multifaceted geopolitical challengers may result in varying responses to international and domestic policies. It gets even more challenging for the United States and the European Union to put forward a coherent plan to unify their strategies towards international affairs, such as climate change and security threats.

Woven together with broader political discourses is identity politics alongside social values which will remain influential in determining and anticipating future developments. Renewed nationalism coupled with debates around multiculturalism, immigration, and social integration show how difficult it is to find agreement on transatlantic policies.

From the analysis of these patterns, it is evident that a proactive approach aimed toward dialogue and cooperative actions among partners across the Atlantic is essential as the political landscape evolves. It is crucial to foster understanding, regard, and compassion from different political angles to bridge gaps and advance common interests.

While embarking on the analysis of the 21st century politics, it is important to mould and adapt heavily in order to solidify the relations between transatlantic unions. The tailor-made approach which involves a wider range of participants and more active empathy-based reasoning possesses the potential required to design in an effective manner to the challenges and opportunities made available by shifting political circumstances.

17

Future Scenarios

Navigating an Uncertain World Order

Summary of the geopolitical challenges and conflicts today

The contemporary geopolitical climate incurs the attention of international policymakers due to the multitude of greatly significant, emergent, and pre-existing tensions. The primary concern centres on the available power resources by the strongest competing states in alliance and their intelligence organisations, and the relations among them is reshaping the alliances or confrontational blocs and active diplomacy affected these confrontational groups. During their interactions, these states will always encounter other factors, including economic dependency, technological development, spatial ideological schisms, and regional conflicts, which work together toward forming the future geopolitical scenario. The latest shifts indicate the existing new global power centres – the return of dips in some previous powers – tend towards the multi-polar world, where previously accepted standards of control and authority are undergoing change. This shift in the balance of global power leads to strategic competition and collaboration along with the development of collective security policies as states try to cope with an increasingly uncertain interdependent international system.

The adoption and development of artificial intelligence, cyber capabilities, and space capabilities has added further complexities to geopolitical relations while simultaneously creating opportunities and exposing previously unconsidered vulnerabilities. Climate change and resource depletion, associated with ecological decline, have transformed nations into superpowers and primary players in the global arena, as countries seek to address these central challenges. Ongoing disputes and conflicts continue to dominate the discourse within international relations and counteract global order and humanitarian principles while raising concerns over the success of diplomacy and multilateral collaboration. With the intensification of these issues, it's clear that the international geopolitical situation requires more focus from strategists and analysts so they can implement appropriate measures and foster readiness in global affairs to achieve long-lasting peaceful international relationships.

Scenario planning: Methodologies and frameworks

Scenario planning is a strategic tool for organisations and governments for forecasting and preparing for possible future outcomes in light of ever changing global circumstances. This process entails assessing a number of diverse and plausible scenarios corresponding to different combinations of external factors and internal decisions. The focus is not on accurate prediction, but rather building a framework to guide decision-making within a solid context of uncertainty. Effective scenario planning incorporates diverse methodologies and frameworks that enable stakeholders to explore and assess diverse alternative future pathways. One of the approaches is the 'probable, possible and preferable' framework, which groups scenarios based on likelihood and how much they are wanted. Another well-known methodology is 'driving forces' analysis, which focuses on the key contour trends and uncertainties of the future. This technique helps to determine critical driving forces of change and enables strategy development to address those forces.

The cross impact matrix technique enables one to analyse the interrelations of various factors and events which reveals possible risks and opportunities. Straiptow takes into account events with low probability, but high impact which can disrupt the anticipated future and refers to them as wild cards, as they can change global dynamics. Fostering participation in the scenario planning stage, especially from people with varying experiences and knowledge bases can greatly enhance the structural strength and thoroughness of the analysis. For example, alongside experts in environmental science, bringing in geopolitics and economics would help further develop technologies that have already been devised. There is a need for scenario planning to be iterative as well as flexible so that it can extract, incorporate and utilise new available information to modify and enhance scenarios that are considered. Organisations and policymakers become more flexible and responsive to emerging situations such as problems and opportunities. In conclusion, scenario planning is a powerful instrument in addressing ambiguity and enables decision-makers to become proactive as they are well equipped to face the rapidly evolving challenges of the globe.

Changes in Global Influence: The Multipolar World

With regard to international geopolitics, multipolar describes a world where there are many centres of power as opposed to one or two that predominate. This marks a shift from the presence of a superpower or a bipolar system like the one that existed in the 20th century. During the 21st century, the rise of developing economic and political forces has enabled the diffusion of global influence, making the global power dynamics more intricate and interdependent. The contemporary equation of power—dominated by the United States and the European Union on one side and fast-growing economies of China, India, and Russia on the other—is in the process of re-distribution and reconfiguration, which transforms the global balance of power. The consequences of such a shift are enduring and impactful for international relations, security affairs, and global governance. One major defining feature of a multipolar world is the increasing diversification of strategic partnerships and coalitions. Countries tend to identify and foster a greater number of relations to ensure their interests are protected and advanced in different parts of the world. This scenario accounts for the increased number of regional groups and multilateral forums that compete for hegemony and try to craft the new order.

At the same time, there has been an increase in competition among the world's major powers in many areas such as commerce, technology, and security. The amalgamation of various competing interests and values has produced intricate diplomatic solutions alongside strategic conflicts, further complicating the governance of international relations.

Small and medium-sized states are likely to benefit from the opportunistic advantages associated with the multipolar world, but they also face the danger of being caught in conflicts between global powers. Moreover, the reconfiguration of power dynamics shifts the boundaries of global institutions and norms, as frameworks for international cooperation and governance undergo significant changes responding to the ever-increasing and diverse demands from various global actors. To sustain effective cooperation in the international system, the multipolar institutions must be adaptable to the reality of competing powers. Progressing through these power shifts will involve careful diplomatic juggling alongside proactive participation in multilateral activities. From a domestic perspective, it is important for policymakers, companies, and citizens to remain alert to the emerging trends in global power structures, utilising them to strategically align themselves within this evolving context.

Technological advances and their global impact

Technological development in the 21st century has achieved a remarkable level. It has changed the way of living, working and socialising at the global level. The impacts of advanced artificial intelligence, machine learning, quantum computing, and biotechnology are expected to produce fundamental changes to the order of the world. The application of Information and Communication Technologies [ICT] in health care, transportation, telecommunication and manufacturing has significantly increased competitiveness or productivity, but it has also created sophisticated issues regarding privacy, security, and ethics. The growing reliance on digital assets has redrawn the geopolitical map, with cyberwarfare and information waging becoming widespread risks. Through this transformation, countries have been positioned in an environment containing both opportunities and vulnerabilities.

The influence of technological advances impacts the world at large, beyond societal growth and economic development. Technology continuously disrupts traditional industries, and therefore issues surrounding skill upgrading, job displacement, and the digital divide must be urgently addressed. The competition for technological superiority, for instance in autonomous vehicles and 5G networks, poses an overarching concern in regard to the economic and geopolitical relations of particular countries, greatly shaping their international business strategies. New modes of international collaboration and competition arise with advancements in digital technology. Lastly, environmental technological advancements alongside renewable energy solutions greatly aid the efforts to mitigate climate change, achieving sustainable development goals while paving the way to a more resilient and balanced world.

The regulatory and ethical ramifications of new technologies are now poised as critical issues in almost every area of governance and policy-making. The innovation 'pursuit paradox' whereby legal frameworks, policies, and ethics voiced by society simultaneously fits into the boundaries toward the law presents a huge challenge for any policymaker. Asphyxiating the categorical imperatives of international cooperation and uniform requirements are issues such as data privacy, bias-fuelled algorithms, and technological militarisation. Genomic engineering, artificial intelligence, and surveillance technology advances pose moral arguments that require attention by intergovernmental bodies, entrepreneurs, productive citizens, and social activists for social debate.

From another perspective, the paradigm defining contouring changing with the aid of powerful advances, tools, or instruments of modern
technology is controversial/emancipating together and unleashing boundless powered with unparalleled and redefining freedom facilitating con-
cepts/ideas/revolution for profound transforming on an international
scale – international territory/area/aspect enabling or guiding states with
further integrating the unprecedented design. On the other hand, capa-
bilities/need for strategic in surmounting the problems turn out warm
collaboration, expand the combined to run to profitable use of modern devices while responsibly setting international innovative relations toward a
common goal. Astute promotion of cross-state arrangements – offer inter-
changeable device/retract or reduce hands, covered dealing with obstacles
turned to be features of globalised unity move forth empowering perpetual
betterment targeting enabled development and aid acquisition for people
globally united in technology progression. The world set free, strengthened to serve/aged for also claim responsible for social and humane main-
tenance/modern aid propelled dedicate boundless achievements prosper
social bridges advancing reality under aid under raw unity propelled bridging the tramping empathy to touch empower human unbound progress,
turning aid becoming centre of unacclaimed universal harmony, claiming
human breaking of modern techs as soars the oats.

Economic Forecast: Trade, Markets and Innovation

In the contemporary context of the world economy, trade, markets, and innovation have become more interdependent and more powerful relative to
each other. To understand the implications of the transatlantic relations,
it is important to analyse the economic forecasts. The trade relations of the
US and EU continue to remain at the epicentre of their economic wellbeing, wherein, tariff negotiations, market access, and regulatory frameworks
dominate the opportunities for growth and stability on both sides. The
shifts in the global market due to new competitors, particularly from Asia,
have transformed traditional investment and trade patterns and pose both

risks and opportunities for Western economies. Initiatives like the Belt and Road Initiative has altered the trade map due to changing geopolitical factors, which need to be strongly addressed by developed economic powers. During these shifts, the most fundamental change is through economic innovative technologies. The digitisation of technologies, AI, and automation has fundamentally transformed production and supply chains, consumer behaviour, and whole new industries, which has created new economically disruptive opportunities. The traditional boundaries of industries have begun to fade away and international competitiveness has transformed with the growth of the digital economy.

Additionally, it has created new concerns regarding data privacy, cybersecurity, and the ethics of technology advancements which must be thoughtfully integrated into future economic policies. In this context, innovation, particularly in the form of new products and business models, has emerged as a critical competitive advantage on the international stage. To unlock poised entrepreneurial activities, R&D, and collaboration across various domains, and for persistent competitive edge and economic growth, it is crucial to create the right environment.

Issues pertaining to climate change and sustainable development

Climate change and environmental issues are phenomena that have been gaining significance in the world today. The socioeconomic impacts and global human effects of these environmental issues are some of the most pressing challenges. The problem begs for a more integrated approach in terms of policy-making, technological advancement, and even diplomacy.

With respect to the current energy and economic context, climate change places a lot of emphasis on reducing the emission of greenhouse gases while increasing the use of renewable energy. Nations and regions are coming to understand how adopting clean energy policies, carbon neutral practices and transitioning to sustainable industry brings positive societal and financial outcomes. In addition to creating new opportunities for businesses and investors, such steps help to limit the effects of climate change.

Environmental preservation can no longer be wholly disentangled from the bigger geopolitical picture. The struggle over natural resources, including freshwater and cultivated land, is bound to heighten an already tense regional war situation and violence. There is a need for policies to be designed that can prevent further destabilisation of the already vulnerable regions by fostering a cooperative approach towards resource management, conservation, and equitable distribution.

Apart from mitigation strategies, adapting to the consequences of climate change is of pivotal importance. Agricultural practices, water resources and infrastructures are being affected by the climate changes and, as a result, disruptions are being experienced by communities across the globe. Implementing resilient infrastructure, preparing for disasters, and utilising nature-based approaches can enhance the ability of societies to absorb shocks and recover from damages.

Fighting climate change is something that must be done in unison and as such, the international community uses treaties and agreements to do so. The Paris Agreement, even though it is currently facing barriers, still provides a basic structure to facilitate intended global actions. In order to achieve the set goals and help the vulnerable states that make efforts to adapt and enhance self-sufficient capacity building, collaboration is needed to provide adequate sought-after support.

Change in the environment is driven by technology and innovation with a primary emphasis placed on it. Advancements in renewable energy sources, as well as in agriculture and carbon capture, provide remarkable opportunities to protect the environment by reducing emissions. The application of artificial intelligence, big data and predictive modelling can be used to identify, understand and study processes of the environment, leading to better policy measures to enhance implementation.

In the end, it is clear that addressing climate change and other environmental issues requires advanced strategy, collective action, and fore-sighted thinking. The adoption of sustainable practices, promotion of environmental care, green innovations, and prioritisation of environmental management will propel the international community towards a more adaptable and low-carbon future.

Subregional conflicts and the challenge of peacebuilding

In relation to transatlantic connections and within the context of the world order, peace continues to face considerable threats of destabilisation and violence. The turbulence in the Middle East is only one of the numerous ongoing conflicts; there are also existing tensions in Eastern Europe and Asia. These issues require comprehensive study related to the building of useful relations through peace. We pay attention to the regional dynamics of conflicts to design frameworks for effective peacebuilding.

The Middle East is a core part of the world's most problematic regions, having several unresolved differences and endless power struggles. The passive and active involvement of non-sovereign entities and proxy wars make peaceful settlements even more difficult. The rivalries in the region have worsened because of increasing competition for energy resources, resulting in significant shifts in the global geopolitical equilibrium. In light of such a situation, strategies for fostering enduring peaceful relations have to deeply understand the multifaceted dimensions of the cultures, history, and religion of the regions.

In the context of Eastern Europe, the military conflict in Ukraine and its consequences epitomise the nature of disputes across the region. The interplay of ongoing competition for control of the territory in question and deep-seated historical hatred prompted both external factors and excessive militarism, which strained diplomacy. It is critical to look for solutions aimed at relieving tensions and fostering lasting peace in the region.

As far as Asia is concerned, unresolved boundary lines and conflicting claims to sea areas raise international tensions, especially in the South China Sea. The competition among regional powers for control of strategically important areas and crucial resources has created the need for conflict prevention policies and active diplomatic engagement. The ever-present danger of nuclear arms being deployed on the Korean Peninsula makes the necessity for effective mechanisms for peacebuilding in that region even more pressing.

When looking at the possibilities for implementing peacebuilding, it seems that international institutions and coalitions play a crucial part. Organisations such as the United Nations, European Union and NATO do possess the knowledge and means required to guarantee peace and undertake conflict resolution. They can also provide support for mediation and prevention efforts.

Sustainable peace processes require prioritising inclusion and dialogue at the local level. Peacebuilding ownership is nurtured and enduring violence resilience is built by engaging civil society organisations, local leaders as well as affected populations in conflict regions.

These days and in the future, fostering preemptive regional conflict solutions and promoting a proactive perspective for peacebuilding as core to international security and cooperation is fundamental. Addressing these conflicts in a comprehensive, multilateral manner allows the transatlantic community to make substantial strides toward peace and stability in troubled areas of the world.

The functions of international institutions and alliances

International institutions and alliances greatly influence the contemporary geopolitics of world regions because they are important tools of cooperation, conflict resolution and goal achievement. Moreover, international institutions and alliances assist to sustain and enhance peace and stability through dialogue, negotiation, and consensus building.

The use of warfare to resolve conflicts is harshly condemned by the UN and most international institutions. The primary reason behind this belief is that modern weapons capable of mass destruction do not spare anyone, regardless of their individual allegiance, and can lead to a global disaster. Multi-national institutions, along with regional blocs and alliances, strengthening economic and political ties, not only ensure peace at a global level, but regional and local levels as well.

Military conflicts pose major threats to humanity and the United Nations, along with other international institutions, urge the use of diplomacy at a multi-national level to dictate pacifist policies. Countries have devolved advanced systems of communication, enabling constant multi-lateral dialogue. The capability to conduct consistent global communication allows for effective cooperation, which is further boosted by the aid and alliances offered by international institutions, bestowing authority and influencing other nations to follow suit.

The European Union, along with the African Union and the Association of Southeast Asian Nations, work towards regional integration and ensure stability through international treaties. These treaties work towards de-escalating hosts of battles that negatively impact humanity while encouraging economic growth. The North Atlantic Treaty Organisation dedicates its resources and collaboration to defend its members and strengthen socio-economic ties while the Collective Security Treaty Organisation focuses on preventing attacks.

The World Trade Organisation (WTO), International Monetary Fund (IMF), and the World Bank are examples of multilateral economic institutions that control global economic balance, oversee trade liberalisation, and aid in development. These organisations manage the negotiations on trade agreements, grant fiscal assistance to ailing states, and crudely encourage sustainable development initiatives globally.

The effectiveness of supra-national institutions or international alliances is anchored in trust, cooperation, and solidarity between countries. They create mechanisms for dialogue, collaboration, collective action, and numerous other modalities which help construct the policies, criteria, treaties, and statutes to be adhered to and followed by the countries in the international system. They provide the most effective means of conflict prevention, mediation, and post-conflict reconstruction by alleviating the consequences of regional conflicts and humanitarian disasters.

As the world works to overcome complicated issues like climate change, cyber and health pandemics, international institutions and alliances are emerging as crucial components in the fight against these problems. Focus is required from member states to enhance the effectiveness, legitimacy, and credibility of these bodies by implementing strategic reforms to strengthen the operational capacity of the institutions and embrace multilateralism and collective defence.

Public opinion and influence on global policies

Public opinion remains a major factor when making global policies and affecting international relations. In a world that is as interconnected as ours, public opinion in one country may extend beyond its borders and impact a number of diplomatic relations, trade relations, and even military interventions. As important as it is for policymakers, diplomats, and leaders to understand these complex geopolitical considerations, it is equally important to comprehend the existing public sentiment and its implications on international politics. Public opinion can greatly depend on a myriad of factors such as media coverage, cultural narratives, economic conditions, as well as historical experiences. In this case, policymakers will be able to analyse the factors that influence diverse populations, resulting in informed and well-thought-out decisions.

In the global scope, the sentiment among citizens of a nation acts as a measure of the government's credibility along with a substantial undertone towards its dealings internationally. Ignoring public opinion is often counterproductive for any government as it creates internal strain while also diminishing reputation outside the country. With the advent of the Internet and social media, information is available to the public without restriction and is accessible all over the globe. This has empowered everyday citizens and social movements to take leaders and systems into account while giving them the right to speak and openly advocate for political change. In the contemporary world, where globalisation has become a norm, public sentiment becomes universal, giving rise to cross-national alliances and movements. Social movements against the alteration of natural conditions like climate change or violation of human rights or even taking part in humanitarian efforts have unified people all across the globe to actively campaign for change on an international battlefield. The impact of public perception on global decisions can have both positive and negative consequences. On one hand, decision-makers run the risk of capitalising on the approval to impose unilateral policies that are deemed essential for international relations. Conversely, decision-makers dealing with policies must carefully consider the diverging opinions and conflicting interests of different populations. Public and citizen diplomacy requires carefully crafted informed strategies that help bridge communication gaps alongside working with differing opinions.

As mentioned earlier, public opinion is not something that is fixed and can be changed with new information, changes in society, or events. It is therefore critical to keep track of public sentiment if one aims at remaining relevant on the world stage. Public sentiments are dynamic, and therefore policies need to be crafted alongside proactive communications with clearly defined goals and priorities. In the end, ensuring that public sentiment is integrated as an input in the making of global policy is important for achieving responsive, sustainable, and inclusive solutions to global problems while fostering cooperation at the international level.

Conclusion: Approaches to Managing Unpredictability

To manage an unpredictable world order, one requires different approaches and keeps in mind the depth of global problems and how they are interrelated. Throughout this book, we have seen how public opinion significantly impacts policy and international relations, but it does not single-handedly shape global governance or decision-making systems. In summary, something needs to be done about unpredictability concerning world governance, and one can think of a few approaches. One approach involves promoting dialogue and collaboration across multiple sectors, such as governments, NGOs, business, and the citizenry. If participation and transparency are fostered, there is a greater chance to build agreement on the most pressing issues and on how to address them. Another impor-

tant approach is the need for a shift in mindset or change in practices regarding diplomacy and foreign policy; they need to be more pragmatic and
flexible. Because of the rapid pace of change and new geopolitical shifts,
countries will have to be able to recalibrate their methods and strategies as
situations change. Such flexibility also includes the use of new technologies
and innovations in tackling global problems.

Fostering new forms of diplomacy, utilising advanced technologies such
as artificial intelligence and big data analytics, and developing sustainable
technologies promotes quicker, more effective responses to the global order.

Fostering multilateralism and reinforcing international institutions is
still vital in countering the volatile nature of global relations. Together
with the United Nations and the regional organisations, the World Trade
Organisation promotes collective efforts and creates mechanisms for controlling action, fostering disputes, and conflicts. Moreover, forming strategic partnerships, alliances with countries sharing similar views, supports
building stability and resilience amid uncertainty.

Anticipating and being prepared for possible interruptions is made easier through proactive risk management and scenario planning. Through
deep analyses of future possibilities, risks, and opportunities, a response to
unexpected developments can be achieved. Cultivating a culture of empathy, understanding, and respectful relations is important for reducing
tensions and building lasting peace. Empathic diplomacy that understands
different perspectives and centres human security helps bridge divides
and encourages cooperation. Overall, responding to the emerging world
order requires multi-pronged approaches while collaboration, flexibility,
and foresight are foundational imperatives.

18

Case Studies
The War in Ukraine and Energy Security

The conflict in Ukraine: Overview and a historical perspective

The roots of the conflict in Ukraine are very much entwined with the historical occurrences which have transformed the political order of Eastern Europe. To comprehend the existing conflict, it is important to reflect on the developments and events that led to it. One such historically significant event is the dissolution of the Soviet Union in 1991, which marked the onset of Ukraine's independence. Post-independence, it faced the struggle of defining a national identity alongside an orientation towards Russia or the West. The 2004 Orange Revolution, or the Revolution of Dignity, is another critical event which was a culmination of protests driven by perceived rampant election fraud. These events are also a precursor to the eventual deadlock between the country's pro-European and pro-Russian factions.

Russia's annexation of Crimea in 2014 alongside the armed conflict in eastern Ukraine exemplifies the deepening geopolitical tensions and struggles for dominance in the region. The combination of Ukraine's history with Russia, alongside its wish for greater relations with the European Union, continues to influence the conflict. Marked by a history of geopolitical strategizing and competing nationalistic agendas, the Ukrainian conflict is best described as a culmination of various power struggles and historical narratives within the region. Geopolitical importance: Ukraine's role in global power dynamics

Ukraine's geostrategic location makes it a focal point of conflicts between world powers as it sits between the borders of Europe and Asia. Moreover, Ukraine's complex history in addition to its ethnically diverse population makes it an attractive global power arena. Geostrategically, Ukraine's position is crucial given its geography and relationships with neighboring states. The aforementioned relations determine the border conflicts along with the global geopolitical struggles. Economically, Ukraine serves as a battleground between Russia and Europe. Ukraine's predominant geographical importance serves as a bridge aiding in controlling the access of maritime routes such as trade across the Black Sea. Furthermore, the majority of the country is positioned bordering rich resources aiding it in becoming an essential agricultural ground serving as the breadbasket of Europe. These resources are economically competing internationally which allows the country to be targeted for foreign energy powers.

Ukraine's geographic position serves as a conduit for the transportation of energy resources from Russia and as a recipient of economic benefits from Russia and Western countries, escalating Ukraine's economic significance. The combination of internal problems faced by the country, including the political turmoil, has magnified the degree of external influence, revealing the weakness of its structures and deepening fault lines. The EU's relationship with Ukraine, which has included attempts by Ukraine to adopt Western values, along with its relations with Russia have, from the side of Moscow and Western capitals, turned Ukraine into a contested symbol of opposing ideologies and spheres of influence. These factors jointly highlight the geostrategic, economic, and geopolitical interests of Ukraine and explain its primary position on the global stage, thus drawing attention from policymakers and analysts in order to understand the un-folding realities in Ukraine.

Primary Stakeholders: Examination of US, EU, and Russian interests

The conflict in Ukraine appears to be one of the most important foci of interest for the strategies of the world global players USA, EU, and Russia. It is in America's interest to actively defend Ukraine's sovereignty and territorial integrity because Ukraine is considered the frontline of influence contest in Eastern Europe. The United States seeks to balance the overpowering Russian influence in the region as well as sustain its alliance with the Eastern European countries. The European Union focuses on the stability and the promotion of democracy in its neighbourhood and sees the Ukrainian crisis as an opportunity to demonstrate its influence in the region.

The EU grapples with economic issues stemming directly from the ongoing war in Ukraine due to its reliance on Russian gas, which raises tensions around energy supply security and geopolitical interests. From Russia's perspective, Ukraine is historically and strategically viewed as a core part of its influence, and Russia aims to block its integration into the Western sphere of influence. Russia also views Ukraine as a critical buffer zone for its national security and a means of influence over Eastern Europe. The conflict enables Russia to leverage negotiations with the EU concerning energy policy and gas transit infrastructure and, thus, enhance its role as the primary supplier of energy to Europe. The clash of deals and the geopolitical maneuvering of the major players show the intricate balance of political, economic, and security interdependencies around Ukraine, which not only affects the regional balance of power but also the global balance of power.

Energy dependencies: Europe's reliance on Russian fossil fuels

The ongoing geopolitical tensions with Moscow have historically centred Europe's energy structure around its dependency on Russian gas. EU Member States consume natural gas in exceeding amounts and remain heavily dependent on its availability. This poses serious risks regarding energy security and the geopolitical balance in the area.

Europe's geographic location is both a blessing and a curse for many of its countries since Russia, its neighbouring state, has a ready and cheap supply of natural gas. But this intimate energy relationship poses potential risks of supply scarcities and political pressure on Europe by Russian forces. The conflicts between Russia and Ukraine, which resulted in the stopping of gas supply to European countries via Ukraine, serve as a classic example of the dangers of dependence.

Even as Europe and Russia engaged in trade relations focused on energy, geopolitical maneuvering and heavy-handed meddling were present. As a leading supplier of gas, Russia has relentlessly pursued its strategic interests, usually dominating the foreign energy market, serving as a means to impose control and as a weapon to enforce policy. This made the EU concerned over the possible abuse of dependency on energy resources for political means alongside the need to diversify available energy sources.

In recent years, there has been a concerted effort aimed at reducing dependency on Russian gas in the European Union. The initiatives aimed towards the diversification of energy resources include the construction of LNG terminals, interconnecting gas pipelines, and the promotion of renewable energy sources. Strengthening cooperation with other gas-producing nations and looking for alternative transit routes has also become an EU initiative to reduce dependency on conventional Russian gas routes.

The aim of improving energy security and protecting nations from possible supply interruptions or geopolitical threats is the primary reason for seeking energy diversification. The dependence on Russian gas creates vulnerabilities that need addressing through energy contracts, infrastructure development, and regulatory frameworks. To ensure energy security, the EU needs to promote a discrepant and clear competitive energy market to curb external propensities and threats to energy markets.

Europe requires stronger diplomatic relations, investments, and amendments in policies to resolve the dependencies relating to Russian gas. Implementing a more balanced and diverse energy fusion will ensure Europe's energy security and protect it from external threats and pressures. The focus remains on providing uninterrupted and consistent energy access to citizens and industries while searching for alternative sources of energy.

Analysing the strategy of imposing sanctions: Their effects

It has been noted that sanctions have become a strategic response to the Russia-Ukraine conflict as well as a concern for global energy security. The case of Russia and Ukraine has led to the imposition of economic sanctions by the United States and the European Union. These sanctions were aimed at Russia's economy in critical areas such as finance, energy, and defence which in principle sought to further expropriate aggression and enforcement of international laws and agreements. The uses of these sanctions have brought about diverse effects. These sanctions have economically subdued the growth of Russia by disrupting investments and curtailing access to international capital markets. There are already several parts of Russia's economy that are on a downward slope thanks to these sanctions and one of them is the energy sector which now finds it difficult to exploit and develop oil, gas and other crucial energy infrastructure projects. On the other hand, the sanctions have demonstrated the strength and solidarity of the Western allies. Nonetheless, there is still uncertainty on these sanctions yielding the sought after political outcomes.

Although they certainly caused some damage to the economy of Russia, they did not result in Russia fundamentally changing its policies concerning Ukraine or its strategic goals.

The sanctions have led the Russian authorities to seek different avenues for trade, partnership, and investment, thus escaping the Western markets. This has created new geopolitical headaches for the West because it makes it much more difficult to maintain a cohesive approach in their sanctioning policies. One cannot ignore the effects of sanctions on the European economies. The interconnectedness of global markets implies that sanctions aimed at Russia will also impact Europe, industries, businesses, and trade relations. The impacts and effectiveness of the sanctions need to be scrutinised more deeply, considering both the intended impacts and consequences that arise from other underlying factors. In the case of Ukraine and energy security matters, a strategic combination of calibrated sanctions, advocacy, and a shift in the focus on energy will be at the centrepiece of transatlantic relations dealing with the complex situation.

Diversification efforts in Europe: alternative energy solutions

In response to the problem of energy insecurity caused by overreliance on Russian gas, Europe has taken extensive measures to diversify its sources of energy and thus reduce its vulnerability. One major initiative is the Southern Gas Corridor, which plans to transport gas from the Caspian Sea through pipelines in the Southern Gas Corridor into Europe. The project comprises the Trans-Adriatic Pipeline (TAP) and the Trans-Anatolian Pipeline (TANAP), which are aimed at replacing Russia as a source of natural gas for Europe. The development of liquefied natural gas (LNG) terminals across Europe has made it possible for LNG to be sourced from different global suppliers, thereby reducing dependency on a single supplier. Another strategy that has been used to diversify the European energy mix is the emphasis on renewable energy sources. Countries like Germany have invested heavily in solar and wind power with an aim of minimising their reliance on traditional fossil fuels.

Cross-border energy transmission capacity has been increased by interconnections and infrastructure improvements, which in turn promote flexibility and better integration within the European energy market. This is evident in the financial support provided by the European Union to such undertakings as well as the regulatory frameworks that have been put in place for this purpose. However, there are also several challenges associated with alternative energy solutions. For example, renewable sources can be intermittent, hence necessitating efficient storage and backup systems to guarantee a steady supply of power.

Long-term investment and planning are necessary due to high upfront costs associated with infrastructure development and technology deployment. The implementation of diversification projects may be complicated by geopolitical considerations as well as competing interests among European countries and external energy suppliers. In order to succeed, therefore, it is essential for collaborative efforts between the EU, Member States, and transatlantic partners to be made. Europe can expand its portfolio of energy sources while mitigating risks related to dependence on a single supplier through technological innovation, regulatory alignment, and investment coordination. As such, economic, environmental and geopolitical implications must be assessed alongside alternative energy solutions' evolution in order to maintain Europe's top priority on energy security amidst changing global dynamics.

Transatlantic Cooperation: Common Approaches to Energy Security

The spectre of energy insecurity is hanging over Europe; hence, transatlantic cooperation becomes more and more important in order to solve this intricate issue. Energy security is not only a matter of economic stability but it is also closely linked with geopolitical stability and national defence. The United States and the European Union must develop joint strategies for mitigating these vulnerabilities that emanate from dependence on external energy supplies since they recognise their interdependence in terms of energy systems.

One of the most important elements of transatlantic cooperation in enhancing energy security consists of the diversification of routes and sources of energy supply. The development of alternative energy infrastructures such as liquefied natural gas (LNG) terminals and gas pipelines can help reduce Europe's vulnerability to disruptions in gas supply. Joint investments into renewable energy projects and advanced technologies are also showing promise for reducing the continent's reliance on fossil fuels from potentially unstable regions.

To facilitate efficient energy exchanges and promote market competition, it is necessary to harmonise energy policies and regulatory frameworks on both sides of the Atlantic. Optimising resource allocation, fostering innovation, and ensuring fair access to energy resources can be supported by closer cooperation on energy governance. Transatlantic efforts towards environmental protection and sustainable energy practices can be strengthened through aligning standards.

Information sharing, technology transfer and capacity building are important in enhancing transatlantic partnerships for greater resilience in terms of energy. In order to enhance the overall efficiency and reliability of energy systems on both sides of the Atlantic, there should be collaborative research and development initiatives in areas such as grid modernisation, storage technologies and energy efficiency.

The US-EU partnership needs to use its combined diplomatic influence to negotiate transparent and equitable agreements with external suppliers. A joint position that supports open competitive markets for electricity can help prevent coercive tactics in the field of gas supply or undue political influence by exporting countries.

The cooperation between the United States and Europe in terms of energy security goes beyond just bilateral relationships to include multilateral platforms and international organisations. In this regard, engaging in constructive dialogues at the International Energy Agency (IEA) and G7 can help align global efforts to enhance energy resilience and address common energy challenges.

In order to ensure collective energy security and contribute to global stability, the US and EU should pursue a comprehensive approach that combines resource diversification, policy coordination, technological innovation as well as diplomatic alignment. In an ever-changing energy landscape, a united transatlantic front will be necessary for navigating through the complex dynamics of energy security in an increasingly interconnected world.

The role of NATO: security measures and military assistance

NATO's role in providing security measures and military assistance to its member states and partner countries is now more closely scrutinised as the conflict in Ukraine continues. As an intergovernmental military alliance, NATO has a primary duty of ensuring that its members' security and territorial integrity are maintained through collective defence and deterrence. In response to the Ukrainian crisis, NATO has initiated several programmes aimed at enhancing eastern allies' security posture and countering potential threats from the war.

To begin with, one of the major responses by NATO has been increasing its military presence in Eastern Europe especially in Poland and the Baltic States. Notably, this includes deploying multinational battle groups under the Enhanced Forward Presence (EFP) initiative which is a visible demonstration of NATO's commitment to deterring any possible aggression. Moreover, it has conducted numerous joint military exercises as well as training missions within this region so as to enhance interoperability among allied forces thereby demonstrating their readiness to respond collectively to any security challenges.

NATO has also prioritised the enhancement of its strategic capabilities and resilience to hybrid warfare tactics in addition to physical presence of NATO forces. These include enhancing cyberdefences, countering disinformation campaigns and strengthening intelligence-sharing mechanisms for better identification and response to potential threats from the Ukrainian conflict. To this end, NATO has provided advisory services and capacity-building support to the Ukrainian armed forces to enable them improve their ability to protect themselves against external aggression.

The ongoing conflict in Ukraine has exposed the need for NATO to re-view its security policies and reaffirm its commitment to collective defence. In this respect, member states of NATO have reiterated their commitment towards allocating sufficient resources on defence spending as stated by Wales Summit Declaration and subsequent agreements. The aim is ensuring that NATO maintains a credible deterrent posture while being capable of responding effectively to any security challenges that may arise within the region.

Beyond its member states, NATO's role in military assistance includes its partnerships with non-member countries within the Euro-Atlantic region. Through programmes such as Partnership for Peace and the Euro-Atlantic Partnership Council, NATO has enabled engagement with Ukraine and other countries affected by the conflict, providing support in areas like defence reform, military training and infrastructure development.

In short, NATO's response to the conflict in Ukraine reflects the Alliance's commitment to security and stability in the Euro-Atlantic area. By putting robust security measures in place and giving military assistance to Allies and partners, NATO seeks to deter aggression, strengthen defences and contribute towards resolving the crisis through a comprehensive and unified approach.

Media Narratives: Information Warfare Influence

Information warfare influence has become increasingly widespread in-fluencing public perceptions as well as narratives on global conflicts. In relation to the war in Ukraine and energy security, media narratives have played a central role in escalating tensions while spreading propaganda from various stakeholders involved in the conflict. The weaponisation of information through traditional media sources, social media platforms as well as disinformation campaigns have blurred lines between truth and misinformation thereby contributing to a complex landscape of competing narratives.

Manipulation of public opinion is often fuelled by the role of state-backed media and dissemination of fake news, which has led to polarization and increased mistrust among global audiences. Propaganda is strategically disseminated in order to undermine opposing narratives, creating an environment where truth becomes subjective and open to manipulation.

The immediacy and reach of information through online platforms in the digital era has intensified the impacts of this information war. The rapid spread of false information combined with sophisticated psychological operations has sown division and discord, thus calling into question the ethical responsibility of media organisations as well as democratic societies' resilience.

The militarisation of information goes beyond influencing public opinion; it includes cyber-attacks and computer hacking aimed at destabilising communication channels, infrastructure, and electoral processes. These tactics underscore the interrelatedness between information warfare and wider geopolitical strategies, hence necessitating strong defences and international cooperation against such threats.

To counteract information warfare, efforts to promote media literacy, fact-checking initiatives, and transparency in reporting are crucial to arm the public with the necessary critical thinking skills for differentiating between factual information and manipulative narratives. It is important that governments, technology companies, and civil society work together to fight disinformation and protect journalistic integrity so that information ecosystems remain intact.

In conclusion, understanding and addressing the multiple dimensions of the information war is essential in order to minimise its negative impacts on public discourse, conflict resolution, and the stability of transatlantic relations. By examining power dynamics behind media narratives vis-à-vis geopolitical interests, stakeholders can help make information ecosystems more resilient whilst creating a more educated global audience.

Lessons Learned: Implications for Future Conflict

The conflict in Ukraine and the concurrent information war have offered important lessons that can influence future approaches to global conflicts. One of the most significant outcomes is the realisation of how disinformation and propaganda can shape public opinion and affect political decisions. Policymakers, media, and the general population need to understand the power of information warfare and its potential dangers in a globally interconnected world.

The Ukrainian conflict demonstrated that unity among transatlantic allies is key when dealing with external aggression as well as destabilising actions. It also showed that security challenges such as hybrid threats, which combine traditional military tactics with non-military means like cyber attacks or disinformation campaigns, require a coordinated approach.

Energy security has been brought to light by this conflict as an essential part of geopolitical strategies. The dependence on Russian gas by Europe shows why there is an urgent need for diversification and resilience in energy supplies. The Ukrainian crisis should be a wake-up call for reinforcing energy independence through alternative sources and routes to ensure stability and reduce vulnerabilities.

The response to the Ukrainian conflict has shown how effective and ineffective economic sanctions can be as a tool of coercive diplomacy. This is because, as experience shows, while they can put pressure on the target and impose costs on them, they may also attract countermeasures and unintended consequences. Hence, future strategies must weigh possible outcomes with a view to adopting a comprehensive approach that integrates diplomatic, economic, and military elements.

The Ukrainian experience has demonstrated the need to enhance defensive capabilities and resilience in vulnerable states. It has underlined the importance of strategic partnerships, security assistance, and capacity building for enhancing nations' ability to deter aggression and protect their sovereignty. The war has initiated debates on reforming and adapting international institutions and alliances to effectively respond to emerging security challenges.

Ultimately, lessons from the Ukrainian conflict highlight the need for anticipating hybrid threats; improving energy security; strengthening transatlantic partnership; reassessing traditional diplomatic tools as well as coercive ones. These lessons are invaluable for policymakers and stakeholders who should take these into consideration while formulating proactive strategies that will help them navigate through complex future conflicts, ensuring global peace and stability.

19

Conclusion

Prospects for USA-EU Relations in the 21st Century

Highlight of the key concepts

Across the previous chapters, this book has analysed the changes and intricacies of the United States and European Union relationship in the contemporary world. We studied the past, which captured important milestones like the challenges from the 9/11 attacks, the 2008 financial crisis, and all the diplomacy from American presidents in the succeeding years. We further included the major domains of cooperation and rivalry such as economic relations, security, climate policies, and geopolitical challenges. The main focus was to analyse the dynamics of transatlantic relationships, revealing the many drivers that define the contours of this partnership. By integrating this extensive scrutiny, we sought to formulate some profound considerations on the future of US-EU relations amid the challenges. The interplay of historical legacies, changing global contexts, and domestic political factors makes for a compelling case to rethink and enhance mechanisms for bilateral relations.

Analysis of the previous chapters helps us to discern opportunities for strengthening cooperation, collaboration, noting patterns and underlying tensions. With this in mind, it is crucial at the outset to highlight the comprehensive character of all the issues raised and their bearing on the prospect of transatlantic relations beyond bilateral engagements. This analysis is intended to deepen the dialogues aimed at understanding how the lessons of the past can inform constructive forward-looking approaches, providing elements for strategic reasoning while also inviting critical thought. Accordingly, from this standpoint, we can analyse profound historical movements and discern the paradigms of EU and US relations essential to the 21st century, best characterised by flexibility and durability, balancing the interests of both sides.

Assessing historical lessons for future cooperation

The interplay between the United States and European Union is characterised by complex struggles and progress successes, each of which have intricately shaped the transatlantic partnership. The relationship, starting from the aftermath of two incredibly devastating world wars towards periods of dynamically growing economies and shifting international powers, paints a selvedge of worldlines. Looking towards the future, it is crucial to study the very intricacies of historical relationship, remembering core features bound to cooperation aimed for sustainable development and understanding mutual aid obligations focused towards societal enrichment around alliances. The turn of the globe-marked international surge marked by post-world war shifted the perception of systems globally. The Burning Point zero showcased The Marshall Plan and new order came into view alongside schemes of international relations, cooperatives and NATO. The dynamic international systems formed allies with perceived unions advocating allies. Both the Cold War's end, along with the dissolution of the Soviet Union mark a highly transformative epoch portraying the EU along with showcasing the blooding currency designed to illustrate the resiliency of maintained EU transatlantic relations.

One must examine how previous instances of international cooperation, conflict, and resolution have influenced the diplomatic evolution of the United States and the European Union.

Evaluating historical events helps us appreciate the methods utilised in building trust and cooperation while avoiding certain pitfalls. During discord in the past, a re-evaluation of the transatlantic relationship has often been possible. Factors such as differing views on the Iraq War, or trade disagreements have acted as a diagnostic measure highlighting cracks in the cohesive alliance. These differences have taught us the need for diplomacy and understanding towards common ground. Through studying the history of relations between the United States and the EU, we note there is a delicate approach in the dynamics that exists which requires deeper relations. At last, the historical context of transatlantic relations offers a rich source of advice for collaboration that enables us to design future relations for the start of the 21st century.

Strategic alterations: Embracing new international shifts

By the start of the 21st century, the United States and the European Union are simultaneously going through notable changes in their international relations—these have undergone alterations concerning the partnership between these two strategic regions of the globe. New power phenomena, changes of the geographic economic focus and modernisation of the security challenge approaches compel the two entities to review their relations. One of the primary elements of a shift of this kind is the acknowledgement of international order, where previously concentrated spheres of international relations are being contested by a number of emerging nations. Hence, both the USA and EU need to change their policies towards international relations, commerce and security in regard to the new world powers.

The revival of great power competition has heightened the necessity for coordinated action from the transatlantic partners. This entails formulating policies to safeguard shared ideals and values, protect democracy, and confront emerging threats like cybersecurity breaches, hybrid conflicts, and sophisticated propaganda attacks. Another critical aspect of the international strategic shift concerns the rapid technological advancements and digital changes as they intersect with global relations. Both the US and the EU need to collaborate on the consequences of such advancements on governance, commerce, and social relationships.

Disruptive technologies such as artificial intelligence, quantum computing, and biotechnology require the reconsideration of regulatory, legal, and ethical frameworks for collective action and standardised policies. Additionally, the world's economy and global shifts in the economy call for devotion to refocus strategies. These strategies should include addressing emerging vulnerabilities from international supply chain dependence and financial instability by strengthening economic relations between Europe and America. Specifically, investing in international trade needs to be prioritised to enhance the reliability and sustainability of the transatlantic trade and investment economy. These challenges require supporting changes for active partnership between the United States and the EU and inclusive collaboration to ensure swift manoeuvring. Regardless, accepting these adjustments will allow transatlantic partners to find ways to mitigate international threats and work together for a more peaceful and equitable international system.

Bilateral mechanisms institutional reforms: changes

The changes facilitate enhancement of bilateral mechanisms within USA and EU relations. The genesis of transatlantic cooperations has served well in the past, however, there is a need to rework strategies for the present time international relations shifts which require more attention towards institution revitalisation and modernisation.

Evaluation of existing policies' effectiveness and decision-making agility in multinational collaborative frameworks enhances policy agility to emerging issues. Optimisation of existing forums and councils will augment competitiveness and problem-solving capabilities of the US and EU.

This might require altering the structure of committees, working groups, and task forces so they can proactively respond to geopolitical, economic, and technological changes.

It is necessary to enhance integration and increase overlap among areas of policies. This requires the merging of regulations, customs, and their benchmarks in areas like trade, finance, energy, and even security. The coordination of strategies to deal with shared issues, like cybersecurity and other issues such as sustainable development, is required to meet the strategic goals of the transatlantic partnership. So, there is a need to institutionalise reforms that focus on integration and alignment of policies, enhancing the synergy and joint impact of initiatives.

The challenges and opportunities presented by the digital world require new forms of governance and cooperation. The further development of AI, data privacy, and cyber defence requires works in these areas to be modernised to digitised frameworks and foster multi-sectoral institutional cooperation. This means creating special channels for dialogue and collaboration on digital governance, establishing collaborative projects and initiatives in research and innovation programmes, and developing transatlantic frameworks to address the transformative impacts of emerging technologies.

Accountability, transparency, and inclusiveness are critical for effective institutional reforms. The involvement of diverse stakeholders such as civil society organisations, think tanks, and academia enhances the quality of transatlantic dialogues and increases the legitimacy and ownership of cooperative efforts. Through recalibrating mechanisms to be more participatory and inclusive, the United States and the European Union are able to tap into a wider array of expertise and perspectives, thus making their collaboration more enduring and relevant.

To conclude, reforms aimed at augmenting bilateral mechanisms constitute an effective approach to strengthen the enduring partnership between the United States and the European Union. With regard to these improvements, flexibility, coherence, creativity, and inclusivity will enable transatlantic relations to respond to 21st century challenges and opportunities with renewed vigour and purpose.

Potential for Collaboration and Technology Advancement

In the twenty-first century, technology has emerged as the anchor of US-EU relations, significantly influencing them in diverse ways. On one hand, the acceleration of new inventions provides ample opportunities, while on the other, challenges that necessitate collaboration to unlock their complete potential. The phenomena of digital transformation, artificial intelligence (AI), and the advancement of cybersecurity underscored the importance of the transatlantic partnership. Harnessing the benefits of these developments demands strategic foresight and regulatory balance in framework innovation. Controlling the ethical use of AI, data privacy, and data flows is imperative for the United States and the European Union in maintaining shared values and protecting their citizens' rights.

Joint research, investment, and cooperation in quantum computing, biotechnology, and space exploration fosters collaboration and economic growth. Clean energy technologies and climate change sustainable practices indicate that efforts towards combating climate change synergistic potential as well. The identification of common standard systems will facilitate interoperability, enhancing trade and reducing barriers. The interconnectedness created through the deployment of 5G and IoT infrastructure enhances resiliency, connectivity, digital inclusion, and reduces the digital divide. Partners across the Atlantic with recognition of the potential from emerging technology industries have the ability to restructure global competitiveness by innovation while capitalising on the available skills and resources. Global market competition, however, intellectual property rights, market access, and fair competition policies require a transparent dispute-focused dialogue. Collaborative efforts targeting technological advancement alongside human capital focused investments, STEM education, and a skilled workforce to address the exponentially increasing demands of the digital economy are essential.

The potential for collaboration in research and development, along with technology transfer agreements, is beneficial for the overall welfare of the US-EU alliance. Hence, implementing a strategically proactive position on convergence of technologies provides multiple avenues for the creation of trust and enhancement of resilience and innovation-driven economic growth in the transatlantic area.

The forecasted economy: Trade and investment issues

In the 21st century, trade and investment form a critical component in the multifaceted relationship between the US and the European Union. The economies of these powerful players are interlinked, presenting numerous challenges that need creative strategies to navigate. Both sides make efforts to cope with change in order to maintain economic growth and stability, as geopolitical factors put stress on traditional frameworks. A determining aspect of regressive trade relations is the varying scope of international supply chains. In a more integrated world, a region's trade conflict or natural catastrophe can set off a chain reaction across continents. It also demands an examination of how robust and how diversified a supply chain can be, which between the US and the EU offers avenues for partnership.

Trade frontier for the digital economy. Issues such as data privacy, cybersecurity and digital taxation require harmonized standards and regulations and, as a result, cross-border action. Because innovation moves more quickly than regulations, there is an urgent need to establish a unified approach to leveraging opportunities and addressing challenges posed by the digital age.

The spectre of protectionism looms large on the international trade stage. Both the United States and the European Union face pressure from domestic stakeholders seeking to safeguard industries and employment opportunities. Balancing the imperatives of free trade with the needs of local groups requires skilful diplomatic manoeuvring and a nuanced understanding of common objectives. At the same time, investment challenges encompass a range of considerations from regulatory frameworks to capital flows. Increased scrutiny in sectors such as technology, infrastructure and healthcare highlights the need for transparent and predictable investment environments. Alignment of standards and practices can strengthen investor confidence and facilitate mutually beneficial capital deployment. The issue of asymmetric market access and the promotion of fair competition remain central themes in the development of future economic collaboration between the United States and the EU. In the future, the convergence of emerging markets and the evolution of geopolitical dynamics will introduce a degree of complexity into the trade and investment landscapes. Exploiting synergies while mitigating risks requires flexible strategies and strong partnerships. Ultimately, charting the economic future requires recalibrating approaches to trade and investment, strategically aligning policies, and capitalising on synergies across sectors and regions.

Regardless of the challenges, the opportunities that can arise from the collaboration between the United States and the European Union remain highly prominent and offer mutual wealth and global economic equilibrium.

As the 21st century accommodates powerful technologies and complexities, security issues have become one of the most important aspects for developing relations between the United States and the European Union. Both the EU and the US have to deal with an increasing set of complex, multi-dimensional challenges, from classical ones to non-state actors and cyber warfare.

Exchanging mutual defence pledges, constituting NATO, focuses on the common responsibility of guaranteeing the respect of conventional domination over authority and sovereignty of member states. This focus also includes fighting regional hybrid instabilities and promoting diplomacy and active conflict resolution, enhancing military readiness of forces. The US and EU must cooperate in the combat against international terrorism, the prevention of the proliferation of weapons of mass destruction and the rise of arm peace.

The combination of new technologies and asymmetric warfare has made strong cyber defence capabilities essential. Cybersecurity collaboration between the US and the EU is critical to combating cyber threats, safeguarding vital infrastructure, and minimising the dangers of state-funded cyber operations. Joint intelligence, counter-intelligence, and policing efforts are necessary to meet the demands of transnational security.

Apart from conventional military security threats, transatlantic allies should also focus on non-conventional threats such as pandemics, climate change, and the depletion of resources. These challenges will require coordinated efforts for responding to disasters, public health resilience, and environmental preservation.

EU and US relations should incorporate the increasing convergence of security concerns and technology, highlighting the need for ethical frameworks and policies in emerging technologies, artificial intelligence, and space. The purpose is to promote advanced forms of innovation while safeguarding against the development of military technologies and advanced systems that could be misused.

The intercontinental shifts in policies need astute foresight, flexibility, and rational planning as obstacles are bound to arise. Stricter alliances need to be formed, the exploitation of mutual resources aggrandised, and trends in security structure should be predicted and worked upon jointly by the United States and the European Union in order to handle the contemporary intricacies of the global security mechanisms in partnership with each other.

Preserving the climate is a critical challenge that the European Union and the United States of America have struggled with in the 21st century, and at the same time a mutual responsibility that has been neglected by both. Both parties have historically shown how significant mitigating the climate crisis is, and have actively looked for ways to reduce its impacts on a global level; for example, the Paris Agreement has been one of the landmarks of the world in uniting to slow the global warming effects. The US and the EU are willing to emphasise their commitment towards protecting the environment not only as international figures but also as collaborative allies in conserving Earth's ecosystems.

The need for cooperation when tackling climate change comes from the acknowledgement of the relationship between the economy, political relationships, and the environment. The United States and the European Union have individually nationalised climate policies within their jurisdictions, but the synergies that exist between the two powerhouse economies can be extremely beneficial. Cooperative efforts include almost everything from the transfer of clean technology, clean fuel strategies, and even clean energy weapon development. The United States and the European Union can use their extensive resources and combine their knowledge in order to further the efforts in climate change which can serve as a global benchmark.

A convergence on climate goals increases the probability of transatlantic initiatives regarding global climate governance. Addressing the growing intricacies of environmental issues, the United States and the European Union partnership terms the spearhead in promoting sustainable and resilient development at the international level. With adequate climate policy coalition building, both sides can influence international climate meetings for broader participation, enabling unified approaches to climate policy. These joint actions are necessary towards developing a more coherent and inclusive approach to climate change mitigation that goes beyond borders and accommodates different societal and ecological needs.

At the same time, agreeing on the need to tackle climate change may present contextual gaps with other potential divergence areas. Political priorities, regulatory policies, and public opinion can be impediments to cohesive action. Balancing unity and diversity while addressing each entity's climate agenda is crucial. In this context, treating climate change as a collective challenge requires converging opposing views through dialogue. The ability to find and deal with opposing issues will enhance the efficiency and robustness of United States – European Union collaborative actions towards climate change, thus making them more effective.

Citizen engagement: The role of public diplomacy

Public engagement is one of the most important factors in shaping US-EU relations in the 21st century. This is because the world is becoming increasingly interconnected. In fostering dialogue, mutual understanding, and cultural relations, public diplomacy is important. Both sides of the Atlantic need to be engaged effectively if lasting relationships and support for transatlantic relations are to be cultivated. Public diplomacy gives rise to a number of initiatives which include exchange programmes (both educational and cultural), media diplomacy and even digital diplomacy. They all endeavour to overcome differences, debunk misconceptions, and promote shared ideals and collective hopes. With public diplomacy, there is a need to capture the attention of people from different ages, socio-economic statuses, and regions to impart more understanding towards each other's views. Public diplomacy strengthens the ties between states while promoting peace and stability across the world. Through collaborative projects and direct interactions, public diplomacy achieves this goal.

Through public diplomacy, democratic values, human rights, and the rule of law are advanced, strengthening the common values that transatlantic relations are founded on. In this digital era where communication is continuously evolving, the use of social media and other digital platforms for public diplomacy is becoming increasingly important. With creative approaches to storytelling, interactive multimedia, and virtual exchanges, entire communities can be engaged to inspire constructive dialogue between diverse cultures.

Integrating public diplomacy approaches with contemporary issues such as climate change, gender equality and social justice helps to better capture the hopes and concerns of citizens on both sides of the Atlantic. Maximally leveraging public diplomacy offers a challenge when it comes to realising the growing potential that public diplomacy has for investment, coordination, and collaboration among government, civil society, academia, and the private sector. Through the development of a wide network of transatlantic partnerships and collaborations, public diplomacy can effectively meet both the new challenges and emerging opportunities which deepen the relations between the US and the EU. It is important to note that the rhetoric surrounding public diplomacy is too often in danger of downplaying the role that public diplomacy plays in fostering cross-citizen relations, where the most effective ties are created through empathy as well as a shared vision for a strong transatlantic community.

Visionary Pathways: Projecting the Future of U.S.-EU Relations

When considering the contemporary trends in the relations between the United States and the European Union, it is evident that visionary pathways are necessary to secure a sustainable partnership that is advantageous to both parties. In the 21st century, there are challenges and opportunities that have never been seen before, thus requiring a proactive approach that employs collaboration and innovation while exhibiting adaptability along the way. While designing the roadmap for U.S.-EU relations, there are certain fundamental aspects that come to mind. First, shared values as a renewed commitment to transatlantic partnership will provide the framework for the envisioned future. Embracing diversity along with democratic governance and human rights as core values will help foster cohesion and resilience amid geopolitical flux.

Strategic use of technological innovations promises to enhance the relations and cooperation among countries. The use of cyber diplomacy, cyber resilience, and new technologies can adapt to constantly shifting security and economic demands. Fighting climate change and ensuring environmental sustainability is a critical aspect of the intended partnership. Proactive approaches toward sustaining the environment, fostering economic growth, energy transition, and strengthening climate resilience will create economic interdependence and shared wealth while reducing environmental risks. Solutions to trade and investment issues require an integrated approach consisting of strengthening multilateral systems, regulatory alignment, and supportive inclusive growth policies. With a focus on open markets and competition, the relationship between the U.S. and the European Union will allow for adaptation to intricate economic systems.

An explicit commitment to strengthening citizen engagement and people-to-people ties is paramount for the further development of the transatlantic partnership. Boosting civil society, facilitating greater educational exchanges, and enhancing cultural dialogue will deepen understanding and create lasting social bonds. As the United States and the European Union manage geopolitical uncertainties and fluid global dynamics, it is critical to re-evaluate security obligations through the lens of collective defence and shared accountability. Joint action against hybrid threats, cyber warfare, and strategic deterrents will build the transatlantic security architecture, defending the shared interests of peace, stability, and international relations. In order to proactively develop the relations between the US and the EU, advanced visions for US-EU relations should be developed by adopting a stance calling for global leadership grounded in multilateral cooperation while engaging emerging powers to strategically shape a rules-based international order. By espousing well-grounded principles of diplomacy and conflict resolution and crisis management, transatlantic allies can constructively shape and advance international efforts towards shared goals and common interests. Initiatives directed at the identified areas and boldly strategised can alter the trajectory of relations between the European Union and the United States towards a future of lasting relevancy, enduring resilience, and rich mutual prosperity.

20
Selected Bibliography For Further Reading

Abdelal, R., & Krotz, U. (2024). *Estranged allies: Transatlantic relations in the post-Trump era*. Princeton University Press.

Alcaro, R. (2023). The transatlantic dimension of European strategic autonomy. *International Affairs*, 99(2), 567-584.

Anderson, P. (2020). *The European Union and the United States: A troubled partnership*. Routledge.

Art, R. J. (2017). *A grand strategy for America*. Cornell University Press.

Ash, T. G. (2019). *Free world: Why a crisis of the West reveals what it means to be European*. Atlantic Books.

Asmus, R. D. (2005). *A little war that shook the world: Georgia, Russia, and the future of the West*. Palgrave Macmillan.

Bacevich, A. J. (2002). *American empire: The realities and consequences of U.S. diplomacy*. Harvard University Press.

Bacevich, A. J. (2013). *The limits of power: The end of American exceptionalism*. Metropolitan Books.

Baldwin, R. E. (2006). *The euro's trade effects*. In R. E. Baldwin (Ed.), *The euro and the dollar in a multipolar world* (pp. 45-78). VoxEU.org.

Balfour, R., & Toygür, I. (2024). Finding a new balance: European strategic autonomy and transatlantic relations. *Journal of European Integration*, 46(1), 79-96.

Beck, U. (2005). *Power in the global age: A new global political economy*. Polity Press.

Beckley, M. (2023). *Rivals: How the power struggle between China, India, and Japan will shape our next decade*. Oxford University Press.

Bergsten, F. (2019). *The United States and the world economy: Selected papers of C. Fred Bergsten, 1984–2019*. Peterson Institute for International Economics.

Berliner, D. T. (2011). *Understanding the European Union*. Lynne Rienner Publishers.

Biscop, S. (2019). *European strategy in the age of geopolitics*. Egmont Institute.

Baker, P., & Glasser, S. B. (2020). *The divider: Trump in the White House, 2017-2021*. Doubleday.

Brzezinski, Z. (1997). *The grand chessboard: American primacy and its geostrategic imperatives*. Basic Books.

Brooks, S. G., & Wohlforth, W. C. (2024). The end of US hegemony? Unipolar anxiety and American power. *International Security*, 48(3), 7-43.

Burwell, F. G. (2021). *The future of the transatlantic relationship*. Center for Strategic and International Studies.

Burwell, F. G. (2023). *Transatlantic relations in transition: The future of US-European cooperation*. Routledge.

Calleo, D. P. (2001). *Rethinking Europe's role*. *Journal of Common Market Studies*, 39(1), 1-19.

Cohen-Tanugi, L. (2008). *The shape of the world to come: Charting the geopolitics of a new century*. Columbia University Press.

Colgan, J. D., & Keohane, R. O. (2023). The liberal order is rigged: Fix it now or watch it wither. *Foreign Affairs*, 102(4), 28-38.

Cooper, R. (2003). *The breaking of nations: Order and chaos in the twenty-first century*. Atlantic Books.

Danchev, A., & MacMillan, J. (2023). *The US-European relationship: Historical foundations and contemporary challenges*. Cambridge University Press.

Daalder, I. H., & Lindsay, J. M. (2003). *America unbound: The Bush revolution in foreign policy*. Brookings Institution Press.

Daalder, I. H., & Lindsay, J. M. (2024). *America and Europe: Partners and rivals in the 21st century*. Yale University Press.

Dinan, D. (2014). *Ever closer union: An introduction to European integration*. Palgrave Macmillan.

Dombrowski, P., & Reich, S. (2017). *Does democracy matter? Uniting the democracies in a changing world*. In P. Dombrowski & S. Reich (Eds.), *The end of grand strategy* (pp. 101-125). Cornell University Press.

Drezner, D. W. (2007). *All politics is global: Explaining international regulatory regimes*. Princeton University Press.

Duchêne, F. (1972). *Europe's role in world peace*. In R. Mayne (Ed.), *Europe tomorrow: Sixteen Europeans look ahead* (pp. 32-47). Harper & Row.

Eichengreen, B. (2011). *Exorbitant privilege: The rise and fall of the dollar and the future of the international monetary system*. Oxford University Press.

Eichengreen, B. (2023). The dollar and its discontents: American currency and power in the 21st century. *Foreign Affairs*, 102(1), 42-50.

Emmott, B. (2017). *The fate of the West: The battle to save the world's most successful political idea*. Portfolio.

Fabbrini, S., & Marchetti, R. (2024). Beyond the transatlantic relationship: Europe's search for strategic autonomy. *Journal of European Public Policy*, 31(2), 234-251.

Ferguson, N. (2008). *The ascent of money: A financial history of the world*. Penguin Books.

Friedman, T. L. (2005). *The world is flat: A brief history of the twenty-first century*. Farrar, Straus and Giroux.

Fukuyama, F. (2023). *The end of the end of history: Politics in the twenty-first century*. Profile Books.

Gaddis, J. L. (2005). *Strategies of containment: A critical appraisal of American national security policy during the Cold War*. Oxford University Press.

Garton Ash, T. (2004). *Free world: America, Europe, and the surprising future of the West*. Random House.

Giddens, A. (2007). *Europe in the global age*. Polity Press.

Gordon, P. H. (2006). *A certain idea of Europe*. Princeton University Press.

Gordon, P. H. (2020). *The United States and Europe: Beyond the Bush era*. In P. H. Gordon (Ed.), *The end of the Bush revolution* (pp. 123-150). Brookings Institution Press.

Gordon, P. H., & Shapiro, J. (2024). *The transatlantic alliance in a multipolar world*. Columbia University Press.

Gray, C. S. (2009). *Hard power and soft power: The utility of military force as an instrument of policy in the 21st century*. Strategic Studies Institute, U.S. Army War College.

Hamilton, D. S. (2014). *The United States and Europe: Rethinking the transatlantic relationship*. Center for Transatlantic Relations.

Hamilton, D. S. (2023). *Transatlantic relations: Converging or diverging?* Routledge.

Hoffmann, S. (1966). *Obstinate and obsolete? The non-Community Europe*. In S. Hoffmann (Ed.), *The state of war: Essays on the theory and practice of international relations* (pp. 89-105). Praeger.

Huntington, S. P. (1996). *The clash of civilizations and the remaking of world order*. Simon & Schuster.

Ikenberry, G. J. (2001). *After victory: Institutions, strategic restraint, and the rebuilding of order after major wars*. Princeton University Press.

Ikenberry, G. J. (2024). The end of liberal international order? *International Affairs*, 100(1), 7-23.

Joffe, J. (2006). *Überpower: The imperial temptation of America*. W.W. Norton & Company.

Jones, E., & Matthijs, M. (2023). Rethinking integration and sovereignty in the European Union. *Survival*, 65(4), 31-58.

Kagan, R. (2003). *Of paradise and power: America and Europe in the new world order*. Alfred A. Knopf.

Kagan, R. (2023). *The jungle grows back: America and our imperiled world* (2nd ed.). Knopf.

Katzenstein, P. J. (2005). *A world of regions: Asia and Europe in the American imperium*. Cornell University Press.

Keohane, R. O., & Nye, J. S. (2012). *Power and interdependence revisited*. *International organisation*, 66(4), 705-734.

Kennedy, P. (1987). *The rise and fall of the great powers: Economic change and military conflict from 1500 to 2000*. Random House.

Kissinger, H. A. (2014). *World order*. Penguin Press.

Kupchan, C. A. (2002). *The end of the American era: U.S. foreign policy and the geopolitics of the twenty-first century*. Alfred A. Knopf.

Kupchan, C. A. (2010). *No one's world: The West, the rising rest, and the coming global turn*. Oxford University Press.

Kupchan, C. A. (2024). *Divergence and convergence: The future of the Atlantic alliance*. Oxford University Press.

Larres, K. (2023). *Uncertain allies: Nixon, Kissinger, and the threat of a united Europe*. Yale University Press.

Leonard, M. (2005). *Why Europe will run the 21st century*. PublicAffairs.

Leonard, M., & Shapiro, J. (2023). Strategic sovereignty: How Europe can regain the capacity to act. *European Council on Foreign Relations Policy Brief*, 25(3), 1-24.

Levy, D., & Pensky, M. (2024). *Cosmopolitanism and the new world order: European and American perspectives*. Polity Press.

Mearsheimer, J. J. (2011). *The tragedy of great power politics*. W.W. Norton & Company.

Mearsheimer, J. J. (2023). The inevitable rivalry: America, China, and the tragedy of great-power politics. *Foreign Affairs*, 102(2), 48-67.

Moravcsik, A. (1998). *The choice for Europe: Social purpose and state power from Messina to Maastricht*. Cornell University Press.

Mounk, Y. (2023). *The great experiment: Why diverse democracies fall apart and how they can endure*. Penguin Press.

Nye, J. S. (2002). *The paradox of American power: Why the world's only superpower can't go it alone*. Oxford University Press.

Nye, J. S. (2004). *Soft power: The means to success in world politics*. PublicAffairs.

Niblett, R., & Vinjamuri, L. (2024). The liberal order isn't coming back: What next? *Survival*, 66(1), 7-24.

Posen, B. R. (2023). The rise of illiberal hegemony: Trump's surprising grand strategy. *Foreign Affairs*, 102(3), 20-27.

Putnam, R. D. (1988). Diplomacy and domestic politics: The logic of two-level games. *International organisation*, 42(3), 427-460.

Rifkin, J. (2004). *The European dream: How Europe's vision of the future is quietly eclipsing the American dream*. TarcherPerigee.

Ruggie, J. G. (1998). *Constructing the world polity: Essays on international institutionalization*. Routledge.

Schmidt, V. A. (2006). *Democracy in Europe: The EU and national polities*. Oxford University Press.

Serfaty, S. (2010). *Bridging the transatlantic gap*. Rowman & Littlefield Publishers.

Shapiro, J. (2003). *Alliance management: How to forge effective transatlantic cooperation*. Council on Foreign Relations Press.

Soros, G. (2023). *In defense of open society: The crisis of liberal democracy and the path ahead*. Public Affairs.

Stiglitz, J. E. (2002). *Globalization and its discontents*. W. W. Norton & Company.

Stokes, D. (2024). Trump and the crisis of liberal hegemony. *International Affairs*, 100(2), 319-336.

Telhami, S. (2013). *The world through Arab eyes: Arab public opinion and the reshaping of American foreign policy*. Basic Books.

Toje, A. (2023). *The European Union as a small power: After the cold war*. Palgrave Macmillan.

Van Oudenaren, J. (2005). *America against Europe: From rivalry to partnership*. Rowman & Littlefield Publishers.

Walt, S. M. (2018). *The hell of good intentions: America's foreign policy elite and the decline of U.S. primacy*. Farrar, Straus and Giroux.

Wright, T. (2023). *All measures short of war: The contest for the 21st century and the future of American power*. Yale University Press.

Youngs, R. (2024). *Europe's Eastern crisis: The geopolitics of asymmetry*. Cambridge University Press.

Online References

Aleshin, A. (2024). The EU–NATO cooperation after the start of the special military operation. *Современная Европа*, 5(126), 189–200. https://doi.org/10.31857/s0201708324050152

Arbatova, N. (2024). Relations of the European Union with the United States and NATO: Dilemmas of euro-atlanticism. *Полис*, 4, 105–118. https://doi.org/10.17976/jpps/2024.04.08

CIOATĂ, I.-S. (2024). Transatlantic partnership – Political developments and transformations in the new geostrategic framework. *Strategic Impact*, 91(2), 48–65. https://doi.org/10.53477/1842-9904-24-8

Demertzis, M., & Fredriksson, G. (2018). The EU response to US trade tariffs. *Intereconomics*, 2018(5), 260–268. https://doi.org/10.1007/S10272-018-0763-2

Erichsen, E. R., & Salajan, F. D. (2014). A comparative analysis of E-learning policy formulation in the European Union and the United States: Discursive convergence and divergence. *Comparative Education Review*, 58(1), 135–165. https://doi.org/10.1086/674095

Filipec, O. (2023). The cooperation between EU and NATO in response to hybrid threats: A retrospective analysis from the institutionalist perspective. *Slovak Journal of Political Sciences*. https://doi.org/10.34135/sjps.230102

Hart, N., & Casey, C. A. (2024). Transatlantic leadership in an era of human rights-based export controls. *Journal of International Economic Law*. https://doi.org/10.1093/jiel/jgae005

Hrubinko, A. (2024). The genesis of the NATO — EU relationship in the context of the historical transformations of the world security system. *Україна Дипломатична*, XXV, 784–794. https://doi.org/10.37837/2

707-7683-2024-33

Justo-Hanani, R., & Dayan, T. (2016). Explaining transatlantic policy divergence: The role of domestic politics and policy styles in nanotechnology risk regulation. *Global Environmental Politics*, 16(1), 79–98. https://doi.org/10.1162/GLEP_A_00337

Kerremans, B. (2022). Divergence across the Atlantic? US skepticism meets the EU and the WTO's appellate body. *Politics and Governance*, 10(2), 208–218. https://doi.org/10.17645/pag.v10i2.4983

Larres, K. (2020). Trump's trade wars: America, China, Europe, and global disorder. *Journal of Transatlantic Studies*, 18(1), 103–129. https://doi.org/10.1057/S42738-019-00040-Y

Leonelli, G. C. (2022). Transatlantic divergencies in the regulation of uncertain risks: Co-production, normative frames and ideal evidence-based and socially acceptable risk approaches. *German Law Journal*, 23(5), 769–799. https://doi.org/10.1017/glj.2022.47

Mormann, F. (2021). Of markets and subsidies: Counter-intuitive trends for clean energy policy in the European Union and the United States. *Transnational Environmental Law*, 10(2), 1–17. https://doi.org/10.1017/S2047102520000394

Mulleti, N. (2023). EU-NATO cooperation in the area of crisis management: Case of Kosovo. *European Journal of Economics, Law and Social Sciences*, 7(2), 64–70. https://doi.org/10.2478/ejels-2023-0009

Nikitin, A., & Klinova, M. (2024). Doctrinal aspects of the US, NATO and EU policies in military space. *Сравнительная Политика*, 13(4), 45–64. https://doi.org/10.46272/2221-3279-2022-4-13-45-64

Prikhodko, O. V. (2023). US-EU trade and economic relationship in the age of global rivalry. *Politics*. https://doi.org/10.31857/s2686673023120015

Ratti, L. (2023). The enduring relationship between NATO and European integration (pp. 308–344). Cambridge University Press. https://doi.org/10.1017/9781108780865.013

Struthers, C. L., Hare, C., & Bakker, R. (2020). Bridging the pond: Measuring policy positions in the United States and Europe. *Political

Science Research and Methods*, 8(4), 677–691. https://doi.org/10.101 7/PSRM.2019.22

VLADU, M. (2023). Considerations on the NATO and EU approach to critical infrastructure protection. *Romanian Military Thinking*, 2023(3), 176–183. https://doi.org/10.55535/rmt.2023.3.10

Wellenstein, E. (1986). Political implications of US-EC economic conflicts (I)* Euro-American turbulence—The trade issue. *Government and Opposition*, 21(4), 387–395. https://doi.org/10.1111/J.1477-7053.198 6.TB00027.X

Yalcin-Ispir, A. (2023). NATO and EU strategic security environment (pp. 43–57). https://doi.org/10.1007/978-3-031-44584-2_3

Yoon, S. (2018). Trump's 'America First' trade policy and the EU's two-fold responses. *Journal of Eurasian Studies*, 15(4), 233–252. https://doi.org/10.31203/AEPA.2018.15.4.012